PORSCHE 911 STORY

By the same author:
On the Starting Grid
Starting Grid to Chequered Flag
Competition Driving
The Racing Porsches: A Technical Triumph
Porsche Racing Cars of the 70s

PORSCHE 911 STORY

Paul Frère

Foreword by Professor Ferry Porsche

PATRICK STEPHENS LIMITED

First published in 1976
Second edition 1980
Third edition 1984
Fourth edition 1989

British Library Cataloguing in Publication Data

Frère, Paul
    Porsche 911 story.
    1. Porsche 911 cars, to 1984
    I. Title
    629.2′222

    ISBN 1-85260-128-0

Patrick Stephens Limited is part of the
Thorsons Publishing Group, Wellingborough,
Northamptonshire, NN8 2RQ, England

Printed and bound in Great Britain by
Butler & Tanner Ltd, Frome and London

10 9 8 7 6 5 4 3 2 1

Contents

List of illustrations

Foreword by Professor F. Porsche

Twenty-five years have gone since the Porsche 911, still under the short-lived type number 901, was first exhibited in the Frankfurt Motor Show. For Porsche, this was a big step ahead. It was the first car designed and developed from scratch by our company which had previously produced only the 356 model, largely based on mechanical units developed from the Volkswagen Beetle.

We had not taken the easy way, having opted for an individualistic design featuring a completely new air-cooled flat-six, overhung in the car's tail. There were many problems which we had to solve without being able to benefit from other manufacturers' experience. But events indicate that the way we had chosen was right. The 911 proved itself to be not only a practical road-going sports car, but also the most versatile competition car ever to roll on the world's roads and tracks. Be it in near standard or specifically modified form, it has won nearly every event for which a sports car is eligible, being as much at ease on the snowbound roads of the Monte Carlo Rally as on the desert tracks of the Paris–Dakar, on the winding roads of the Targa Florio or in the gruelling Le Mans and Daytona 24-Hours Races, all of which it won.

Never could we have imagined that, after being produced for 25 years in which more than a quarter million were built, it would still be, more than ever, one of the world's most respected sports cars. Thanks to continuous development, both in atmospheric and turbocharged versions, it has maintained its position among the leaders of the sports car world. In production models, its power output rose from 130 to 300 hp and even 450 hp in the limited production 959 directly developed from the 911, while racing engines developed from the basic 911 produce more than 700 horsepower.

But the end is still not in sight. Under the timeless shape my son originally designed, there is still room for further developments. In the second quarter century of its life, the 911 will benefit from the very latest developments of automotive and production engineering, ensuring the continuation of its exceptional career.

Paul Frère has remained in close contact with our company ever since, in the 'fifties, we invited him to drive our racing cars on various occasions, and as an engineer he has closely followed our growth and the evolution of our products. It is a great pleasure for me that he has written a new version of his excellent *Porsche 911 Story* to celebrate the 25th anniversary of this evergreen model.

Professor F. Porsche.

Author's introduction

Very few cars remain in production for 25 years without major change either in shape or in basic mechanical specification, and those few which do are usually very obviously dated. This certainly does not apply to the Porsche 911 and its derivatives. After its teething troubles had been sorted out, the 911 became one of the most coveted sports cars ever built and its prestige has increased ever since, in spite of strong competition from other high class sports cars, including those marketed by the Porsche company itself. This is due both to the ceaseless development from which it has benefited, thanks to the efforts of a team of purists who — without ignoring the imperatives of cost — have set themselves technical excellence as their major target, and to the brilliant successes the car has achieved in many branches of motor sport. In fact Porsche consider racing and rallying as the indispensable complement to their own magnificent proving ground and development facilities and run racing and production developments in close co-operation and under the same top management.

The 911 is a perfect example of how racing improves the breed, and the reader will find innumerable examples of how Porsche's sporting activities have led to progress that has been quickly incorporated in the production car, the 'Turbo' being an obvious case in point. But a virtue of the development staff is that they recognised that, however much a well-engineered sports car can benefit from racing, a road car must fulfill some basic requirements not directly related to the sport, such as comfort, flexibility, silence, durability and, more recently, fuel economy. The blend achieved from these requirements is what makes the Porsche what it is today and its development story so fascinating that we felt it deserved to be told.

Obviously this book could not have been written without the full co-operation of those responsible for the development of the car, and I am deeply indebted to them for the help they provided. Porsche's PR department has been extremely helpful, but I would like to thank particularly Prof Ferry Porsche himself, past and current Managing Directors Prof Ernst Fuhrmann, Peter W. Schutz and Heinz Branitzki, Technical chief Prof Helmuth Bott and all his close collaborators such as Dipl Ing Peter Falk, currently head of the Racing Department and Dipl Ing Fritz Bezner, in charge of 911 development who have kindly provided a lot of internal information on failure as well as success and even on matters usually kept secret, such as the latest developments in the racing field.

Paul Frère
Vence, France, 1988

NB. In this book the turbocharged version of the 911 is sometimes referred to as the 911 Turbo, sometimes as the 930 Turbo. Both denominations apply to one and the same car, 911 Turbo being the commercial designation and 930 Turbo the technical description.

Chapter One

Birth of the 911

As is now well known, the first batch of Porsche 356 models was hand built in a small workshop in Gmünd, a beautiful little resort in the Austrian province of Kärnten where Prof Ferdinand Porsche and his son 'Ferry' (now Professor F. Porsche) temporarily transferred their activities before returning to Stuttgart. Those first cars had all-aluminium bodies and, as they were lighter than later production models, they were kept by the company for use in competition or sold to some selected competition drivers. They were fundamental in establishing the sporting reputation of the young company.

By 1950, production was transferred to Stuttgart-Zuffenhausen where it was housed in wooden barracks, while assembly took place in a workshop rented by Porsche at Reutters, the body builders. The Zuffenhausen-built cars mainly differed from the Gmünd cars in having an all-steel body of generally similar shape. One development prototype was built before the start of the actual production and run for two months before the first production car was delivered.

Those early Type 356 cars were what we would call today 'Volkswagen Specials', of which many were built in the early 'fifties — and are still built today — mainly in the form of 'Dune Buggies'. The body structure was entirely original but, except for a few engine details, all the mechanical units were standard Volkswagen products. The engine, however, was fitted with special cylinder heads, having inclined valves of larger diameter than the Volkswagen's, with a special camshaft and twin single choke carburettors, while the cylinder bore was reduced from 75 to 73.5 mm to bring the car down into the 1100 cc class. The bottom end, cooling fan, etc, were unaltered. In this form, the engine developed 40 (DIN) bhp, an increase of 15 bhp over the 'Beetle' of the period.

A major contribution to the new car's success was the fact that an agreement was concluded with Volkswagen to sell and service Porsche cars through their own organisation, while further confidence was inspired because the new sports car was developed by the creator of the Volkswagen himself and his design team, rather than being more or less amateurishly evolved from somebody else's original design. Also, of course, Prof Porsche (1875-1951) was known as one of the world's leading automobile engineers and the creator of the immensely successful mid-engined Auto-Union racing car from which many basic VW features were borrowed.

As soon as production had started in Zuffenhausen, the Type 356 was under constant development and improvements were made from year to year: engine capacities went up from 1100 to 1300, 1500 and finally 1600 cc and there were 'normal' and 'S' variants in all sizes except 1100 cc. A gearbox incorporating an early version of the famous Porsche synchromesh system replaced the VW 'crash' box at the end of 1952, while brakes, steering and running gear were improved in various steps, disc brakes being fitted when the 356 'C' series was introduced in July 1963. Meanwhile, a baulking mechanism had been added to the synchronising system. There were some styling changes, too, like the replacement of the V-shaped windscreen by a curved one in 1953, a larger rear window in 1961 and various bumper styles, though the basic body shape which originally had a remarkably good drag coefficient of around 0.38 (progressively rising to 0.41 for high bumper models) remained unchanged throughout.

A comparatively small number of 356 models was also produced with the four overhead camshaft 'Carrera' engine, designed by Porsche's later Managing Director, Dr Ernst Fuhrmann, which had nothing in common with the original VW engine. This was first conceived as a racing engine and was used successively in 1500 and 1600 cc forms, both with roller bearings, then in 2 litre form with plain bearings, in the years 1957-1963.

Though by the end of the 'fifties little was left of the Type 356's VW ancestry except the basic design, even in the pushrod models, it was clear that the development was quickly catching up with the limits of the basic concept. Though good for 125 mph, the Carrera could remain only marginally competitive, since it offered little room and comfort for its very high price, while the fastest pushrod model of 1960, the 'Super-90' with a top speed of 115 mph and capable of reaching 60 mph in about 11 seconds, was getting a bit pressed by the much more comfortable and quiet higher class saloons of the period, like the Mercedes 220 SE and the Jaguar 3.4s and 3.8s which also handled no worse than the Porsche. Even the Citroën DS was a problem on the Autobahn, as it was not really safe for the Porsche's engine to be cruised indefinitely at over 100 mph.

At that time, however, nobody in the factory really knew exactly what form an eventual replacement for the 356 should take. More room was certainly required,

Left *After more than 20 years with Porsche as Finance Manager, Heinz Branitzki became Porsche's Managing Director in January 1988.*

Right *Several examples of this Type 745 air-cooled pushrod 2 litre 6 cylinder engine were built, but the project was abandoned as too noisy, too unreliable and too wide. It had a four-bearing crankshaft, 40 per cent heavier than the eight-bearing shaft of the 901 engine.*

calling for a longer wheelbase which would also help to improve ride comfort, and the first steps towards an evolution were styling projects by Dr Porsche's son Butzi. These eventually matured into a project internally known as 'Type 7', the styling of which is clearly recognisable as a direct forerunner of the 901, soon to be renamed the 911.

The project was eventually handed over to one of the company's long-standing members, body engineer, Erwin Komenda, to give the design a proper structure and build a number of development prototypes, still using the 356 swing axle rear suspension, the object in mind being mainly to finalise the shape and the internal dimensions. At the front, however, a MacPherson layout with torsion bars replaced the twin trailing link suspension of the 356. This was quite a revolution, for since the earliest Auto-Union Grand Prix car days, back in 1934, all Porsche designs had used a parallel trailing link front suspension with transverse torsion bars. But the need for more luggage space in the front boot of a rear-engined car dictated its abandonment in favour of a MacPherson layout in which only the dampers were incorporated in the struts, the springing medium being longitudinal torsion bars, so as to reduce the overall diameter of the struts. This left the largest possible boot width available between them. The MacPherson layout also has the advantage of allowing the designer more freedom in the choice of the suspension geometry and, more specifically, camber variations. It is not without interest that, while the 901 was being developed, the Porsche trailing link front suspension gave way to transverse wishbones on the factory's racing cars, from which the development engineers gained useful experience with front-end geometries.

Altogether, three or four prototypes of the Type 7 were built, each differing a little more from the original design and each a little larger than the previous one, Komenda holding the opinion that mankind is progressively increasing in size and that the new car would have a better future if it was fairly large to start with! In the

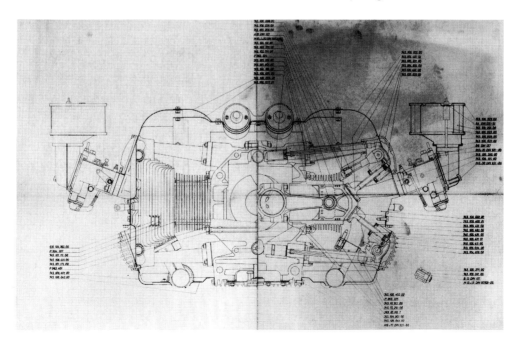

end, the project became a full four-seater and a new six-cylinder engine was designed to propel it with the briskness expected from a Porsche. It was a 2 litre push-rod design based on the contemporary Porsche four-cylinder of VW derivation.

For this engine, designed under Klaus von Rückert who was soon to move to BMW, there were several projects. One had oil cooled cylinders and two camshafts located at the bottom of the crankcase (as in a Lancia Flavia), operating the valves by pushrods and rockers, the intake valves being parallel with the cylinder axis and the exhaust valves at an angle, as in the 356 engine. Oil cooling for the cylinders was supposed to be a cheap and efficient way of quietening the engine, of which the cylinder heads remained air cooled, but no prototype of this novel engine was actually built. Instead another version was produced with one camshaft above and one camshaft below the crankcase with valves set in V formation, operated by pushrods and rockers.

The engine had a dry sump and was fully air cooled by two small axial impellers. Bore and stroke were 80 x 66 mm, as for the yet to be designed 901 engine and a margin was provided to permit the use of 84 and even 89 mm bore cylinders to increase the capacity to 2.2 and 2.5 litres. Engines with those bore and stroke dimensions were also built in what was to become the 911 range, the former size in production, the second as an experimental racing engine. Side draught carburettors were used, making the engine very wide. It was finally rejected for several reasons, but mainly because of the noise created by the valve gear, the difficulty of securely anchoring the rocker fulcrum pin in the alloy head, and the bulk of the engine and its large timing gears. One such engine is preserved in Porsche's own museum.

The development of the 901

'The Type 7 my son had originally designed was a 2+2 seater and we were determined that it should remain so,' said Professor Porsche in an interview I had with him. 'The four-seater it had been developed into was not in the same market as the 356 and it was not our intention to compete with Mercedes in their own speciality.' And as Komenda insisted on following his own ideas, rather than the instructions given to him by the head of the company, Porsche contacted Reutter bodies to develop a structure closely following the lines and dimensions of Butzi Porsche's original Type 7.

By that time, the main requirements which the new car was to fulfil had become more clearly defined:

1   It was to be a true '2+2', less cramped than the 356 in which the occasional rear seats had been added as an afterthought after two years' production, but it was *not* to be a full four-seater, in order to keep the dimensions and the weight down.

2   It was to have more adequate luggage space, big enough to carry golf clubs — a requirement often expressed by customers.

3   It was to offer better comfort and handling.

4   It was to combine the performance of the 2 litre Carrera with the quietness and good manners of the lowest-powered pushrod 356, the 60 bhp 'Lady' as it was known on account of its refined behaviour.

5   There should be no grease nipples and routine maintenance was to be drastically reduced.

When he realised that he was going to be short-circuited, Komenda changed his mind and willingly co-operated in the project for which a new semi-trailing link rear suspension was still to be developed, using the same transverse torsion bar layout as the old swing axle suspension. This type of suspension was adopted because it required comparatively little space, was reasonably inexpensive and lacked the obvious limitations of the 356's swing axle suspension.

Neither the rear engine position nor the air cooling were really questioned when the new design was laid down, as the current strict limitations on noise did not exist at the time and the development engineers felt they could easily master the handling problems by using the semi-trailing links to good effect. Perhaps they were a bit presumptuous on this point, though in fact most of the difficulties they were to experience really came from the front end.

The most important decision of all was probably taken when Ferry (now Professor) Porsche opted to forget about pushrods and to go ahead with the development of a completely new six-cylinder engine with an overhead camshaft for each bank of three cylinders. Refinement was the main reason for having six cylinders, while the overhead camshafts were dictated by the requirement of a lower noise level, of a high specific power output and consequently high crankshaft speed, and with an eye on future developments, both for road use and for racing purposes.

One detail which involved a lot of thought and discussions with the Technical Director of the period, Ing Tomala, was how to drive the camshafts. The existing four-cylinder Carrera engine, which had been developed mainly for racing, used a shaft and bevel gear drive — an efficient but noisy means of driving camshafts, prone to vibration periods. The two alternative solutions were chain drive and toothed rubber belt. At the time, only the small Glas company had been brave enough to trust a toothed belt for driving an overhead camshaft. The system was ideally simple: silent and flexible enough to take care of the heat expansion of the engine without requiring an automatic tensioner. But even though reports on the reliability of the system had been encouraging, it was still very much an unknown quantity at the time and it was finally decided not to take the risk.

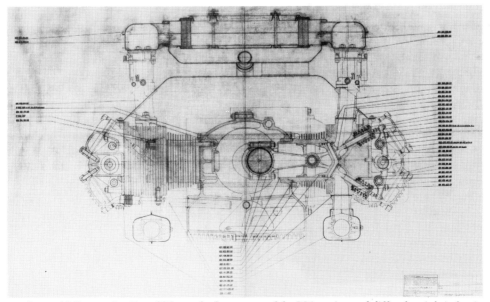

Experimental 2 litre engine Type 821 was the forerunner of the 901 engine and differed mainly in having a wet sump.

This left chain drive as the only possible solution, even though reports from the Porsche importer in the United States, Max Hoffmann, who also handled Jaguars, indicated that the XK engine's timing chain gave more than its fair share of trouble. In order to run clear of those, Ferry Porsche insisted that only the best chains available in the world—Reynolds—were to be used, in conjunction with hydraulic tensioners — one per chain — to obviate vibration problems. First-quality chains were essential because of the high inertia forces in a high performance engine having a very light flywheel, and thus subject to very high accelerations and decelerations.

In order to achieve the performance target, yet keep the new car in a class accessible to most of the existing Porsche customers, 2 litres was considered to be the right size for the engine, but it was deliberately designed with a margin sufficient to accommodate possible capacity increases at a later date if market developments or performance requirements warranted it. Even at that stage, it was considered that the basic dimensions were large enough to allow for a capacity increase up to about 2.7 litres, though complete drawings to prove it were not made. 'Had I known, at that time, that the unit could actually be stretched to 3.3 litres and still be completely reliable, even in racing form, I would almost certainly have decided that it was unnecessarily large and heavy, and would have asked the designers to scale it down', says Professor Porsche, 'Now I am glad I didn't!'

The pushrod, four-cylinder engine had used Chromal cylinders (aluminium alloy with a chromium-plated working surface) and later Biral cylinders (cast iron with light alloy fins cast around it) in its more highly tuned versions (1600 Super and Super-90) and light alloy for all its structural parts. Similarly, the structural parts of the Type 901 engine were at first all made in aluminium alloy. Pre-production models had cast iron cylinders, but Biral cylinders were used as the car was put into normal production.

Oil surge is a particularly difficult problem with flat engines. Fast cornering tends to throw oil into one bank of cylinders, unless the sump is deep enough, which means raising the engine higher above the ground. A flat sump causes the oil pump intake to be starved when the oil is centrifuged by side forces. In the pushrod engine of VW derivation, a system was developed incorporating two oil pump pick-ups and inertia valves closing whichever was likely to aspirate air rather than oil, but for the new six a larger volume of oil was wanted and, though a wet sump engine had been on the drawing board, it was decided to adopt a dry sump lubrication system. This had already been used by Porsche in the four-cylinder Carrera and in the eight-cylinder racing engine introduced in 1962 for Grand Prix and sports car racing.

But the four-cylinder Carrera engine, first seen in the 'Spyder' designed for sports car racing in 1954, had been conceived mainly with racing in mind and with little consideration for accessibility or ease of servicing when fitted to a Type 356 body shell. (Owners of Type 356 Carreras will remember that changing plugs and adjusting valves were major servicing operations.) The six-cylinder, Type 901/01 engine, however, was developed specifically for a production car. The plugs are very accessible and so is the ignition distributor, and the single camshaft-per-bank arrangement with valves operated by easily adjustable rockers makes valve clearance setting a straightforward operation.

Another important difference, compared with the old pushrod engine, was the use of an axial-flow, rather than a radial-flow cooling fan. The radial-flow cooling fan the old engine had inherited from the Volkswagen was not only cheap to make, but also very cheap to buy from VW. The efficiency of a radial-flow fan is lower than for an axial-flow fan however, and, when used for a flat engine turning clockwise, more air reaches the left-hand bank of cylinders than the right-hand bank, as cooling the latter involves additional ducting. To compensate for this, the cooling fan of the 'Beetle' and of Type 356 Porsches is offset to the right of the engine axis.

For all these reasons, a change was made to an axial-flow fan when the 901 engine was designed. Thanks to its good efficiency, a comparatively small light alloy impeller wheel, co-axial with the 490 watt alternator housed within the impeller wheel hub and belt-driven from the rear end of the crankshaft at 1.3 times crankshaft speed, could be used. From the light alloy blower housing, the cooling air was ducted with a maximum output of 1,390 litres per second at 6,100 rpm engine speed to the cylinders and heads by a neat one-piece plastic moulding entirely covering the upper part of the engine. From this duct, on either side of the cylindrical part matching the impeller housing, some of the air blown by the fan was diverted to heat exchangers surrounding the exhaust manifold, on either side of the engine, where it was heated. From these, flap valves controlled from the cockpit allowed the air either to escape into the atmosphere, or to be directed into the body, after passing through silencers built into the door sills. Thus the position of the flap valves controlled the amount of heated air which was forced into the body. This body heating installation remained substantially unchanged up to and including 1989 models, though there were some detail changes, to be discussed later. The other air ducts around the cylinders and heads were made of sheet metal because of the rather high temperatures reached.

The cast aluminium crankcase was split vertically along the crankshaft axis, supporting seven steel-backed lead-indium bearing shells and one additional hard lead bush supporting the crankshaft nose at the rear end of the engine. The two crankcase halves were held together by through-bolts. Long studs retained the individual light alloy cylinder heads and the cylinders in the seats provided for them in the crankcase. The three-bearing camshaft boxes also containing the valve rocker mechanisms were one-piece aluminium castings common to each bank of three cylinders and bolted to the cylinder heads. The exhaust valves were hollow and sodium-filled for better cooling, and valve adjustment was by the usual screw and lock-nut, carried by the rocker. The first 3,069 engines made had hollow camshafts to which oil was fed under pressure and escaped through small holes to lubricate the cams. As from engine No 9013070, the cams were lubricated by a holed ramp parallel to the camshafts, this system providing a better control of the oil feed.

Steel connecting rods running on big end bearings of similar lead-indium material to the crankshaft bearings were used, and the cast aluminium pistons had two upper compression and one lower oil scraper rings, the upper compression ring being chrome-plated.

The fully counterweighted forged crankshaft carried a pinion at its rear end, between the 7th and the 8th bearing, driving a half-speed shaft running directly below the crankshaft. This shaft carried the two sprockets for the two camshaft driving chains and drove, through an intermediate shaft, the scavenge and the pressure oil pumps. The scavenged oil was pushed through an oil cooler bolted to the crankcase, in the cooling air stream delivered by the blower before returning to the tank located in the right rear wheel housing.

Carburation was by three single choke 40 Pl Solex overflow carburettors mounted on a common base plate for each bank of cylinders, fed by a Bendix electric pump and scavenged by twin mechanical membrane pumps driven off the rear end of the left-hand camshaft.

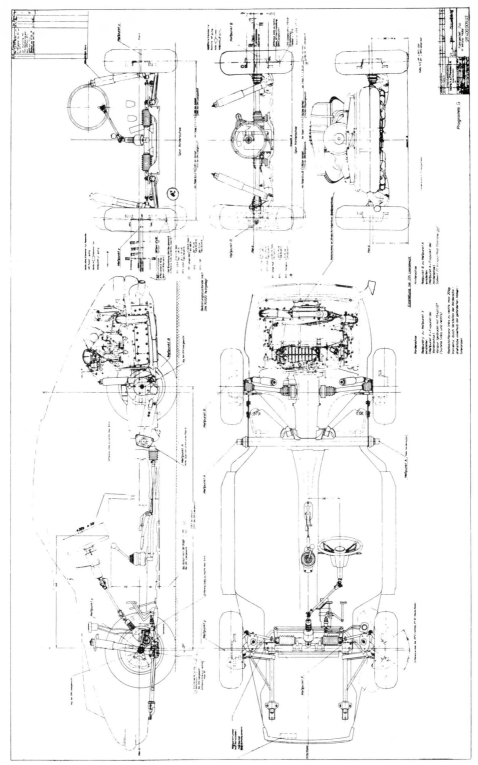

General layout of Porsche 911 exemplified by a G-series model.

This first version of the 2 litre 911 engine, Type 901/01, developed 130 (DIN) bhp at 6,100 rpm and a torque of 17.8 mkg (128.8 lb/ft) at 4,200 rpm on a 9:1 compression ratio and weighed, complete with its 215 mm diameter single disc diaphragm clutch, 184 kg (406 lb). Its minimum fuel consumption was 225 gr/bhp/hour at 3,400 rpm.

The drive was taken through the aforementioned 215 mm diameter Fichtel & Sachs single disc diaphragm clutch to a 5-speed 'transaxle', one single aluminium housing containing the clutch, the two-starwheel, spiral bevel differential and the main gear clusters. The front cover contained the outrigged first and reverse gear sets, the speedometer drive and the front end of the gear selector rod, while a lateral cover allowed the insertion of the differential unit. Both the gearbox shafts ran in two bearings, rollers being used at the rear (engine and differential) end and ball bearings also taking the longitudinal thrust at the front end.

Only the second gear input pinion was integral with its shaft (so that a change of the second gear ratio necessitated the replacement of the input shaft) and all gear sets could be chosen individually, though when the model was announced one standard gear set was available: first 12/34, second 18/32, third 23/28, fourth 26/25 and fifth 28/23, with a 7/31 crownwheel and pinion ratio. Engagement was by the well-known Porsche split-ring synchronising system and selection was by a central gear lever with second, third, fourth and fifth gear in the usual H pattern, while first and reverse were selected in a plane to the left of the H, first by moving the lever backwards. The lever was spring loaded to return to the central (second-third gear) plane.

The drive shafts to the wheels were Hooke-jointed at the wheel end but had an interesting variation on the Hooke joint, allowing an axial movement of the shaft, on the differential end, making a splined shaft redundant. This joint was manufactured by Nadella.

Space considerations had dictated the use of a MacPherson-type front suspension and to make the struts as small as possible in diameter torsion bars were used as the suspension medium. They were enclosed in the tubular base of the triangulated wishbone, to which they were anchored at the forward end, their adjustable abutment being just aft of the rear wishbone bush carried by a tubular transverse member bolted to the body shell. This also carried the ZF-made, but Porsche-designed rack-and-pinion steering box. The lower wishbone was pivoted in 'Flanblocks' (a variety of Silentblocs, with additional axial thrust washers) after 'Fluidblocks' had proved unsuitable in the development stage because of uncontrollable friction characteristics under heavy and changing loads.* The front suspension was supplemented by an anti-roll bar of 13 mm diameter connected to the wishbones by a lever and rubber-bushed rod at either end.

This type of suspension allows the widest possible luggage compartment to be inserted between the front wheels. It is also worthy of note that the steering pinion is in the centre line of the car, so that no change is necessary for right-hand drive cars. In addition, the universally jointed steering column running at a considerable angle to the vehicle centre line was a very efficient means of minimising steering column

---

* Fluidblocks, developed by Boge, are made up of two concentric metal bushes separated by rubber. But rather than being bonded to the metal and working in shear, the rubber glides on the metal bushes. It is fully floating and a permanent lubricant ensures that the relative motion occurs with a minimum of friction.

A scantily camouflaged 911 (then 901) undergoes its final development tests before going into production.

intrusion in the case of a crash, at a time when very little thought was given to such safety features. The overall steering ratio was 16.5:1. The steering box itself was a very elaborate design. To obtain automatic adjustment for play, the pinion was carried in two ball bearings in a housing carried by the rack and was spring loaded against the latter. This assembly could float vertically in the main steering housing, made of aluminium, which carried the rack at either end.

At the rear, a semi-trailing link geometry was used for several reasons. One is that Porsche had a vast experience of that sort of suspension, used in a much cruder form, in connection with ordinary 'swing axles', on both the Volkswagen and the Type 356. A lot of development had been done on the Type 356, but its design had obvious limits. For the Type 901, the tubular cross member housing two torsion bars anchored at its centre and each controlling a spring steel trailing arm of great beam, but little torsional stiffness, was maintained. But instead of being carried by the half shaft, each wheel hub was carried by a suspension arm pivoted on a bracket welded to the tubular cross member, the rubber-bushed pivot being located near the centre line of the car and slightly rearward of the cross member. Eccentric adjustments were provided for both camber and toe-in. This arrangement provided a much longer virtual swing-arm for the wheels, with correspondingly smaller variations of both camber and toe-in than in the swing axle system. The double acting dampers were anchored to the rear of the hub centre line, providing increased travel.

The other two main reasons for using this type of suspension were that it was comparatively cheap and also very compact, leaving room for the occasional seats in the rear body compartment. No anti-roll bar was used at the rear, which seemed logical in a rear-engined car with a natural tendency to oversteer.

Whereas Porsche had developed their own disc brakes with internal caliper for racing, late 356 models and the 911 were fitted with normal disc brakes of ATE manufacture, also used on Porsche racing cars from 1964. The calipers were of cast iron with two pistons and quick-change pads. They were operated from the master cylinder by a single circuit. At the rear the disc was mounted on a small diameter drum incorporating the parking brake, operating on the Bendix Duo-Servo system, to obviate the usual leverage problem and consequent poor efficiency of parking brakes working on the disc.

For a firm so closely connected with racing as Porsche it may seem strange that the 165 HR 15 tyres were fitted to rims as narrow as 4½ inches. This can partly be explained by the fact that, at the time, there was a line of thought prevailing in the factory that comparatively narrow tyres with a rounded tread profile were in a better position to accommodate the camber variations which were both inevitable and desirable to obtain the desired handling characteristics. It must also be remembered that 4½ inch rims were the widest recommended by tyre manufacturers for 165 tyres at the time. It took three years to step up the rim width to 5½ inches and another

This is how the 911 began its successful career. Ferdinand Alexander Porsche, who gave it its shape, seems satisfied with it.

year to 6 inches which remained the standard wear for all models up to the K-Series (1977 models), except Carrera and Turbo.

With a wheelbase of 2,211 mm (87.05 in), a front track of 1,353 mm (53.27 in), a rear track of 1,321 mm (52.0 in), an overall length of 4,163 mm (163.90 in) and an overall width of 1,610 mm (63.39 in), the 901 was still a very compact model, being slightly longer than a Type 356 C, but actually narrower, as the lateral overhang of the body over the wheels was much less. At the time it was also commendably light in relation to its power, the DIN weight (which means with all accessories and full tanks) of 1,080 kg (2,381 lb) giving a power/weight ratio of 8.3 kg/bhp (120.4 bhp/ton). And though the body was never tested in the wind tunnel before it went into production, it proved to have a very good drag coefficient, compared with most contemporary cars, the actual figure being around $C_D = 0.38$. Of course, this was not just chance, for if harmonious shape was a primary consideration when Ferry Porsche's son Butzi designed the car's shape, the requirement of a low drag and low lift were constantly kept in mind, past racing experience having indicated how important these were.

Owners of 911s who have suffered when trying to get their luggage into the rear compartment will surely be interested, if not comforted, to know that the car was originally planned with a lift-up rear window to facilitate handling the luggage, but the body engineers at Reutter, who had made most of the bodies until their company was bought up by Porsche, raised so many objections about the practicability of the scheme, suggesting it would be next to impossible to make the opening rattle-free and water-proof, that the idea was finally abandoned. 'Now we know they were wrong' says Professor Porsche regretfully today. 'Such an opening works quite satisfactorily on many modern cars, even quite cheap ones.'

Chapter Two

Early problems and progress

Problems began even before the first cars were delivered, but one was in the nature of red tape: unbeknown to Porsche, Peugeot had, long before the war, registered all three-figure numbers, of which the central one was an '0', for the designation of car models, and the French company objected to 901 (actually Porsche's design office project number) being used by Porsche to identify their new car. Consequently the 901 became the 911 before it reached the hands of the first customers, though internally the number 901 continued to feature prominently to identify parts and units.

Other problems were much more worrying and handling was probably the most important. Any car with an overhung rear engine carries more weight on its rear than on its front wheels and consequently has an inherent tendency to oversteer, to be unstable at speed in a straight line and to be very sensitive to side winds, due to the fact that the centre of aerodynamic pressure is far ahead of the centre of gravity. To a certain extent, these undesirable features can be corrected by appropriate suspension design and aerodynamic aids. Today's most powerful racing cars carry anything between 65 and 70 per cent of their weight on the rear wheels. Examples include the over-1,000 hp Porsche 917 'Turbo' Can-Am car, one of the best handling racing cars ever made, while the 935 which earned four World Championship titles for Porsche proves that, properly tuned, basically standard 911 suspension can even cope with a rearward weight bias of 69 per cent. But this is with powerful aerodynamic aids and the help of racing tyres, of which the rear ones are on rims very nearly four times as wide as those of early 911s!

Early 911s stood on 4½ inch wide rims front and rear, which did not make things any easier, and with identical tyres front and rear the only way of preventing fierce final oversteer and getting acceptable straight line stability is to match the front and rear suspension in such a way that the car will understeer quite vigorously when submitted to moderate side forces. In the case of the 911, the weight of the engine finally turned out to be quite a lot higher than the design office had anticipated. This increased the rearward weight bias, and when the suspension settings were finalised the understeer under moderate lateral forces turned out to be enormous. It was further emphasised by the considerable slip angles developed by the narrow tyres. These also increased the yaw angle variations caused by varying the driving torque and resulting from the rear wheel camber change taking place with rear-end lift as the throttle was closed: when cornering at high speed, lifting off would cause immediate and severe oversteer. This was bad enough, but even more worrying was the fact that the reaction was quite often different on right- and left-hand bends. Even in a straight line, some examples would react directionally to the throttle opening.

In the prototype stage, when cars were built individually by highly skilled mechanics, handling was said to be still quite acceptable, but once the car was assembled on the line it proved to be extremely sensitive to inevitable slight production inaccuracies, so much so in fact that some cars leaving the line were real beasts. It is strange indeed that originally no production tolerances, or only impossibly small ones, were allowed for in the running gear, as testified by the original 911 instruction book in which the following data is given: Camber, front +4' (yes, four *minutes* of arc!), rear 1°6'; toe-in, front 15 to 20', rear 0 to −2' (!); castor 7°45'.

Such close tolerances had little meaning if they could not be maintained in production. Ing Tomala, under whom the 911 was designed and developed, insisted that the upper anchorage points of the front MacPherson struts, which govern castor and camber, need not be adjustable if, in production, the holes were actually drilled *after* the whole suspension had been assembled, so as to make up for any production inaccuracy. But in practice the results were disastrous. Furthermore, straight line stability, handling and throttle reactions proved to be very sensitive to the weight actually carried by each individual wheel and depending upon torsion bar settings, but there were no means available to check this on the production line.

A quick remedy had to be found, especially to cure the poor straight line stability and the sensitivity to side winds. Somebody suggested that adding weight at the front might improve matters, and front bumper overriders were experimentally filled with lead. It was found that their weight had virtually no effect when the overriders were just carried in the front part of the luggage compartment, ie, near the longitudinal axis of the car, but that they made a considerable improvement when mounted near the extremities of the bumpers. In practice, lead being expensive, cast iron lumps weighing 11 kg (24.5 lb) each were made and inserted in production in the far ends of the front bumper. Officially they were known as 'bumper reinforcements' and there was at least one advantage to this rather inelegant and empiric solution: 'reinforced bumpers' could easily be fitted to existing cars if their owners complained. In fact many cars were burdened with the extra 22 kg without their owners ever knowing about it!

The effect of the weights was, of course, to increase the polar moment of inertia of the car around both its vertical and longitudinal axes. The increase is so small that it seems unlikely to cause any noticeable difference, especially where the increase around the longitudinal axis — the most likely to have any effect at all — is concerned. Yet development chief Ing Helmut Bott, responsible for chassis development at the time, says the difference was quite obvious and he could step into any 911 and say if it carried the weights or not, just by driving it up and down the road!

This is an episode Porsche's engineering department is not particularly proud of and does not like to remember. It certainly hastened the resignation of Ing Tomala, who had come to Porsche in 1962 as Technical Director with many advanced and excellent ideas, but no previous experience of the car branch. He succeeded Karl Raabe as head of the design office and also took Klaus von Rücker's place as chief of development. The successful Type 904 racing coupé was developed under his direction.

Ing Tomala finally left the factory in 1966 to be succeeded as chief of development by Dr Porsche's nephew, Ferdinand Piëch, who had been in charge of the engine development for about two years and had a much more scientific approach to development problems. He was later to become the driving force behind Porsche's access to the highest racing honours. After heading the Audi development team for

15 years and masterminding the Quattro, he was promoted to the Managing Director's seat as from January 1988.

The weighted front bumper certainly made the 911 less unpredictable and, despite its narrow wheels and tyres, it could be cornered quite surprisingly fast. So fast, in fact, that after I had had one of those early 911s for a prolonged road test, when it was used mainly in Germany and Italy, I wrote that on the road cornering speeds were generally limited by visibility and traffic, rather than by the actual cornering power of the car. In a later chapter we shall see how the 911 running gear was developed and how the ballast in the bumper was eventually discarded.

Carburation problems

Another obvious fault of early 911s was the carburation. A very neat arrangement of three carburettors mounted on a common base plate and with a common manifold ducting air from the filter had been designed by Solex specially for the 911 engine, which used one set for each bank of three cylinders. These carburettors were of the overflow type, without float chamber, for which there was no room. The overflow chamber was kept filled by a Bendix electric pump, while twin mechanical pumps driven off the left-hand camshaft scavenged the overflow back to the main tank. Unfortunately, the development of these carburettors was not completed when the 911 went into production and almost all cars had a very bad 'flat spot' starting just short of 2,500 rpm and lasting up to over 3,000 rpm. This was all the more infuriating because, in the experimental department, identical engines ran perfectly on triple Weber carburettors with a float chamber.

In view of the excellent co-operation that had always existed between Porsche and Solex, however, the works management insisted that every effort should be made to make the Solex carburettors work, and engineers from Stuttgart were actually dispatched to the Solex factory to co-operate with their technicians. But no immediate solution could be found. Already every Porsche 911 involved in serious competition and every Type 901 engine developed for racing was fitted with Webers. As from February 1966, the production 901/01 engine was superseded by the 901/05 engine, which was identical except for the use of two triple-choke Weber 40 IDA 3C and 40 IDA 3C 1 carburettors (these likewise being identical except for inverted controls) on appropriate inlet manifolds, and the deletion of the twin mechanical fuel pumps which had become redundant with the use of normal float-chamber carburettors. The performance data of the engine remained unchanged, including the minimum specific fuel consumption of 225 gr/bhp/hour at 3,400 rpm, but the bad flat spot had gone and the engine was consequently much more flexible.

Unlike the Solex, the Weber carburettor had not been developed specially for the 911* and it had its three chokes slightly closer together, requiring the two external pipes of the inlet manifold to be slightly more inclined. A new and neater air filter was also designed to fit the new carburettors.

Lower gearing

Another early modification was the use of a different set of gear ratios for the otherwise unchanged five-speed gearbox, the final drive ratio of 7/31 (providing a step down of 4.428:1) remaining as it was. Every single ratio was lower geared to make better use of the engine's safe revolution limit of 6,800 rpm. Whereas with the

*They were originally designed for the Lancia Flaminia V6.

early box in fifth gear the claimed maximum speed of 210 kph (130.5 mph) was reached at an engine speed of 6,400 rpm, ie 400 rpm below the safety limit though 300 beyond peak power, it was now geared for the engine to run at 6,700 rpm at the same speed. There was now also a lesser gap between second and third gears, but according to the diagrams published by the manufacturers there is only an insignificant difference in through-the-gears acceleration between the two gear sets, though pick-up on any of the gears must obviously be better.

The gearbox with the new gear set was known as the Type 902/1 and was used on all 911s built to European specification after July 1965, ie, for the 1966 model year. Here is a comparison between the ratios of the early 901/0 and the later 902/1 boxes:

	901/0	902/1
1st	12:34	11:34
2nd	18:32	18:34
3rd	23:28	22:29
4th	26:25	25:26
5th	28:23	28:24

Early road test data

As already mentioned, I was able to borrow an early example of a 911 Coupé, still fitted with Solex carburettors and the Type 901/0 gearbox. Being a factory demonstrator, it suffered less than most from the Solex flat spot which I found to be much worse on other examples of the same models I drove. An idea of the performance can be gained from the following figures:

Mean maximum speed	131 mph
0-60 mph	8.5 sec
0-100 mph	22.7 sec
Standing ¼ mile	16.1 sec
Standing kilometre	29.3 sec

Chapter Three

Twenty years of flat-six development

The 911 S engine

After the first urgent problems, such as the unsatisfactory carburation, had been solved, attention turned to developments of the basic 901 engine to widen the choice of models to be offered to the public. But even before that a racing development programme had been started, running parallel with the development of the original production engine. In fact, only seven months after the new production car started rolling off the assembly line, in September 1964, a Porsche 904 experimentally fitted with a racing version of the flat-six earned its first laurels by finishing second in the 1965 Targa Florio.

Apart from the modifications usually made to production engines to increase the specific power, the racing engine Type 901/20, which we shall discuss in more detail at a later stage, mainly differed from the Type 901/01 production unit in the use of magnesium alloy instead of aluminium for most of its castings, except for the cylinder heads and cam boxes (in which the camshafts ran directly). The connecting rods were made of titanium and the engine also had twin ignition. The same type of Weber carburettors as were later to be used in production were fitted. It developed 210 bhp at 8,000 rpm.

Pressurized camshaft chain tensioner, as used in all 911 engines from 1984 models on.

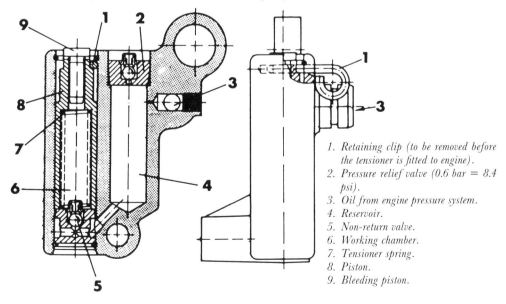

1. Retaining clip (to be removed before the tensioner is fitted to engine).
2. Pressure relief valve (0.6 bar = 8.4 psi).
3. Oil from engine pressure system.
4. Reservoir.
5. Non-return valve.
6. Working chamber.
7. Tensioner spring.
8. Piston.
9. Bleeding piston.

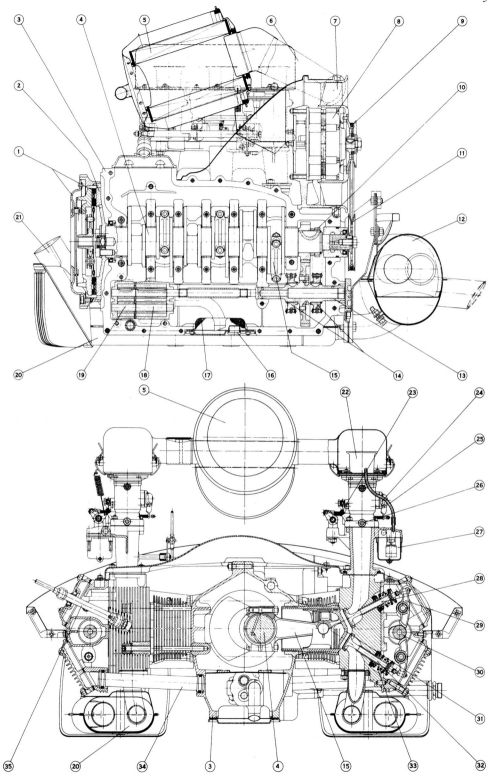

As this racing engine proved itself to be very reliable during the course of the 1965 season, the factory obviously had the know-how to increase the rather conservative power output of the production engine without impairing its reliability, and this is what was done to produce the Porsche 911 S, publicly announced on July 25 1966.

Compared with the 901/05 engine used at the time in the 911 (the type number was changed from 901 to 911 before the first production cars were delivered), the Type 901/02 engine fitted to the 911 S differed in the following main points:

The compression ratio was raised from 9:1 to 9.8:1, by using a higher piston crown.

Different camshafts were used, considerably increasing the valve overlap.

The diameter of the valves and ports was increased.

Slightly modified Weber carburettors, type 40 IDS (rather than 40 IDA) were used.

The ducting of the exhaust system inside the heat exchanger for the body heating system was modified, providing a gain of nearly 10 hp.

These modifications raised the engine's output from 130 (DIN) bhp at 6,100 rpm to 160 (DIN) bhp at 6,600 rpm, the safe limit going up from 6,800 to 7,300 rpm. Simultaneously the maximum torque went up from 17.8 mkg (128.8 lb/ft) at 4,200 rpm to 18.2 mkg (131.7 lb/ft) at 5,200 rpm. The minimum specific fuel consumption was unchanged at 225 gr/bhp/hour, but strangely was obtained as low as 2,000 rpm, rather than at 3,400 rpm.

To maintain the engine's reliability, in spite of the higher stresses imposed by the higher mean effective pressure and the increased revving ability, the following modifications were made:

The pistons were light alloy forgings rather than castings.

The connecting rods, identical in shape, were soft nitrided.

The little end bushes were turned from solid copper alloy instead of being rolled bronze.

Apart from the better exhaust manifolding, the main power increase obviously came from the much increased volumetric efficiency derived from the larger valves and considerably increased valve overlap.

	901/01 & /05 (911)	901/02 (911 S)
Valve diameter (inlet/exhaust)	39/35 mm	42/38 mm
Valve lift (inlet/exhaust)	11.55/10.57 mm	11.6/10.3 mm
Inlet opens/closes	52°btdc/62°abdc	64°btdc/76°abdc
Exhaust opens/closes	64°bbdc/44°atdc	64°bbdc/44°atdc

(All data with 0.1 mm valve clearance.)

1964: The original Type 901/01 engine. 1 — Clutch disc, 2 — Flywheel, 3 — Crankcase, 4 — Crankshaft, 5 — Air filter, 6 — Air intake pipe, 7 — Cooling blower wheel, 8 — Generator, 9 — V-belt, 10 — Distributor drive pinion, 11 — Belt pulley, 12 — Exhaust silencer, 13 — Intermediate shaft, 14 — Toothed wheel for camshaft driving chain, 15 — Connecting rod, 16 — Oil drain plug, 17 — Oil intake filter, 18 — Oil scavenging pump, 19 — Oil pressure pump, 20 — Heat exchanger, 21 — Hot air exit, 22 — Intake trumpet, 23 — Idle adjusting screw, 24 — Acceleration pump, 25 — Air passage to float chamber, 26 — Throttle valve shaft, 27 — Float chamber, 28 — Intake valve, 29 — Rocker, 30 — Camshaft, 31 — Piston, 32 — Exhaust valve, 33 — Valve spring, 34 — Oil cooler, 35 — Radio interference screening cap.

The transmission of the 911 S was exactly the same as for the contemporary 911, except for a slightly higher geared fifth gear, a wheel set of 29:23 being standard, compared with 28:24 for the 911.

With a claimed maximum speed of 225 kph (139.8 mph) reached at an engine speed of 6,700 rpm, the 911 S was some 15 kph (just over 9 mph) faster than the 911, but it is interesting to note that in his speech introducing the 911 S to the press, development engineer Bott mentioned that part of the gain in maximum speed was due to the increased tyre pressures recommended. These were 25 psi front and 28 psi rear for the 911, and were increased to 31 and 34 psi, respectively, for the 911 S. It appears that at the car's maximum speed, the reduction in rolling resistance amounts to a saving of more than 9 hp — at the obvious cost of some comfort.

Contemporary instruction books mention a weight (with full fuel tank) of 1,030 kg (about 2,271 lb) for the 911 S, compared with 1,080 kg (about 2,381 lb) for the normal 911, but there seems to be very little reason why the 'S' model should have been so much lighter and the weight quoted rather looks like an attempt to convince the authorities governing motoring sport to homologate the car at the lower weight. Anyway, in his speech of introduction, Ing Bott mentions a weight of '1,030 to 1,100 kg according to the equipment' and quotes the following comparative acceleration figures 'for cars of equal laden weight':

	911	**911 S**
0-100 kph (62.5 mph)	8.6 sec	7.4 sec
0-150 kph (93 mph)	18.2 sec	15.8 sec
0-200 kph (125 mph)	47.6 sec	34.4 sec

Some of the lessons learned in the course of the development of the Type 901/02 engine for the 911 S were, of course, applicable to the normal 911 unit. A good example is the heat exchanger boxes in which the exhaust gases heat up the air directed into the cockpit for heating the body interior. There was no reason why the more efficient design evolved for the new model should not be used on the normal 911 ... except that the power would have gone up from 130 to 140 bhp and the edge of the 911 S over the cheaper model would have been too small. Consequently, the new heat exchangers were not used for the normal 911 until November 1966, when new camshafts providing considerably less valve overlap were introduced simultaneously, in order to restrict the power to its former value. The modified engine bore the type number 901/06 and its valve timing compares as follows with the 901/01 and 901/05 engines previously fitted:

	901/01 & /05	**901/06**
Inlet opens/closes	52°btdc/62°abdc	43°btdc/57°abdc
Exhaust opens/closes	64°bbdc/44°atdc	65°bbdc/31°atdc

In conjunction with the new heat exchangers, these new camshafts left the engine's key performance data (power, torque and specific consumption) unaltered.

The 911 T engine

Some time after the original 911 had been introduced, the 356 series was discontinued and replaced by the 912, introduced in April 1965. Except for some simplified equipment, the 912 was virtually a 911 in which the six-cylinder engine was replaced by the 1600 cc pushrod flat-four of the top 356 model, the 356 SC, developing 90 (DIN) bhp with the 911 exhaust system. Thanks to its lesser overhung weight at the rear, it handled rather better than a 911, but it was notably more expensive than the 356 series and, considering the price, the performance was anything but overwhelming. It is thus not surprising that just over two years after the 912's introduction, the flat-four of still very obvious VW ancestry finally disappeared, its place being taken by a detuned version of the flat-six.

The reason for using a less powerful variant of the Type 901 engine for what was to be the cheapest car of the range, to be called the 911 T (T for Touring), was not only a marketing one for, by detuning the engine, it could also be produced cheaper. The thermal stresses being less, the aluminium-finned 'Biral' cylinders could be replaced by plain cast iron cylinders, while less power and a lower rotating speed meant reduced loads on the bearings. Consequently a different and cheaper crankshaft could be used with no counterweights to reduce the loads on the main bearings. It is generally known that counterweights are not necessary to obtain perfect balance in a six-cylinder engine, but they can be used to relieve stress in the main bearings. At the maximum permissible rotating speed of 6,500 rpm, the forces acting upon the main bearings did not require the use of balance weights to ensure longevity, and they could thus be deleted. But the resultant higher stresses on the crankcase itself made the engine noisier than it would have been with the fully counterbalanced crankshaft of the other models. The deletion of the counterweights saved about 6 kg (13.5 lb) on the crankshaft weight. Another cost-saving change was the replacement of the steel rockers by similar ones made of cast iron. They were so satisfactory that they were adopted for all production engines the following year.

The expensive Weber carburettors were still used, however, and — at first sight very strangely — the cylinder heads were identical with those of the 911 S, featuring larger ports and valves than the normal 911 head. The reason for this was that, in contradiction with the official factory handbooks, the less luxuriously equipped 911 T was the lighter car of the three and it was the factory's intention to use this model for competition tuning. The power was restricted mainly by the use of a lower compression ratio of 8.6:1 (compared with 9.0:1 for the 911 and 9.8:1 for the 911 S) and camshafts providing a 'softer' valve timing:

Inlet opens/closes	40°btdc/56°abdc
Exhaust opens/closes	66°bbdc/22°atdc

This gave a maximum power of 110 (DIN) bhp at 5,800 rpm with a maximum torque of 16.0 mkg (116 lb/ft) at 4,200 rpm — strangely enough at the same engine speed as for the 911 — but the specific fuel consumption was noticeably lower at 210 gr/bhp/h between 3,000 and 3,500 rpm. The 'T' engine, internally known as 901/03, had a much flatter torque curve than the contemporary 901/05 engine of the normal 911 and would easily pull in high gear from as low as 1,200-1,300 rpm, its torque at 2,000 rpm being some 10 per cent higher. Consequently some cost could also be saved on the gearbox by providing only four ratios rather than five, though the five-speed transmission was optional and was probably fitted to the vast majority of 911 Ts built.

Of the three basic Type 901 engines built in 1967, ie , 901/03 for the T, 901/05 for the normal 911 and 901/02 for the S, new variants were put into production in July 1967 for the 'A' series of cars when the semi-automatic 'Sportomatic' transmission was announced. They were, respectively, 901/13 for the T, 901/07 for the normal 911 (now called the 911 L), and 901/08 for the S. They differed from the basic engines only by having some attachment lugs required by the Sportomatic transmission. At the same time two special versions of the 911 L engines were marketed specially for the USA, in order to meet the emission requirements. They differed from the European engines mainly by the addition of a V-belt-driven air pump blowing into the exhaust manifolds when the throttle was closed. These engines were known as 901/14 with manual transmission and 901/17 if fitted with the attaching lugs for the Sportomatic transmission.

The first major development of the engine came in July 1968, when the 1969 (B-series) models were put into production. Since 1966, racing versions of the Type 901 engine had been using a sequential fuel injection system in which the Bosch six-plunger injection pump was driven by a diminutive toothed belt off one of the camshafts and the injectors were located in the inlet ports. This increased the engine's power from 210 to 220 bhp and it was decided similarly to equip the two top versions of the production engine.

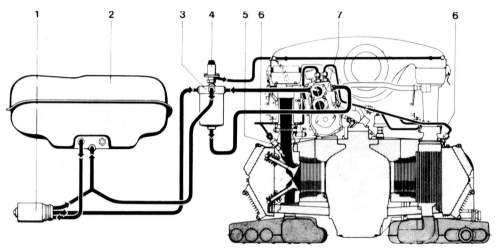

Principle of the Bosch-Porsche plunger pump fuel injection system introduced on E and S, B-series models and still used on racing engines. 1 — Fuel feed pump, 2 — Fuel tank, 3 — Microfilter, 4 — Solenoid pump for cold starting, 5 — Injector, 6 — Injection pipes, 7 — Injection pump.

Basically, the layout was very similar to the one used for racing in 1968, when the injection pump incorporated an engine speed sensitive 'space cam', making the quantity of fuel injected sensitive to both throttle opening and engine speed, providing very much better fuel economy than when the quantity of fuel injected was governed only by the throttle opening. As usual with plunger pumps, the quantity of fuel injected was regulated by a rack turning the grooved plungers as they moved up and down towards fixed ports or away from them. This rack was moved not only by the space cam controlled by both the engine-sensitive centrifugal governor and the accelerator, but also by a barometric corrector, a thermostat enriching the mixture as long as the engine was not thoroughly warm, a starting solenoid slightly enriching the mixture as long as the engine had not reached its normal working temperature, and a stop solenoid cutting off all fuel feed as long as the engine ran at higher than idling speed with the accelerator released.

From the plunger pump, belt driven off the front end of the left-hand camshaft, the fuel was directed by six equal length pressure pipes to the injectors screwed into

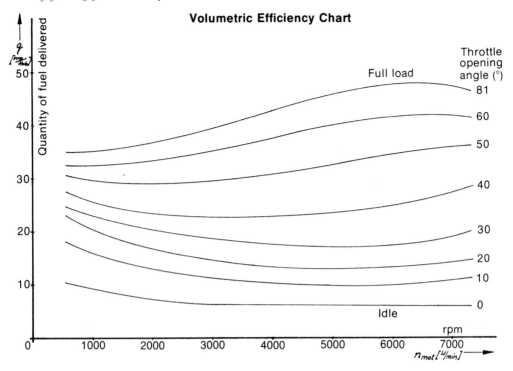

Fuel delivered by space cam injection pump in 2 litre 911 S engine, in function of throttle opening and engine speed. Fuel delivery scale indicates the plunger stroke in millimetres.

the cylinder heads and spraying the fuel into the inlet ports. Their opening pressure lay between 15 and 18 bar (approx 215-250 psi).

Other changes which the switch from carburettors to injection involved were the replacement of the Bendix pulsating fuel pump with a continuous-flow rotating pump of the roller cell type, also electrically operated, and the incorporation of a very fine fuel filter in the line between the fuel feed pump and the injection pump in order to protect the injection pump from any impurities. The new type of fuel pump was also used on the 911 T, which retained its carburettors. The higher current requirement of this pump and the newly introduced heated rear window led to the use of an alternator giving a higher output: 770 W instead of 490 W.

Valve sizes and timing remained unaltered for the S model, but for the E model which took the place of the 911 L as the middle-of-the-range car, a reversion was made to the original valve timing used in the Types 901/01 and 05 engines, while the compression ratio was marginally raised from 9.0:1 to 9.1:1. The net result was a gain of 10 hp for both the E and the S engines, in both cases obtained at a slightly higher engine speed. The official figures were now 140 (DIN) bhp (instead of 130 (DIN) bhp) at 6,600 rpm (6,100 rpm) for the E and 170 (DIN) bhp (160 (DIN) bhp) at 6,800 rpm (6,600 rpm) for the S engine. The increase in torque was nil, however, in the case of the E engine (17.8 mkg=129 lb/ft) and was reached at a slightly higher engine speed (4,500 rpm instead of 4,200 rpm), and it was insignificant in the S engine where it rose from 18.2 to 18.5 mkg (134 lb/ft) at 5,500 rpm instead of 5,200. Though the engines would not pull more vigorously in the low and medium speed ranges, one advantage was that they would pull smoothly from lower speeds than before, making them nicer to drive in heavy traffic.

The injection engine also had a higher minimum specific fuel consumption, but in this case the figures are misleading for with the carburettors the curve tended to rise steeply as the engine speed increased, whereas they were remarkably flat for the injection engines. For example, in the E engine, the specific consumption rose from 240 to 260 gr/bhp/h as the engine speed rose from 4,500 to 6,500 rpm — the most important range for this car — while it rose from 239 to 275 gr/bhp/h in the older carburettor engine. In the case of the S, where the most important range lay between 5,000 and 7,000 rpm, the specific consumption rose from 238 to 262 gr/bhp/h instead of from 250 to 280 gr/bhp/h in the carburettor engine. This is a very considerable gain indeed which had its influence on the actual road consumption.

Another advance was made in the ignition sector, where the conventional battery ignition was replaced by a capacity discharge system, still keeping the conventional contact breaker, but providing a higher voltage spark which eliminated occasional plug fouling experienced if the car was run in heavy traffic for long periods. Thanks to the lesser current carried by the contact breaker, service intervals to the latter could be increased.

In view of the very high specific output now reached by the S engine (85 bhp per litre), an additional oil cooler was fitted, supplementing the cooler bolted to the crankcase inside the cowling which ducted air from the cooling blower on to the cylinders and heads. The supplementary cooler was located in the right-hand front wing, just ahead of the wheel, the cooling air being admitted through the small grille next to the direction indicators, which previously only served to provide better cooling for the brakes. This supplementary oil cooler was included in the scavenging circuit and the oil flow through it was governed by a thermostatic valve opening only when the oil reached a temperature of 70-80°C. If the oil temperature was lower, the lubricant was returned straight to the oil tank, by-passing the radiator.

With the switch to fuel injection, another change was made which did not in any way affect the engine performance, and also applied to the otherwise unaltered carburettor engine of the 911 T: the two-piece crankcase was pressure-cast in magnesium alloy instead of being die-cast in aluminium alloy, which saved approximately 10 kg (22 lb) of very important overhung weight. With the introduction of the 1969 models, internally known as the B-series, the wheelbase was increased by 57 mm (approx 2.3 in) by moving the rear wheels back and reducing the rear overhang by the same amount. The car's handling was dramatically improved, especially with the 6 inch wide rims and 70 series tyres fitted for the first time to E and S models.

In the 911 T, the introduction of the magnesium crankcase and of twin valve springs, mainly as a safety measure, was made without changing the engine's type number, which remained 901/03, but new numbers were logically used for the fuel injection engines: 901/09 for the E and 901/11 for the equivalent Sportomatic version, and 901/10 for the S on which the semi-automatic transmission was not available any more. The reason for this was officially that the torque characteristics of the engine were not suitable for a torque converter transmission, but the main reason was probably that there was very little demand for this transmission on the S, those people buying this fastest of Porsches scorning the Sportomatic. There were no special USA versions of the injection engines, which met the Federal and Californian emission standards of the period.

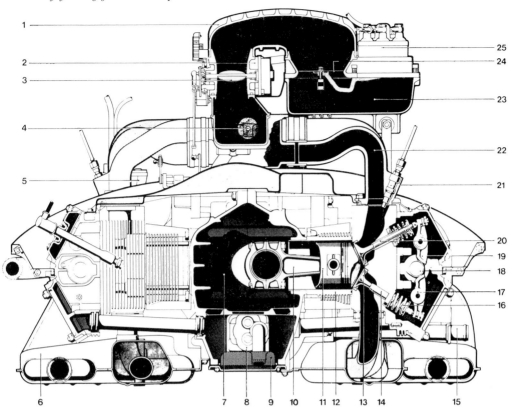

Cross section of 2.7 litre engine with K-Jetronic fuel injection (at the beginning of 1974). 1 — Cover, 2 — Throttle valve control unit, 3 — Throttle valve, 4 — Starting valve, 5 — Temperature sensitive mixture corrector, 6 — Heat exchanger, 7 — Crankshaft, 8 — Oil pump, 9 — Oil intake filter, 10 — Connecting rod, 11 — Piston, 12 — Cylinder, 13 — Exhaust valve, 14 — Valve guide, 15 — Oil connection (from oil tank to oil pump), 16 — Valve spring, 17 — Rocker shaft, 18 — Camshaft, 19 — Rocker, 20 — Intake valve, 21 — Injector, 22 — Intake pipe, 23 — Intake chamber, 24 — Air metering disc, 25 — Mixture control unit.

The 2.2 litre models

In contrast with the normal Porsche policy of leaving the basic data of any new series unchanged for at least two years, refraining from advertising any minor improvement made during the production run, the fuel injection 2 litre engine had a life span of only one year, being replaced in August 1969 by a new version in which the cylinder bores were increased from 80 to 84 mm, raising the capacity from 1,991 to 2,195 cc. This capacity increase also applied to the T engine, which had remained practically unchanged since the introduction of the model, except for the switch from aluminium to magnesium as a crankcase material. It is probably because magnesium is not as good as aluminium as a bearing material that a bush was added to the front end of the auxiliaries shaft which had previously run directly in the crankcase. This shaft, gear-driven from the crankshaft at half its speed, carries the two sprockets driving the camshafts by chains, and also drives the oil pumps from its forward end.

Cylinder heads and valve sizes were now unified and enlarged for all models, the valve diameter being 46 mm for the inlet and 40 mm for the exhaust, and another small change in the cylinder heads was that the plug thread was now cut directly in the aluminium instead of being a 'Helicoil' insert. The cold start solenoid was deleted from the injection pump, the thermostatic control having proved to be sufficient.

Apart from the increase in capacity and the use of larger valves, the most important change made to all three engine versions was the replacement of the 215 mm diameter Fichtel & Sachs clutch by a larger one of the same make having a diameter of 225 mm, in order to take care of the higher torque of the larger engines. In this context, it must never be forgotten that whatever change they make to their production models, Porsche always keep in mind what will be required from major components when the car is tuned for rallying or racing, and from this point of view the capacity increase over the 2 litre class limit offered prospects of considerable increases in power and torque, as the sporting rules would now allow the engine to be stretched up to the upper limit of the 2,001 to 2,500 cc class. The construction of the clutch was different, too, the pressure plate now being driven from the outer case by flexible steel straps rather than lugs, while the diaphragm spring was inverted to obtain a better leverage. More details on these modifications will be found in the chapter on transmission developments.

No other changes worthy of note were made to the S engine, but a new type of triple-choke Zenith carburettor was introduced for the T as a production alternative to the more expensive Weber instruments which soon disappeared, while the use of the capacity discharge ignition system was extended to this engine.

With the bigger valves now used in the E engine, another change of camshafts was made, the one originally fitted to the Type 901/06 engine, providing a lesser overlap, coming into use again. It aimed at providing more flexibility, the 911 E being the more flexible and less fuel-consuming alternative to the 911 S at a sacrifice of only 10 kph (6 mph) in top speed, the maker's figures being 220 and 230 kph (137 and 143 mph), respectively. The speed claimed for the S was confirmed by my own road-test timing, giving a mean speed of 231 kph (143.6 mph).

All cars fitted with the five-speed gearbox had the same transmission ratios, whatever the engine variant used, with a top gear very slightly higher than with the former 2 litre engine (fifth speed gears being 29:22 instead of 29:23), but in view of the better torque of the 2.2 litre engines, the intermediate gears were more noticeably higher.

There was no change in the compression ratio of any of the engines, but the capacity increase raised the power and torque figures as follows:

911 T — 2.2 litre (2 litre figures in brackets)

Max power: 125 (DIN) bhp at 5,800 rpm (110 at 5,800 rpm)
Max torque: 18 mkg or 130.4 lb/ft at 4,200 rpm (16 mkg or 116 lb/ft at 4,200 rpm)

911 E — 2.2 litre

Max power: 155 (DIN) bhp at 6,200 rpm (140 at 6,500 rpm)
Max torque: 19.5 mkg or 141.3 lb/ft at 4,500 rpm (17.8 mkg or 130 lb/ft at 4,500 rpm)

911 S — 2.2 litre

Max power: 180 (DIN) bhp at 6,500 rpm (170 at 6,800 rpm)
Max torque: 20.3 mkg or 147.1 lb/ft at 5,200 rpm (18.5 mkg or 134 lb/ft at 5,500 rpm)

The biggest advance was thus made by the bottom of the range engine, which gained 13.6 per cent in power and 12.5 per cent in torque from the capacity increase and other minor changes. But this was to the detriment of the specific fuel consumption which became some 4 per cent higher over most of the range. For the 911 S the specific consumption was practically unaltered compared with the fuel injection 2 litre engine, and in the case of the 911 E it dropped by some 10 per cent up to 5,000 rpm, above which the curve rises more sharply than before, but it still does not quite catch up with the curve for the 2 litre engine at 6,200 rpm which approximately corresponds to both cars' maximum speed. This is, no doubt, a benefit gained from the softer valve timing used, compared with the preceding 2 litre model.

From the 2.2 litre engines on, the engine type number prefix was changed from 901 to 911, type numbers being as follows:

For the 911 T
911/03 2.2 litre basic engine
911/06 2.2 litre with Sportomatic attachments
911/07 2.2 litre US version with air pump
911/08 2.2 litre US version with Sportomatic attachments

For the 911 E
911/01 2.2 litre basic engine
911/04 2.2 litre with Sportomatic attachments

For the 911 S

911/02 2.2 litre basic engine

Again, no special US versions of the E and S engines were required, and Sportomatic was not available on the S.

The capacity increase from 2 litres to 2.2 litres was the first step towards more flexible and quieter Porsches, though apparently the designers were not yet prepared to sacrifice performance for flexibility and other virtues. In fact, performance had been increased by a handsome margin, the 911 S I tested being able to reach 143.6 mph, as stated before, and to cover a kilometre from a standing start in 27 seconds dead, only 6.7 seconds being required to reach 60 mph from rest. What additional torque had been obtained was only a consequence of the increased capacity, and above-average performance could only be achieved by keeping the engine revving in the higher part of its range by means of continuous gear changing. With the 911 S this meant keeping the engine speed above 5,500 rpm, when the power came surging in: it meant a lot of work and also a lot of noise.

The 2.4 litre engine

As the current sporting regulations allowed the 2.2 litre engine to be increased in capacity up to the limit of 2,500 cc, providing this did not involve a change in the stroke dimension, competition versions of the 2.2 litre engine were soon fitted with 85 mm, then 87.5 mm bore cylinders, still with room to spare between the cylinders for cooling and spigoting the liners to the crankcase. It will be remembered that the original Type 901 engine had been designed deliberately with some room to spare for eventual capacity increases and this proved very valuable. By now a full development programme was in hand for the 911 engine with the object of bringing its capacity progressively up to at least 2.7 litres.

Parallel to this development scheme for the near future, there was a longer-term plan, suggested by the then Technical Director Ferdinand Piëch, to widen the range of engines offered to include 4, 6 and 8 cylinder versions, all based on the very successful Type 908, 3 litre, twin-cam, flat-8 racing engine which had been designed deliberately to be simple and easily adapted to production requirements. A development programme on those lines had already been started when it was recognised that emission standards were becoming stricter everywhere and that highly tuned, high revving engines had little chance of meeting them. Instead, work was started on an entirely new, larger capacity, single cam per bank V8 destined to power a completely new front-engined car, but this was a long-term project which became even longer in term as the general economic crisis reared its ugly head in 1974-75 and the development of the 911 was actively pursued.

With the prospect of tougher exhaust emission laws, especially in the United States of America, the decision was taken slightly to detune the engines, though at no cost in performance, which could only be obtained by further increasing their capacity. If the larger capacity was obtained by further increasing the bore, as had been done in racing versions of the engine, the combustion chamber became excessively flat and further capacity increases in the future became problematical, especially for production engines, as the 87.5 mm bore used for racing was the maximum that could be accommodated when the usual Biral cylinders were used. It had been found, however, that with only small alterations to the crankcase a longer-throw crankshaft could be accommodated, so the stroke was lengthened from 66 mm to 70.4 mm, exactly as had been done to increase the capacity of the Type 917 racing flat-12 from 4.5 to 4.9 litres. The connecting rods were shortened from their original length of 130 mm to 127.8 mm, the other dimensions remaining unaltered.

In fact, racing experience was put to good use, the connecting rod design and dimensions being virtually identical with those of the 917 engine, except that steel was used for the production engine, rather than lighter, but much more expensive titanium. In the case of the 911 S model, a change was made to the treatment of the connecting rods which, instead of being soft nitrided, were now treated by the Tenifer process. Untreated rods were used, as before, in the other model. The new, longer-throw crankshaft, which raised the engine capacity to 2,341 cc, was the same for all models and was fully counterbalanced, there being no difference between the T crankshaft and that used in the engines of higher rating, as had been the case before. From this the T derived a noticeable gain in quietness.

Additional piston cooling was obtained by the provision of six jets fed from the main oil gallery and spraying oil into the pistons. The supply to the jets was controlled by a valve which opened when the pressure in the gallery exceeded a pre-set figure (3-4 bar). There was thus no supply at low engine speeds.

But the boldest move was certainly radically to lower the compression ratio of all engines. The main reasons for this were to reduce the nitrogen oxide emissions and to reduce the octane requirement of the engines in view of the proposed reduction of the lead content of European fuels. The ratio was reduced from 8.6:1 to 7.5:1 for the T engine, from 9.1:1 to 8.0:1 for the E engine and from 9.8:1 to 8.5:1 for the S engine, so that in most European countries all models ran perfectly happily on regular grade fuel — in the first months following the introduction of the new models, much to the amazement of filling station attendants! Officially, the Research Method octane requirement was lowered from 96 for the T and 98 for the E and S models to 91 for all versions.

Valve sizes remained unchanged from 2.2 litre models, ie, 46 mm on the inlet side and 40 mm on the exhaust side but, thanks to the capacity increase and careful attention to the ports, the power output was increased by 5 bhp in the case of the T engine and 10 bhp in the case of the E and S engines, in spite of the lowered compression ratio, with corresponding improvements in torque, the figures now being as follows:

	911 T (Engine 911/57 & /67 Sportom)	**911 E** (Engine 911/52 & /62 Sportom)	**911 S** (Engine 911/53 & /63 Sportom)
Max power (DIN) bhp	130 at 5,600	165 at 6,200	190 at 6,500
Max torque	20 mkg =145 lb/ft at 4,000 rpm	21 mkg =152 lb/ft at 4,500 rpm	22 mkg =159.5 lb/ft at 5,200 rpm

It will be noted that the torque increase is largest (approx 11 per cent) in the case of the T, where the increase in power is smallest, but that in all cases the better torque was much more noticeable in the middle and higher engine speed ranges than in the lower ranges. On the road, though, no Porsche owner is likely to let the revs drop below 3,500-4,000 rpm and the cars — especially the T and the E — felt very much more flexible than before. It is significant that all models of what was internally known as the E series, introduced in August 1971 as the 1972 model range, had a four-speed gearbox as basic equipment, the five-speed box being an option, though it was specified on the vast majority of the cars delivered.

Both boxes were entirely new in view of the higher torque of the engines, to take care of the high loads imposed by ever more powerful racing versions, but both the 7:31 crown wheel and pinion and the 29:22 fifth gear ratio were unaltered from the 2.2 models, so that the full increase in torque was available for top gear acceleration. Moreover, all the lower ratios were slightly *lower* geared, so that the performance, particularly in third and fourth gears, was vastly improved, and noticeably less gear changing was required than before. For the first time, too, top gear ratio was slightly lower (28:23) in the four-speed box than in the five-speed box. In view of the increased torque, a heavier diaphragm clutch spring was used in all versions.

In the T engine, the specific consumption was increased over the entire range, which is what you would expect from lowering the compression ratio by more than one unit, but strangely no such ill-effects are noted in the case of the E and S engines: in the case of the E the consumption is more or less unaltered up to 5,000 rpm and rises much less sharply as the engine speed is increased, while the S consumption curve remains well below that of the 2.2 model right up to 6,500 rpm and does not exceed it even at the governed maximum safe engine speed of 7,300 rpm.

While the timing of the previous S engines was retained for the 2.4 litre version, there were slight alterations to the timing of the T and E engines, their camshafts remaining unchanged:

	T 2.4 litres	**T previous models**
Inlet opens/closes	41°btdc/55°abdc	40°btdc/56°abdc
Exhaust opens/closes	67°bbdc/21°atdc	66°bbdc/22°atdc

	E 2.4 litres	**E 2.2 litres**
Inlet opens/closes	41°btdc/59°abdc	43°btdc/57°abdc
Exhaust opens/closes	63°bbdc/33°atdc	65°bbdc/31°atdc

A small additional modification concerning the S engine was the replacement of the oil radiator, located in the right-hand front wing, by a simpler serpentine, similarly located. This was no doubt less efficient than the former proper radiator, but provided the required temperature drop at lesser cost and was also less vulnerable.

No increase in top speed was claimed for the 2.4 litre models, compared with the corresponding 2.2 litre versions. The main accent was put on the increased tractability and the gain in performance was, in fact, marginal, though the performance, especially of the E and S types, was superb by any standards. I timed a 2.4 litre 911 S electrically at a mean speed of 232 kph (144.2 mph) and at 26.9 seconds over the standing start kilometre — 1 kph and 1/10 second quicker, respectively, than the 2.2 litre. Twelve years later, a 3.2 litre Carrera was only 1 second quicker over the standing kilometre.

There was no special US version of the 2.4 litre E and S engines, despite increasingly stricter emission laws, except that close tolerance injection pumps were selected for US cars. The T engine fitted with twin triple-choke Zenith 40 TIN carburettors

Schematic drawing of K-Jetronic fuel injection system. 1 — Metering unit, 2 — Air flow measuring disc, 3 — Throttle, 4 — Idle adjusting screw, 5 — Mixture adjusting screw, 6 — Fuel tank, 7 — Fuel pump, 8 — Pressure accumulator, 9 — Micronic filter, 10 — Distributor, 11 — Metering piston, 12 — Metering port, 13 — Pressure equalising valve, 14 — Injector, 15 — Pressure regulating valve, 16 — Derivation throttle, 17 — Damping throttle, 18 — Throttle operated valve, 19 — Warm-running regulator, 20 — Cold starting valve, 21 — Micro-switch.

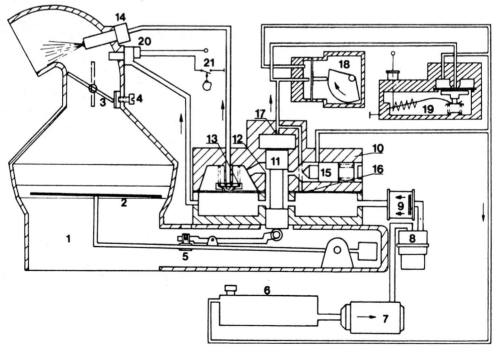

Above *The Type 7 prototype of which presumably four were built, all slightly different from each other, was the forerunner of the 911. It was almost a four-seater on a 2.40 m (94.5 in) wheelbase. The front end is near identical with the 911's, as is the front suspension, but the rear suspension is 356. This example was provisionally powered with a 'Carrera 2' four-cylinder engine, back in the car today, but this car served as a rolling test bed for a 2 litre pushrod flat-six which never went into production.* **Below** *The original 901. Before the first cars were delivered, the type number was changed to 911, the fuel filler trap door was reshaped and a rubbing strip was added on the door sills.*

Above *The very first 901, as it was still known, with those responsible for its creation. Nearest the car are Dr F. Porsche, with (left to right) Ing F. Tomala, Director of Engineering, F. Piëch, Chief of engine development, and Butzi Porsche, styling.*

Below *One of the first production 911s.*

Above left *Dr Ferry Porsche, who set the ball rolling and is today the Chairman of the company, in a characteristically informal pose.* **Above right** *Dr Ferry Porsche with an early 911 in 1965.* **Below** *Paul Frère, having just test driven a Group 4 Carrera RSR on the Weissach track in November 1973, discusses the car with (left to right) Dipl Ing H. Bott, Chief of Porsche Development, Manfred Jantke, Public Relations and Sports Manager, and Dipl Ing Norbert Singer, responsible for the Carrera RSR development.*

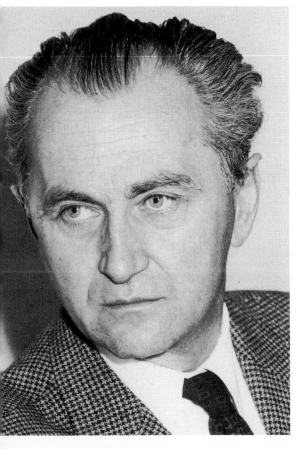

Left *Dr Ernst Fuhrmann, Porsche's Managing and Technical Director from 1972 to 1980.* **Above** *Engine Type 901/01, as fitted to early 911 models.* **Below** *The 911 S was announced on July 26 1966. Its forged alloy wheels were a prominent feature.* **Right** *Early 911 S engine as fitted to O- and A-series. Carburettor engines up to 2.4 litre remained almost indistinguishable from this.* **Below right** *Early 911 models had a die-cast aluminium crankcase, replaced in 1969 by a 10 kg lighter magnesium crankcase (top). With the advent of 3 litre engines, aluminium had to be used again to improve rigidity and fatigue strength (bottom). From 1983 models on, the large inspection opening in the sump was deleted.* **Below far right** *The camshaft driving chain tensioners were one of the 911's Achilles' heels. The photo shows an early, self-contained model in which the spring acting on the jockey pulley is damped hydraulically by oil contained in the cylinder. From 1983 models on, the cylinder containing the spring is pressurized from the engine pressure system, which solved all problems.*

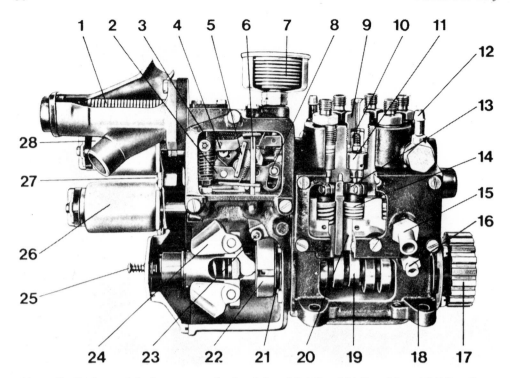

Above *Bosch plunger-injection pump as fitted to 2.2 and 2.4 litre 911 E and S and 2.7 litre Carrera engines. The injection plungers are operated by the pump camshaft. Adjustment of the quantity of fuel injected is governed by rotating the plungers which have a ramp matching with a fuel return port. The earlier the port is uncovered, the smaller the pump output. Rotation of the plungers is obtained by a rack matching with toothed segments carried by the plungers. The position of the rack is controlled by that of the accelerator, the space cam controlled by the engine speed sensitive centrifugal regulator, by the barometric corrector and by the thermostat sensing the engine oil temperature. The stop solenoid interrupts the fuel feed altogether whenever the accelerator is fully released, except at idling speeds. It is operated by a micro-switch and an engine speed sensitive switch. The 2 litre models had an additional cold starting solenoid. 1 — Thermostat, 2 — Correction lever, 3 — Connecting muff, 4 — Rocker, 5 — Pushrod, 6 — Guiding stud, 7 — Barometric corrector, 8 — Guiding ramp, 9 — Connection for injection pipe, 10 — One-way valve, 11 — Plunger, 12 — Fuel inlet, 13 — Toothed segment, 14 — Plunger spring, 15 — Engine oil outlet, 16 — Engine oil inlet, 17 — Cog-belt driven wheel, 18 — Mounting flange, 19 — Camshaft, 20 — Roller tappet, 21 — Pressuring spring for space cam, 22 — Space cam, 23 — Feeler roller, 24 — Bobweight for centrifugal regulator, 25 — Idling fuel control, 26 — Stop solenoid, 27 — Access to control rack adjustment.*

would not meet the latest American emission standards, however, and a special US version was produced, using the same type of six-plunger injection pump as the E and S models. Otherwise identical with the carburettor version of the T unit, it had a 10 hp higher maximum power than the European version, the power being 140 (DIN) bhp at the same 5,600 rpm engine speed as for the carburettor version. The torque figures were unaltered. These US engines were given the type numbers 911/51 in the normal version and 911/61 in the Sportomatic version.

In contrast with the 2.4 litre E and S engines which were made for two years, these engines had a production run of only 16 months. As from January 1973 they were replaced by a different version to comply with the tighter American emission stan-

Above *Front view of fuel injection 2 litre engine, as fitted to B-series E and S models. Nearest the camera are the outlets from the heat exchangers for interior heating.* **Below** *Porsche 911 engines are extremely well protected from dust and sand and keep remarkably clean. This is a 2.7 litre K-Jetronic engine fitted to a 911 owned by the author at the time.*

Above *Type 930/50 3 litre turbocharged engine. The turbocharger is nearest the camera; the pressure limiting valve is on the left. The recirculation valve can be seen linking the compressor's intake and delivery pipes. On top of the engine is the metering unit of the K-Jetronic injection system. Note the stainless steel exhaust system, standard on all Porsches from 1973.*

Below left *Heat exchangers of I-series models. In each of them, the engine exhaust gases enter through the upper three flanges and exit through the three pipes merging into a single tube. Fresh air enters the boxes at the rear end (near the camera) and exits at the front end. The design of the heat exchangers changed several times, but their principle remained unaltered.* **Below centre** *Camshaft and rocker box. All camshaft boxes are machined with four bearings and can take camshafts with either three or four journals, 3.0, 3.2 and 3.3 engines all have four-bearing camshafts.* **Below right** *Carrera 2.7 Nikasil cylinder and forged piston.*

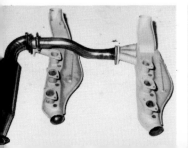

dards introduced that month. Known as the 911/91 (911/96 in Sportomatic version), it was fitted with a completely new Bosch continuous flow injection system, able to meter the fuel supply much more accurately in response to the engine's operating conditions. This system is known, rather misleadingly, as the K-Jetronic, which leads one to believe that its operation is based on electronics. Basically it is a mechanical system, fed under pressure by an electric roller cell pump, with only two additional electric circuits: one operating a valve to enrichen the mixture for a cold start when the hand throttle lever is pulled to its stop, and one to heat a bi-metal blade that progressively weakens the mixture as the engine warms up.

In principle, the system is very simple: the quantity of air aspirated by the engine is measured by a flat disc carried by a partly counterbalanced pivoting lever. The disc can move up and down in a large diameter, conically shaped passage, located upstream of the throttle, through which all the air aspirated by the engine passes. As the flow of air increases, the disc moves with the air stream and since the passage in which it moves is roughly conical, the clearance between the disc and the walls of the passage increases to allow more air to flow through the gap, until a new state of balance is reached. The force opposing movement of the disc is provided by the fuel pressure acting on a piston pushing the lever in the appropriate direction. This piston also acts as a valve metering the fuel flow to the distributor feeding the six individual injectors mounted on the induction pipes. It is easily understood that, as the quantity of air aspirated by the engine increases, the disc moves downstream, progressively opening the fuel metering valve. By correctly shaping the conical passage in which the disc moves, the fuel supply can be matched very accurately to the requirements of the engine. The device incorporates a fuel pressure regulator, but in fact this pressure is not really critical as both the force pushing on the metering lever and the flow of fuel passing through the metering valve are proportional to this pressure. Moreover, no correction for barometric pressure or air intake temperature is required as the ram effect moving the disc is directly proportional to the *weight* of air passing through the chamber containing the disc.

This injection system later became standard for 911 and 911 S models, beginning with the 1974 model year. Apart from its advantage of lower exhaust emissions, it is also cheaper and easier to service than the plunger pump injection system, while the very accurate fuel metering results in a noticeably lower road fuel consumption. It has its limits, however. One is that the metering disc produces a slight throttling of the intake charge, in a similar way to carburettor venturis. Conseqently there is a slight loss in volumetric efficiency, compared with some other systems, including the six-plunger pump system of other Porsches. Another limitation is that it is not really suitable for engines with a large valve overlap, as the blowback of the intake charge at low engine speeds disturbs the flow around the metering disc, creating vibrations and irregular running.

For this special US 2.4 litre K-Jetronic engine a different camshaft was thus used, giving even shorter valve opening periods than before, the timing data being as follows:

Inlet opens/closes	24°btdc/56°abdc
Exhaust opens/closes	54°bbdc/14°atdc

The compression ratio was raised by half a unit to 8.0:1 and the power was unaltered at 140 (DIN) bhp, obtained at 5,700 rpm — 100 rpm more than before.

Thanks to the increased compression ratio, the maximum torque was raised from 20 to 20.5 mkg (148.5 lb/ft) at an unchanged 4,000 rpm.

From 2.4 to 2.7 litres

The 2.4 litre models were built during a two-year period, but an additional model was announced at the beginning of the second year of the production run and given the name Carrera, traditionally used by Porsche to designate a model of particularly high performance. This was a special lightweight version of the 911 S, with slightly widened rear wings to accommodate 7 inch wide rims, a spoiler on the engine compartment lid to reduce aerodynamic lift at high speeds, and an engine of 2,687 cc capacity obtained by increasing the bore from 84 to 90 mm.

The production of this car was prompted by the requirements of competition. Specially prepared 911 S models had been extremely successful in the GT class, both in rallies and races, usually providing the overall winner in the latter, irrespective of engine capacity. But some highly developed Group 2 (so-called Touring) cars were getting embarrassingly fast and some increased competition from larger-engined GT cars was expected, particularly on very fast circuits, where sheer power was more important than agility. The development possibilities of the 911 S were limited by sporting regulations which

a   did not allow the engine to be bored out to a capacity exceeding the limit of the class (2,500 cc in the case of the 2.4 litre);

b   did not allow the car to be lightened beyond the homologated weight of the standard car (995 kg);

c   allowed the wings (fenders) to be extended laterally by only 2 inches on each side to cover wider wheels and tyres which were not to protrude beyond the wings; and

d   did not allow any modification to the body contour above hub level (except for the widened wings), which effectively prevented the use of aerodynamic aids not specified in the standard car.

By producing 500 units of a special version of the 911 S, ie, the minimum number required for homologation in Group 4 (Special Gran Turismo cars), which were lighter, had wider rear wings (providing a wider base from which to further extend them by 2 inches each side), had a rear spoiler to improve high speed rear wheel adhesion and had an engine in the 2,501-3,000 cc class, Porsche considerably opened up the development possibilities of the 911 as a competition car. Despite its spartan equipment to achieve light weight, the Carrera RS, as it was called, was also a commercial success and, instead of the planned small production of 500 units, approximately 1,600 were built. Of these, 1,036 were actually lightweight models (which could be re-trimmed to De Luxe specification by Porsche dealers) so that the model was actually homologated in Group 3 (Production GT cars), while the rest of the production had the normal 911 S trim.

In this chapter we are actually concerned only with the engine Type 911/83 of the Carrera RS which, except for its larger 90 mm bore cylinders and corresponding pistons, was identical in every way with the 911/53 engine used in the 911 S. The cylinders, however, differed not only by their bore, but also in their material. Up to then, all 911 engines, except the T, had always had Biral cylinders, of which the actual liner was cast iron, around which a finned envelope was cast. This results in comparatively thick walls, and as the distance between bores is set by the engine dimensions, it was not possible to provide a 90 mm bore while maintaining the wall thickness resulting from the casting process. But here, once again, racing experience came to the rescue. Since 1971 Porsche's all-conquering Type 917 flat-12 engine used finned aluminium cylinders with bores coated by an electrolytically deposited Nikasil (nickel-silicon carbide) layer used with great success and having excellent frictional properties which had actually created an appreciable increase in the power output. As the Nikasil layer has a thickness of only a few hundredths of a millimetre, the wall thickness was considerably reduced, compared with the Biral cylinders. In fact, at a later stage of development, Nikasil cylinders with a bore of 97 mm were used to bring the engine capacity up to 3.3 litres.

With the same valve timing, port diameter (intake 36 mm, exhaust 35 mm) and valve sizes as the 911 S, and using the same 8.5:1 compression ratio allowing the use of regular grade fuel, the specific output of the Carrera 2.7 litre engine was slightly lower than that of the 911 S though, of course, the total horsepower was increased from 190 to 210 (DIN) bhp at 6,300 rpm (instead of 6,500 rpm for the 911 S). But though the power increase was only 10.5 per cent, the increase in torque from 22 mkg at 5,200 rpm to 26 mkg (188.4 lb/ft) at 5,100 rpm amounted to more than 18 per cent and made the use of a heavier diaphragm clutch spring necessary. The higher torque was very obvious when driving the car, and whereas to make full use of the 911 S engine it was advisable to keep the revs above 5,000 rpm, with the Carrera RS there was little need to change down for really rapid acceleration, as long as the revs did not drop below 4,500 rpm.

In fact, the Carrera had the same torque at 2,500 rpm (20 mkg) as the 911 S had at 4,000 rpm and the maximum torque reached by the 911 S at 5,200 rpm (22 mkg) was available in the 2.7 litre version of the same engine as low as 3,300 rpm. Nevertheless, the Carrera 2.7 litre had superb revving abilities: it just soared up to its 7,300 rpm rev limit and one felt sometimes grateful for the provision of an ignition cut-out preventing an unwary driver from exceeding it.

In the standard car, the two upper ratios of the standard five-speed gearbox were slightly higher than in the other models, but the lower three were the same and the combination of a lightened car and a larger engine resulted in really startling performance figures. I timed a Carrera RS at:

0-60 mph in	5.5 sec
0-100 mph in	13.0 sec
1 km from a standing start in	25.4 sec
Max speed	149 mph

The 2.7 litre Carrera engine, Type 911/83, remained in production for three years, practically without change, until the end of the 1975 model run, and even continued into 1976 for the Australian and South African markets.

For 1974, beginning with the G-series cars which went into production in August 1973 and are easily identified by their larger and higher bumpers designed to meet American requirements, all production Porsches went up to the 2.7 litre capacity obtained by the use of 90 mm bore cylinders. Moreover, the model range which had been widened by the addition of the Carrera RS was narrowed back to three basic models — 911, 911 S and Carrera. Thus the 911 took the place of the 911 T, the 911 S became the middle range car in the position formerly occupied by the 911 E and the Carrera became the highest performance production model. As has been said before, its engine remained unaltered and the car continued to be recognisable by its widened rear wings and wider rear wheel rims and tyres, but the body trim and structure were the same as for other Porsches, with no attempt drastically to reduce the weight compared with other models.

The other two cars, the 911 and 911 S, were both fitted with the K-Jetronic injection system, similar to the installation used for the US version of the 2.4 litre 911 T. The same valve sizes as used in the 2.2 and 2.4 versions were retained, and the basic 911 had the same camshafts as the US version of the 2.4 litre 911 T but retarded 2°. The 2.7 litre 911 S differed from the basic 911 only by its fractionally higher compression ratio of 8.5:1 instead of 8.0:1, intake and exhaust pipes and ports of larger diameter, these being 32 and 33 mm, respectively, for the 911 and 35 mm for both intake and exhaust on the 911 S. Its camshafts provided a longer opening time, considerably less, however, than on the Carrera or the previous 911 S models:

	911 — 2.7	**911 S — 2.7**
Inlet opens/closes	22°btdc/58°abdc	16°btdc/72°abdc
Exhaust opens/closes	52°bbdc/16°atdc	47°bbdc/21°atdc

It will be noted that the exhaust duration is common to both models, only the timing relative to the crankshaft being different.

Performance figures were as follows:

	911	**911 S**
Max power at rpm	150 (DIN) bhp	175 (DIN) bhp
	at 5,700 rpm	at 5,800 rpm
Max torque at rpm	24 mkg (175 lb/ft)	24 mkg (175 lb/ft)
	at 3,800 rpm	at 4,000 rpm

With the 210 (DIN) bhp Carrera, this gave a nicely balanced range of engines to choose from.

The maximum engine speed allowed of 6,400 rpm (the ignition cutout was set at 6,500 rpm ± 200 rpm) did not necessitate the use of specially treated connecting rods or of forged pistons, but for the S engine the additional oil cooling serpentine in the right-hand front wing was retained.

Though the basic 911 engine was the direct successor of the 911 T, the plain cast iron cylinders of the latter were considered to be thermally overloaded by the 150 bhp produced by the 2.7 litre engine, and for the first time this basic engine was fitted with light alloy cylinders identical with those used on the 911 S. The first production models of the 2.7 litre-engined 911 and 911 S were fitted with Nikasil cylinders, as used on the Carrera, but after only a very short time, plain aluminium alloy cylinders (the main alloy material being silicon) were progressively introduced. They were unlinered and had no protective coating of the working surface, but the aluminium alloy pistons were iron coated by an electrolytic process. This was, in fact, only a reversal of the previous material pairing, in which the plain aluminium piston ran in the iron bore of the Biral cylinder. The pistons and cylinders were made by Mahle and Karl Schmidt under Reynolds Aluminium patents, those two suppliers being Germany's largest piston and cylinder specialists.

This was not the first time unlinered aluminium cylinders had been used in connection with iron-coated pistons. In the years 1969-1972 the Chevrolet Division of General Motors had been supplying a few selected racing teams — McLaren being the most important one — with Reynolds Aluminium block V8 engines which had been very successful in Can-Am racing until Porsche intervened with their turbo-charged 917. Following this successful experiment, Chevrolet used a Reynolds Aluminium block with the appropriate iron-coated pistons for their four-cylinder Vega 2300 production car. This is why the plain aluminium cylinders quickly became known among the Porsche development crew as Vega cylinders, though their official name is Alusil cylinders. There were very few problems with their development, and in production they proved to be very reliable and long wearing. Being also considerably cheaper than the Nikasil cylinders, these were quickly abandoned for the 911 and 911 S models, though they were retained on the Carrera and are being used in all engines from 1978 models on.

Though the 2.7 litre 911 S engine effectively took the place of the former E model in the three-model range, its output of 175 bhp warranted the retention of the additional oil cooling serpentine in the right-hand front wing, not fitted to the normal 911.

In view of the higher torque developed by the 2.7 litre K-Jetronic engines, the same clutch diaphragm spring had to be used as for the Carrera. Since the 225 mm clutch had been introduced for the 2.2 litre models the pressure on the clutch disc had been progressively increased by roughly 30 per cent from 600-670 kg to 720-780 kg, and even 795-866 kg on H-series (1975) 911 S and Carrera models, increasing the force necessary to depress the clutch pedal by a corresponding amount. In order to lighten the action, an over-centre spring was introduced in the linkage, beginning with the G-series cars of which production started in August 1973 (the Carrera RS 2.7 litre did not have it). The geometry chosen is so good that the over-centre action is hardly noticeable at all and the system is used even in the racing models.

With the high torque available from the 2.7 litre engines, the four-speed gearbox now became standard equipment on all models, including the Carrera, though the latter was not available with the Sportomatic transmission. The five-speed box was still available, however, and was, in fact, standard equipment for all models on several export markets. This box had the same ratios as used previously on the Carrera RS, which means that fifth and fourth gears were slightly higher than on 2.4 litre models, the fifth gear set being 29:21 instead of 29:22. The same top gear was used in the four-speed box, this being made necessary by the higher power and (in the case of the 911 S) the lower peak speed of the 911 and 911 S engines, compared with the smaller-capacity 911 T and 911 E they replaced. In fact, a 2.7 litre 911 S will reach the ignition cut-out speed (6,500 rpm) in fifth with the 29:22 gear set, as I found out when an engine of that type was dropped into my own E-series car without changing the top gear ratio.

For K-Jetronic engines, top gear was raised slightly and the lower gears more noticeably with the introduction of the H-series cars, mainly in order to meet the stricter US emission tests. The engines themselves remained unchanged, except for the use of an alternator of increased output (980 W) and modified heat exchangers, both required by the improved cockpit heating system. A further refinement was a layer of sound deadening material applied to the exhaust valve covers. For the first time in Porsche history, the US engines were derated compared with the corresponding European versions. In order to meet the 1975 Federal Standards, the 911 S engine had to be fitted with a belt-driven pump injecting air into the exhaust ports, while the K-Jetronic settings were slightly altered. This dropped the power from 175 to 165 (DIN) bhp, while engines meeting Californian Standards were additionally fitted with an exhaust gas recirculation system which cost them another 5 hp, dropping the power to 160 bhp all at the same engine speed as before. Maximum torque dropped accordingly to 23 and 22.4 mkg (166.6 and 162.3 lb/ft), respectively, still at 4,000 rpm. At the same time, the normal 911 was dropped from the American market.

These various 2.7 K-Jetronic engines bore the following type numbers:

	Regular	SpMatic	US	US SpMatic	Calif	Calif SpMatic
911 (G-series)	911/92	911/97		Same as other markets		
911 (H-series)	911/41	911/46	NA	NA	NA	NA
911 S (G-series)	911/93	911/98		Same as other markets		
911 S (H-series)	911/42	911/47	911/43	911/48	911/44	911/49

NA = Not available

The specific fuel consumption figures of the K-Jetronic engines are the lowest obtained since the introduction of the 911. In the normal 911 engine, the curve drops below 200 gr/bhp/hour between 2,800 and 3,500 rpm, while for the 911 S engine it remains below 210 gr/bhp/hour all the way from 2,500 to 3,500 rpm, with an absolute low of 205 gr/bhp/hour around 3,000 rpm. This is why, in ordinary road driving where very high speeds are seldom reached, the K-Jetronic cars are much more economical than the smaller engined, but more highly tuned models which preceded them.

3 litres and K-Jetronic: the logical evolution

With the excellent reliability record of the 3 litre racing engines and of the Turbo, to be analysed in a later section, there was nothing to prevent Porsche from enlarging the cylinder bores to 95 mm also for large scale (by Porsche standards) production engines which could then become full 3 litre units. And with this capacity it became possible approximately to equal the performance of the G- and H-series 2.7 litre Carreras, using the K-Jetronic injection system which provides better fuel economy, improved flexibility and lower exhaust emissions — and is also cheaper than the plunger pump system. To obviate any fatigue problems with the large bore cylinders, the 3 litre Carrera engine (930/02 and 930/12 for three-speed Sportomatic) has a die-cast aluminium crankcase and, for reasons of standardisation, it has Nikasil cylinders similar to the Turbo's. Both the Turbo and the reasons which led to the replacement of the magnesium crankcase by one of aluminium for 3 litre engines will be dealt with in later sections.

As mentioned earlier, the K-Jetronic injection system does not allow the use of extreme valve timing and the air metering disc causes a slight loss of charge which the Bosch sequential injection system used on the Carrera up to the 1975 model avoided. Consequently the capacity increase from 2.7 to 3 litres was not quite enough to make up for the change to K-Jetronic, but by using larger diameter valves (inlet 49 mm, exhaust 41.5 mm, as for the Carrera RS 3.0) and a camshaft providing a larger valve overlap than in other K-Jetronic engines but still compatible with the system, a maximum power of 200 (DIN) bhp was eventually obtained at 6,000 rpm, still with an 8.5:1 compression ratio and on regular grade (91 octane) fuel. This is 10 hp less than the 2.7 litre Carrera production engine, a loss of little significance compared with the considerable further gain in flexibility accruing from the fact that the unaltered maximum torque of 26 mkg (188.4 lb/ft) is produced as low as 4,200 rpm, compared with 5,100 rpm for the 2.7 litre Carrera engine. The specific consumption is almost identical to that of the 2.7 H-series 911 S engine. Following extensive tests, sodium cooling of the exhaust valves was deleted for this new model and this trend was soon followed for the 2.7 litre model, as with the lower specific output of the new engines no such internal cooling was required.

Except for the combustion chamber volume and the intake port diameter, the cylinder heads of the K-Jetronic 3 litre engine (which is identified by a 930 serial number, as is the Turbo engine) are similar to those of the Turbo, but the intake port diameter is increased to 39 mm (Turbo 32 mm, Carrera 2.7 litre 36 mm) and, as with the Turbo, the camshafts run in four bearings directly in the aluminium alloy cam box. They provide the following valve timing:

Inlet opens/closes	24°btdc/76°abdc
Exhaust opens/closes	66°bbdc/26°atdc

For the I-series, beginning with the 1976 model year, Porsche went back to a three-model range, the top model being the Turbo, while the Carrera, fitted with the 3 litre K-Jetronic engine became the intermediate model — albeit a very fast one with a claimed maximum speed of over 230 kph (over 143 mph). At the bottom of the engine range was the 2.7 litre unit previously fitted to the 911 S, now renamed the 'normal' 911, while the 150 bhp 2.7 litre unit was dropped.

Both the I-series 2.7 and 3 litre engines use the larger oil pressure pump (and correspondingly smaller scavenge pump) developed for the Turbo and a new, faster-running cooling fan with only five blades instead of 11, but with the V-belt pulleys stepping up the crankshaft speed by 1.8 instead of 1.3. The reason for the change is to increase the alternator speed at the lower engine speeds. An automatic cold starting device was also added to the K-Jetronic injection system. Those I-series 2.7 litre engines are identified by the numbers 911/81 and (with Sportomatic) 911/86.

Though no change was made to the 2.7 litre engine likely to affect its performance, the power quoted for the I-series is 165 bhp at 5,800 rpm instead of 175 bhp at the same speed for the G- and H-series 911 S models, as it appeared that the previous rating was rather higher than average and only reached by the very best of the production engines. That the power output is no less than before is fully confirmed by a Road Test published in the magazine *Auto, Motor & Sport* of October 25 1975, in which the standing start acceleration figures quoted for an I-series 911 are better throughout than those quoted two years before for a G-series 911 S, with a standing start kilometre time down from 28.7 to 27.9 seconds and 1.5 seconds chopped off the 0-100 mph time. Only the maximum speed was very slightly reduced from 139.8 to 138.1 mph.

The same test report indicates that the loss of 10 hp in the I-series Carrera 3.0 engine compared with its 2.7 litre predecessor is of very little consequence, maximum speed being reduced by a mere 2 mph to a still very useful 146.2 mph, with all standing start acceleration figures practically identical or, if anything, on the better side of it. Flexibility, however, which was already excellent with the 2.7 litre Carrera, shows a quite dramatic improvement, 40 to 80 kph (25 to 50 mph) in fifth gear dropping from 14.1 to 9.4 seconds, the 80 to 120 kph (50 to 75 mph) time from 12.1

to 10.4 seconds, and the 120 to 160 kph (75 to 99.5 mph) time from 12.4 to 10.7 seconds.

Looking back to the earlier 2 litre models, of which the manufacture ceased in July 1969, it can be recognised that Porsche's engine philosophy changed considerably as the 'sixties gave way to the 'seventies. This change of philosophy was no doubt partially dictated by changing laws all over the world: laws to combat noise, laws to combat exhaust emissions, laws introducing overall speed limits in many countries. But as for the change from the old 356 series to the 911 series, commercial competition from roomier, quieter and more comfortable cars of larger engine capacity, but usually of lesser or no higher price, of which the performance progressively increased, certainly played an important part in Porsche's changing engine philosophy. With roads becoming more and more crowded, the highly tuned, high revving engine lost a great part of its appeal for many users, who became fed up with the noise of the high-revving engine and with the continuous gear changing required to live up to the Porsche's performance image.

The specific power of the 911 S engine is very representative of the change in philosophy. It started life as a 2 litre with carburettors in July 1966 (as a 1967 model) with 160 (DIN) bhp and a specific power of 80 bhp/litre. This was increased to 170 bhp and 85 bhp/litre with the introduction of fuel injection for the 1969 model range. So far, this is the highest specific power reached by a standard, unsupercharged Porsche model. It fell to 82 bhp/litre with the introduction of the 2.2 litre model range for 1970, maximum power and torque being obtained at slightly lower revs. This was the first step towards the new generation of engines. Two years later, the 2.4 engine was down to 81 bhp/litre — in fact, still a very high figure in view of the lowered compression ratio of the engine which now used regular grade fuel. In later years, the Carrera 3 litre was down to 67 bhp/litre and the 911 SC of 1980 produced 188 bhp, equal to 63 bhp/litre. As, under Peter W. Schutz's management, the development of the 911 was activated again and benefited from the progress of technology, the specific power of the 911 engine went up again. For 1981, when the 911 SC was readapted to suit premium fuel again, its power rose to 204 bhp, still with a 3 litre capacity, equalling 68 bhp/litre and was further increased to 231 bhp, thanks to both a capacity increase to 3.2 litres and full electronic engine management (Motronic) when the 1984 model (Carrera) was announced in summer 1983. This equals 73 bhp/litre.

From the fuel injection 2 litre 911 S to the Carrera 3.0 litre there is an increase in absolute power from 170 to 200 bhp, a gain of 17.6 per cent, but the torque has risen from 18.5 to 26 mkg, a gain of 40.6 per cent. In fact, the torque of the 3 litre is higher than the peak torque of the old 2 litre over its entire revolution range, from 1,000 right up to 6,600 rpm. This means that, in order to achieve the same road performance as the 2 litre, the 3.0 requires incomparably less work from the driver who gets the additional benefit of even higher performance. Whereas to cover the ground really quickly with the 2 litre S, it was necessary to keep the engine spinning between 5,500 and 7,000 rpm or more, even better results are achieved by keeping the 3 litre between 3,700 and 6,000 rpm. This is not only a much wider range, but it is also much lower and results in less frenzied and much quieter engine operation.

Looking at it from another angle, we see that the enormous gain in flexibility, and the considerable gain in power in the case of the Carrera, have been achieved without in any way increasing either the external dimensions or the weight of the engine. In fact, the 200 bhp 3 litre Carrera engine of 1976 weighs 184 kg (406 lb), ie, exactly the same as the original 130 bhp 2 litre 911, and the 165 bhp 2.7 litre weighs only 175 kg (386 lb) thanks to its magnesium crankcase. Specific weight has dropped from 1.4 kg/bhp for the 2 litre 911 and 1.15 kg/bhp for the 2 litre 911 S to 0.92 kg/bhp for the Carrera 3 litre which will fit straight into the engine bay of a 2 litre car. And while most other manufacturers had to sacrifice power and drivability in order to meet even the current European emission standards, Porsche have recorded considerable gains in both these characteristics. In fairness, however, it must be observed that in 1975, for the first time, cars equipped to meet the extremely strict US emission standards have a slightly reduced power output, compared with European models.

The Carrera RS 3.0 engine

Clever interpretation of the rules enabled Porsche to homologate a further developed version of the Carrera RS lightweight model in Group 3 (Production GT cars) after only 100 units of the new model had been built. With this target in mind it was expected that most of the cars built (in fact, only 106 were made) would be used for serious competition work rather than normal road use. Thus its specification was defined in such way that, as listed, the Carrera RS 3.0, as it was called, was fully competitive in Group 3 racing and that up-rating it to Group 4 specification was a comparatively simple and not outrageously expensive matter. Consequently such items as Type 917 racing brakes, a large oil radiator centrally mounted in the front air dam, a gearbox with an oil pump circulating the transmission oil through a special cooler, and an engine brought up to the 3 litre limit by cylinders of 95 mm bore were all included in the basic specification. Both front and rear wings were extended laterally to cover 8 and 9 inch rims, respectively, and this very elaboraté basic equipment raised the price of the RS 3.0 way above the level of the RS 2.7 it superseded. A new, larger rear spoiler was also used.

Many lessons from racing experience were incorporated in the RS 3.0 engine. The 95 mm bore Nikasil cylinders gave a capacity right at the 3 litre class limit, so that the cylinders did not have to be exchanged for Group 4 racing. The cylinder heads were new, too, with larger ports and valves, the inlet ports being opened up from 36 to 39 mm diameter with an unchanged 35 mm exhaust port diameter, while the valve head diameter was increased from 46 to 49 mm on the inlet side and from 40 to 41.5 mm on the exhaust side. The camshafts (carried in separate boxes, as in other models) were the same as for all earlier 911 S and Carrera engines. The same heads and valves were retained for the engine in Group 4 trim, when a second plug hole was bored in the head for the twin ignition system.

An important modification which does not appear in the general specification is that, for this particular engine, what could be considered a retrograde step was taken by replacing pressure-cast magnesium alloy with die-cast aluminium alloy for the crankcase. The reason for this was that the 95 mm bore cylinders left very little metal between the bores in the crankcase into which the cylinders were inserted, and when the engine was race-tuned to produce some 330 bhp, fatigue cracks were found to develop. Lack of rigidity of the magnesium housing also led to some crankshaft failures in racing engines. These are the reasons why, for the 3 litre, the factory reverted to the heavier aluminium alloy, which provided greater strength than the magnesium alloy used for other models.

Wider wheels and wings gave the RS 3.0 a larger frontal area and higher drag than the RS 2.7. Consequently it was necessary that its engine should have at least enough power to match the speed of its 2.7 litre predecessor. Apparently, despite the capacity increase, the 3 litre engine did not quite make it, so Porsche made an exception to their policy of designing their engines to burn regular grade fuel and reverted to the 9.8:1 compression ratio used on 911 S models up to and including the 2.2 litre series. This gave a power of 230 (DIN) bhp at 6,200 rpm and a maximum torque of 28 mkg (203 lb/ft) at 5,000 rpm, which endowed the RS 3.0 with a straight-line performance almost identical to that of the RS 2.7, as indicated by my own timings of a rather heavier than standard press car:

	RS 2.7	RS 3.0
Max speed	149.1 mph	148.2 mph
0-100 mph	13.0 sec	13.7 sec
1 km from standing start	25.4 sec	25.35 sec

Strangely, despite the use of larger valves to match the capacity increase, and the considerably raised compression ratio (from 8.5:1 to 9.8:1), both the specific power (76.7 bhp/litre) and the specific torque (9.36 mkg/litre) were lower for the 3 litre than for the 2.7 litre engine.

The Type 930 Turbo

The idea of increasing the 911's performance by turbocharging its engine was not prompted by the successful application of turbochargers to the flat-12 Type 917 engine to win two Can-Am championships in 1972 and 1973. Back in 1969, experimental turbocharged Type 901 engines of 2 litre capacity were built for use in both the 911 and the newly-announced Type 914-6 VW-Porsche, but the plan was dropped as being premature. It was taken up again following the turbocharged 917's successes, both for an experimental racing version of the 911 (in fact a sort of laboratory car faced with the opposition of full-blooded racing prototypes from Matra, Alfa Romeo, Gulf and others, which nevertheless finished second at Le Mans and in the Watkins Glen six-hours race) and for a road car to compete directly with the fastest and most exotic machinery from Italy and elsewhere.

Compared with mechanically driven superchargers, a turbocharger has the advantage that the power required to drive it is provided by the heat energy still contained in the exhaust gases when the exhaust valve opens — an energy that is lost in other types of engines — instead of being subtracted from the engine's gross output. It is not entirely a matter of 'getting something for nothing', however, as the turbocharger inevitably increases the exhaust back-pressure, which does reduce the engine's gross output, and as in all supercharged engines the compression ratio must be reduced to prevent detonation, reducing the thermal efficiency of the power unit. On balance, however, from the point of view of thermal efficiency (and fuel consumption, which goes hand in hand with it), turbocharging is the most rewarding method of supercharging.

It has one drawback inherent with its principle, however: when the throttle is shut there are no exhaust gases to keep the turbocharger spinning at full speed, and its rotating speed quickly drops from its normal 80,000-100,000 rpm. When the throttle is opened again, due to the inertia of the turbine and supercharger wheels, it takes some time for the turbocharger to regain its full operating speed, and as the supercharging boost is proportional to the square of the rotating speed some time

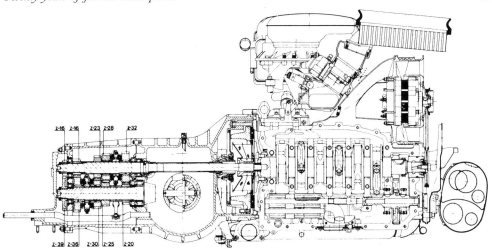

Engine and transmission of Turbo 3.3. Note intercooler and special clutch disc hub.

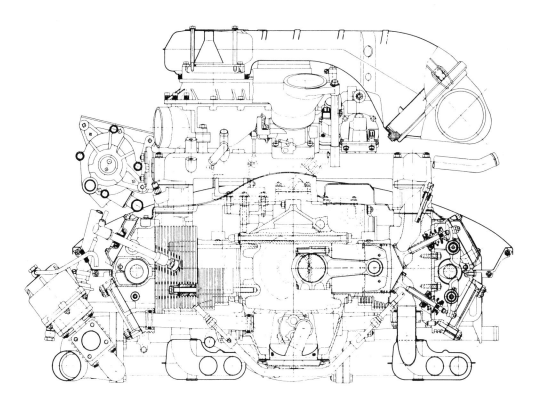

Cross section of 3.3 litre type 930/60 turbocharged engine.

elapses until the full boost pressure is reached, with the result that the full engine torque is not immediately available. By carefully matching the turbo to the engine characteristics the response time can be shortened, but it can never be completely eliminated.

One factor tending to slow the turbo as soon as the exhaust gas supply stops is that when the throttle is closed the blower has to work against the intake pipe pressure. So, in order to keep the turbo spinning as fast as possible during closed throttle periods, and thus to reduce the time necessary for the turbo to resume its normal operating speed when the throttle is reopened, Porsche fitted their racing cars with a flap valve, operated by the accelerator linkage. This is opened as soon as the accelerator is released and drops the pressure in the blower output line to atmospheric. The scheme was very successful, and the lessons learned in the development of the turbocharged 917 engine — and later the turbocharged 911 racing engine — were applied to the turbocharged production car based on the 911, but which was designated Type 930.

Its engine, carrying the type number 930/50 (USA 930/51 with air pump), is derived from the Carrera RS 3.0 (type number 911/77) 3 litre engine. It features the latter's die-cast aluminium crankcase, its 95 mm bore Nikasil cylinders and generally similar cylinder heads with the same valve sizes (49/41.5 mm) but 2°15′ narrower included valve angle than the RS 3.0. In the interest of medium range performance, however, when the boost pressure is low or nil, the intake port diameter is reduced to 32 mm. New camshaft boxes are used, the camshafts running directly in the aluminium cam box, being supported by four, rather than three, bearings — a modification suggested by racing experience. Of course, the camshafts themselves are appropriately modified, and so are the cams, giving the following valve timing diagram:

Inlet opens/closes	20°btdc/60°abdc
Exhaust opens/closes	50°bbdc/18°atdc

The forged pistons are nearly flat to reduce the compression ratio to 6.5:1 and the jets provided in the crankcase to cool the pistons with oil are increased in diameter from 1.0 to 1.5 mm. This increased oil supply to the cylinders and the lubrication requirements of the turbocharger led to an increase in the oil pressure pump capacity which was lengthened by 8 mm, the length of the scavenge pump being reduced correspondingly. Lubricating oil for the turbocharger is derived from the main oil circuit. From the turbo, it goes into a small catch tank from which it is scavenged into the main oil reservoir by a small gear pump driven from the nose of the left-hand camshaft.

For this top model of the Porsche range a fully electronic ignition system, controlled by impulses generated by a trigger disc carried by a conventional advance mechanism inside the distributor, was adopted. This system, which is more expensive than the contact-breaker controlled condenser discharge system used on other Porsches, requires no maintenance whatever and had previously been used for Porsche racing engines. A further important advantage is that there is no contact breaker wear to affect the ignition timing.

Porsche's philosophy on turbocharging is to obtain the required power output by using a comparatively high boost pressure and a comparatively slow-running engine. For the 930/50 engine, a governed maximum boost of 0.8 bar (approx 11 psi) is used, the power peak of 260 (DIN) bhp being reached at only 5,500 rpm, which results in extremely quiet operation. The maximum permissible rotating speed is 6,000 rpm, and as the cooling requirements of the engine are higher than for any other production Porsche the 11-blade cooling fan speed is stepped up from 1.3 (as in other contemporary models) to 1.67 times crankshaft speed.

With a maximum torque of no less than 35 mkg (254 lb/ft) at 4,000 rpm, an entirely new transmission had to be designed and the engine had to be fitted with a larger flywheel to accommodate a larger clutch with a disc of 240 mm diameter instead of 225 mm. In view of the extreme flexibility of the engine, only four forward ratios were provided in the new transmission.

Schematic drawing of Type 930/50 turbocharging installation. 1 — Air filter, 2 — Mixture adjustment, 3 — Intake pipe, 4 — Turbocharger blower, 5 — Recirculating valve, 6 — Pressure delivery pipe, 7 — Throttle housing, 8 — Intake manifold, 9 — Fuel injection pipe, 10 — Exhaust collector pipe, 11 — Turbocharger turbine, 12 — Exhaust silencer, 13 — Pressure regulating valve (waste gate), 14 — Turbine by-pass, 15 — Control pipes, 16 — Closed throttle air control pipe, 17 — Closed throttle air feed valve, 18 — Pressure sensitive safety switch.

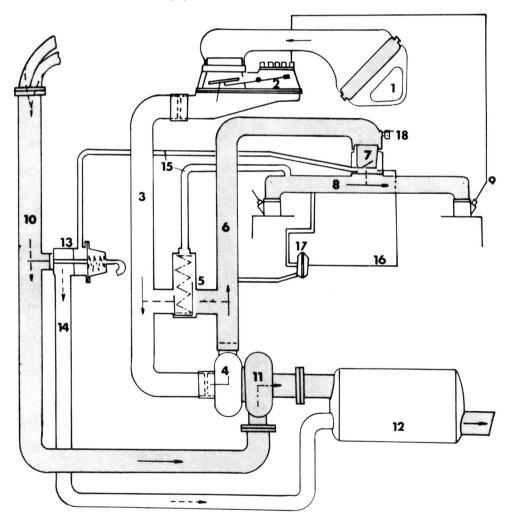

A sample of performance curves illustrating the trend towards more torque and lower specific outputs for practically unchanged engine bulk and weight.

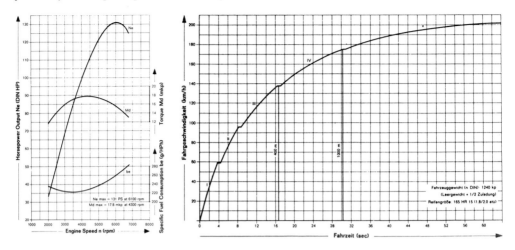

Original 2 litre 911: power, torque and specific consumption curves and acceleration chart. Fuel 98 ROZ.

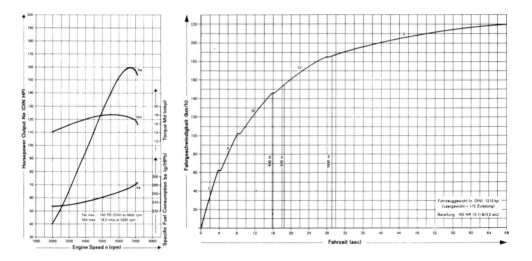

Original 911 S: power, torque and specific consumption curves and acceleration chart. Fuel 98 ROZ.

Whereas turbocharged Porsche racing engines used plunger pump fuel injection, the K-Jetronic system was chosen for the production Turbo because of its simplicity and excellent emission performance. A schematic diagram shows how the installation operates.

When the engine is running, the exhaust gases are directed from the exhaust manifolds of either bank of cylinders, via the pipe (10) to the turbocharger turbine (11), of radial flow construction. Here the heat and kinetic energy still contained in the exhaust gases are used to spin the turbine from where the gases are led into the exhaust silencer (12) and hence into the atmosphere.

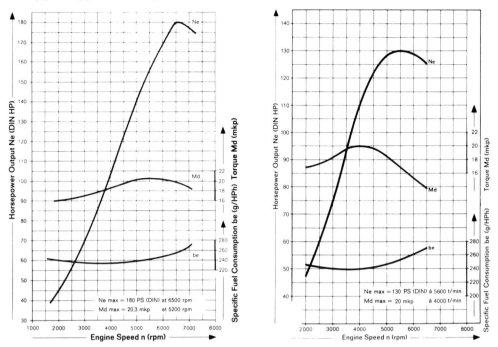

Power, torque and specific consumption curves of (**left**) *911 S, 2.2 litre engine, fuel 98 ROZ and* (**right**)
911 T, 2.4 litre, fuel 91 ROZ.

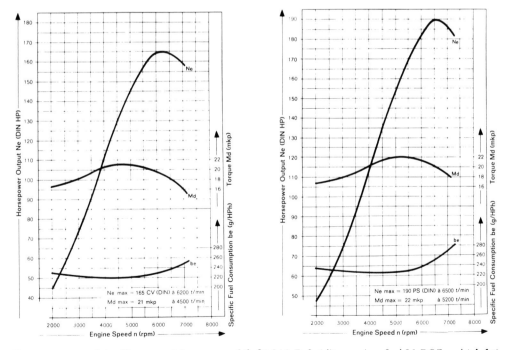

Power, torque and specific consumption curves of (**left**) *911 E, 2.4 litre engine, fuel 91 ROZ and* (**right**)
911 S, 2.4 litre engine, fuel 91 ROZ.

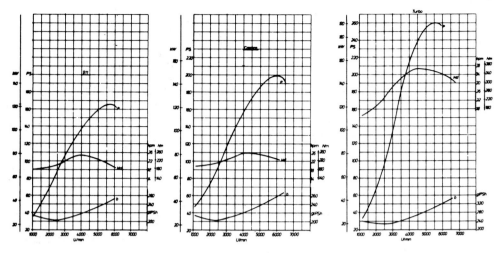

Power, torque and specific consumption curves of 1976 (I-series) engines. **Left to right** *911 /2.7 (fuel 91 ROZ), Carrera 3.0 (fuel 91 ROZ), Turbo (fuel 96 ROZ).*

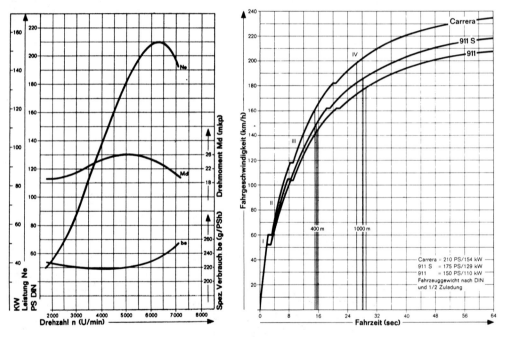

Left *Power, torque and specific consumption curves of Carrera 2.7 engine, fuel 91 ROZ.* **Right** *Acceleration chart, 1974/75 models.*

The turbine shaft also carries the wheel of the centrifugal blower (4). This sucks ambient air through the air filter (1), the metering unit (2) of the K-Jetronic injection system and the intake pipe (3). The metering unit (2) governs the quantity of fuel injected into the engine's ports by the injectors (9). From the blower (4), the air is fed through the blower output pipe to the throttle housing (7) and the engine's intake manifold (8). Two pipes (both numbered 15) transmit the intake manifold

Above left *Cars with the 221 cm wheelbase have the cover giving access to the rear torsion bars very close to the bottom of the wheel arch.* **Above right** *In 227 cm wheelbase cars, the rear wheel arch is moved back from the torsion bar access cover, here partly hidden by the bright aluminium stone guard. Also note the slightly flared wheel opening.* **Below** *At one stage Porsche envisaged adding a full four-seater model to the 911 range, and two prototypes were built based on B-series models. Here is one of them, which served as a factory hack for several years. The other car had longer rear lights, similar in shape to the standard 911's.*

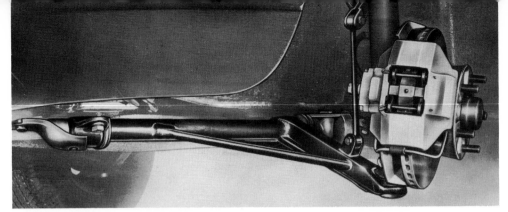

Above *Aluminium 'S' caliper as fitted to 911 S models beginning with the B-series and up to the F-series, to all Carrera 2.7 litre models and to the 930 Turbo.*

Left *The Turbo 3.3 uses the four-piston calipers and perforated brake discs developed for racing.*

Below *E-series 2.4 litre models carried the oil tank in the right-hand body side panel to reduce overhung weight. In the background is a rare VW-Porsche 914-6.*

Above *The original Targa with folding rear window panel. It was introduced with the A-series in August 1967.*

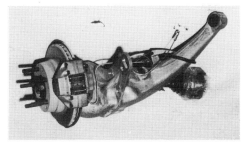

Right *Larger and reinforced cast-alloy inner rear suspension arms are used on the Turbo, providing a wider track. The hub bearings are larger, too.*

Right centre *Aluminium alloy rear suspension arms, as used from G-series on.*

Below *Cast iron 'M' brake caliper as used in several models from the beginning of production.*

Bottom right *Aluminium 'S' caliper as used for 911 S from B- to F-series, on Carreras up to the H-series and on the Turbo 3.0.*

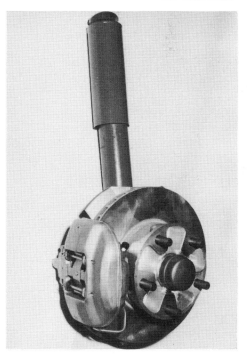

Above *F-series Carrera 2.7 in RS (left) and RSR versions. Note the widened wings and front oil cooler on the RSR.*

Left *G- and H-series Carrera 2.7 cockpit. Note steering wheel incorporating collapsible safety boss.*

Right *Two views of the Carrera RS 3.0 in standard G-series form, and **below** modified to RSR (racing) specification. Note the wider wings with air in- and outlets, and the larger rear spoiler.*

Four development stages of the interior: **Above** *O-series 911,* **Below** *B-series 911 S.*

Above *G-series 911 with lightweight seats featuring integral headrests and steering wheel incorporating collapsible safety boss.* **Below** *From K-series on all 911s have fresh air vents.*

Above *G-series 911 Targa. 1974 was the last model year when pressed steel wheels were standard on the bottom model of the range.*

Below *The front air dam introduced on E-series 911 S and standardised throughout the F-series. It reduced the lift over the front wheels from 183 to 103 lb at 143 mph.*

LEO-ZA 44

pressure to the pressure limiting valve (or wastegate) (13) and the recirculating valve (5). The pressure limiting valve is operated by a diaphragm acting against spring pressure. When the maximum permissible boost pressure of 0.8 bar (11 psi) is reached in the inlet manifold, the pressure acting upon the diaphragm carrying the pressure limiting valve (13) causes the valve to lift and part of the exhaust gases flowing through the pipe (10) escape directly into the silencer (12), via pipe (14), by-passing the turbine (11).

If the throttle is closed during normal driving, a vacuum is created in the intake manifold (8). This has no influence on the pressure limiting valve (13), which remains closed, but it acts, via the pipe (15), on the recirculating plunger valve which it attracts against the pressure of its return spring. This creates a connection between the blower intake pipe (3) and the blower output pipe (6), so that the blower output, which cannot reach the cylinders because of the closed throttle (7), is fed back to the blower intake and recirculates as long as the throttle is kept closed. Thanks to this recirculation, there is no back pressure on the blower to hasten its slowing down and no air goes through the fuel metering unit (2), so that the fuel supply to the injectors is cut off. The installation is completed by the emission control valve (17), a vacuum-sensitive diaphragm valve which diverts a small quantity of air from the blower output pipe to the intake manifold (8), via pipe 16, whenever the throttle is closed at anything but idling speed. This air will allow any small quantity of fuel seeping through the injectors to be burned.

Operation of the 930/50 engine requires 96 octane fuel, which is not particularly exacting, bearing in mind its specific power of 87 bhp/litre. The turbo installation adds some 25 kg to the weight compared with the Carrera RS 3.0 engine using the same, heavier aluminium crankcase; the total weight (which always includes the complete silencing installation) is 207 kg, resulting in the same specific weight of 0.79 kg/bhp (1.75 lb/bhp) as the Carrera RS 3.0 engine. The Turbo being a luxury car engine, rather than a highly tuned sports engine, it would be fairer to compare its specific weight to that of the 1976 Carrera, which is a 3 litre K-Jetronic engine with an output of 200 bhp. This has a specific weight of 0.92 kg/bhp (2.03 lb/bhp).

Despite the fullest possible de luxe equipment, which included air conditioning, an electric sliding roof, electric windows and the most elaborate type of radio/stereo cassette player, the 930 Turbo test car which was put at my disposal was easily the fastest production Porsche I have tried, and certainly reaches the target set by its makers to compete directly with the fastest production cars in the world. Despite a clutch which would not allow a racing start, my test car achieved the following performance figures:

Maximum two-way speed	155.8 mph
0-100 mph	14.2 sec
1 km from standing start	25.15 sec

With a less accessory-burdened car, the very reliable Swiss journal *Automobil Revue* did 0-100 mph in 12.6 seconds, and 1 km from a standing start in 24.2 seconds, the best figures we had ever seen for a production car at the time. But perhaps even more remarkable than sheer performance is the flexibility of the engine, which will propel the car from 60 to 120 mph in 20 seconds in top gear and in a mere 13.5 seconds using only third gear!

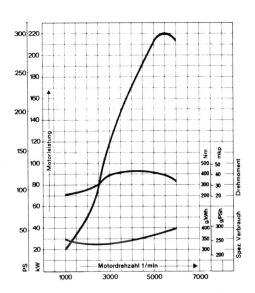

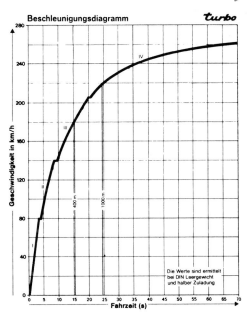

Power, torque and specific consumption curves of Turbo 3.3 litre engine.

Acceleration curve for Turbo 3.3 with full tank, driver and 115 kg payload.

911 SC and Turbo 3.3 litre

The original 'Turbo' engine remained in production virtually unaltered for three years, from September 1974 to August 1977, when it was superseded by an even more powerful engine of 3.3 litre capacity with an output of 300 bhp at 5,500 rpm and 42 mkg (304 lb/ft) torque at 4,000 rpm. The increased power and torque outputs were obtained not only through the increased swept volume, but also thanks to the use of an intercooler between the compressor and the engine. This is located under the rear spoiler, slightly raised to make room for the intercooler through which the circulation of cooling air is activated, even at low speeds, by the engine cooling fan. At normal speeds, the temperature drop in the cooler is 50-60°C, improving the compressor efficiency as well as the engine's volumetric efficiency, while the lower temperature at which the mixture reaches the cylinders has enabled the compression ratio to be increased from 6.5 to 7.0:1. This explains why the increase in power, and especially in torque, is greater than the increase in engine capacity, in spite of the addition of an air pump blowing into the exhaust ports made necessary by the stricter European emission laws implemented in 1978. The pump is driven through a cog belt from the left-hand camshaft.

The addition of the intercooler and the air pump, as well as other modifications enumerated later, have increased the engine's weight from 207 kg (457 lb) to 230 kg (508 lb) for the 3.3 litre, type number 930/60, though the *specific* weight comes down from 0.79 to 0.76 kg/bhp.

In fact, the differences between the type 930/50 and the type 930/60 engine go far beyond a simple capacity increase, the addition of an intercooler and the use of a slightly larger compressor (the turbine of the turbocharger remaining unaltered). More extensive modifications were required to accommodate the longer stroke of

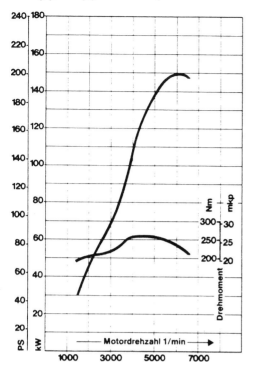

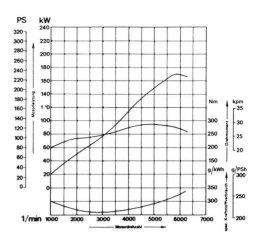

Above *Full load power, torque and specific fuel consumption of type 930/20, 3.2 litre 'Carrera' engine.*

Left *Full load power and torque curves of type 930/10 engine of 1981 model Porsche 911 SC.*

Right *Acceleration curve for Carrera 3.2 with 930/20 engine (two up).*

Below *Full load power, torque and specific fuel consumption of type 930/25 US specification engine with three-way catalyst. The type 930/25 is identical to the 1984–86 type 930/21 engine, except for the different Motronic.*

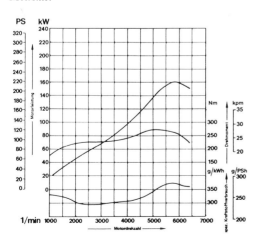

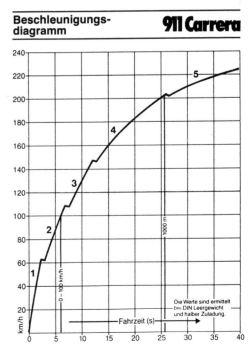

Beschleunigungs-diagramm **911 Carrera**

74.4 (instead of 70.4) mm and the 2 mm larger bore (97 mm) required to bring the engine up to its 3,299 cc capacity while preserving its reliability. To preserve its rigidity, the crankshaft has slightly thicker webs, accordingly narrowing the journals and crankpins, and in order to provide sufficient bearing areas both the main bearing and the big end diameters were increased. Crankshaft bearings Nos 1-7 have their diameter increased from 57 to 60 mm, bearing No 8 from 31 to 40 mm, while the 2 mm narrower big ends (reduced from 23.8 to 21.8 mm) are increased in diameter from 52 to 55 mm. And to accommodate the longer stroke, the con-rods are shortened from 127.8 to 127 mm. Additionally, the crankshaft counterweights have been slightly rearranged to provide even better dynamic balance.

Both to accommodate the larger bore *and* to provide more uniform cooling of the bearing surface of the Nikasil cylinders, these have no cooling fins on the side directly hit by the cooling air, while the fins on the opposite (lee) side are larger than before. The head gasket is deleted, the head now bearing directly on the cylinder's upper face and the cooling fan's speed is raised to 1.8 times engine speed.

Another modification to improve the reliability is the use of an oil pump of larger capacity, the gear width being increased from 43 to 51 mm on the pressure side and from 58 to 80 mm on the scavenge side, in which the aluminium alloy housing was replaced by a cast iron housing to keep the clearance down when the oil is hot. Other modifications not directly related to the capacity increase are an improved timing chain tensioner using different plastic materials for the slides and an ignition distributor of a different type, turning anti-clockwise, with the attendant driving pinions.

With the type 930/60 engine goes a modified clutch in which the spring hub is a Porsche development intended to suppress low-speed gearbox chatter. It is described in Chapter 4. The new hub, which provides 34° of angular movement either side of the static position, is thicker than the original disc and has necessitated moving the engine 30 mm back in the body, so that the weight carried by the rear wheels is increased to 60 per cent of the total, which is also increased by about 66 lb (30 kg) compared with the previous car. To take care of the increased weight borne by the rear axle, the factory recommends that the rear tyre pressure should be increased from 2.4 to 3.0 bar (from about 33.6 to 42 psi).

In my experience, there is no detectable difference in the handling of the Turbo 3.3, compared with its predecessor, while the increase in performance makes the 3.3 the fastest accelerating production car of its time, a better gripping clutch partly accounting for the quicker standing start figures, compared with the 3-litre:

Maximum two-way speed	160.3 mph
0-100 mph	12.0 sec
Standing start km	24.0 sec

When the 928 was added to the Porsche programme, which at the time also included the basic 924, it was obvious that the 911/930 range would have to be reduced and this is what happened with the introduction of the L-series for the 1978 model year. On this occasion an effort was made to standardise the production, replacing both the 911/2.7 and the Carrera 3.0 by a single model based on the Carrera body (with wide rear wheel arches) and running gear and using an engine of 3 litres capacity which had a lot in common with the Turbo 3.3. In this case, too, an air pump was required to meet the new European emission standards (it is driven by a V-belt off the cooling blower hub) and the engine was slightly detuned, compared with the Carrera 3.0, producing 180 bhp (132 kW) at 5,500 rpm, though its maximum torque is up from 188.4 lb/ft at 4,200 rpm to 195.7 lb/ft (27 mkg or 265 Nm) at 4,100 rpm. This was obtained with the use of the Carrera camshafts advanced 6° of crankshaft rotation to give the following timing with the normal 0.1 mm valve clearance:

Inlet opens/closes	30°btdc/70°abdc
Exhaust opens/closes	72°bbdc/20°atdc

Incidentally, the engines for the USA and Japan retained the Carrera's timing.

The cylinder heads (except for the air injection hole in the exhaust port), the port and valve sizes and the compression ratio remained as in the Carrera and one cannot help thinking that the only reason for reducing the engine's power from the latter's 200 bhp to 180 bhp was to prevent the new model, known as the new A-series 911 SC*, from having a higher maximum speed than the much larger engined and more expensive 928.

This 911 SC engine, type number 930/03 (930/13 for Sportomatic) uses the same crankcase as the 3.3 Turbo's 930/60 engine, featuring larger diameter main bearing recesses to take seven 60 mm main bearings and an eighth main bearing, supporting the timing gear, of unaltered 31 mm diameter. Though the stroke (and the bore) are unchanged from the Carrera 3.0, the crankshaft is new and similar in design and counter-weighing to the 3.3 litre's. The webs are not quite as thick, however, so that the connecting rod's thickness is reduced by only 1.2 mm from 23.8 to 22.6 mm, the big end diameter being increased from 52 to 53 mm.

As in the Turbo, a breakerless electronic ignition system is used (for the first time in an unturbocharged production 911), the distributor rotating anti-clockwise. For this engine, a reversion was made to a slightly less efficient, but quieter 11-blade cooling blower wheel of the same diameter (226 mm), running at the same speed as the five-blade wheel.

After two years of production, minor modifications intervened in the A-series 911 SC engine for the 1980 model cars. The modified engine (type No 930/09 — 930/19 for the Sportomatic) has its compression ratio raised from 8.5 to 8.6:1 — still with 91 octane requirement — and uses the same 245 mm diameter cooling blower wheel as the Turbo. The wheel's speed, however, is reduced from 1.8 to 1.68 times crankshaft speed, but the output is increased from 1,380 to 1,500 litres per second at 6,000 rpm crankshaft speed. Apart from the difficult-to-spot larger cooling blower wheel, the new engine is easily recognisable by the new longitudinal ribs on the valve gear covers, designed to reduce vibrations. It is rated at 188 bhp (138 kW) at 5,500 rpm, with unaltered torque rating, and there seems to be little reason for the 8 bhp increase in power. It is, in fact, said that production 930/03 engines mostly turned out to deliver well over the advertised 180 bhp, so the rating was revised with the introduction of the 1980 model. This also features the more resilient Porsche clutch disc hub, though in this case it is smaller than in the Turbo and has not required moving the engine back.

Up to the 1979 models, the 911 SC had retained the gearbox ratios of the Carrera 3.0, both for the five-speed and the Sportomatic boxes, but the 1980 models have a slightly higher geared fifth gear (28/22 instead of 28/23) in the five-speed unit.

The corresponding 3.3 Turbo engine remains largely unchanged, the only significant

---

* Incidentally, 911 SC is a confusing type number, as it had previously been widely used internally to designate Carrera models.

modifications being a more efficient exhaust silencer with twin outlets, said not to increase the back pressure, and the longitudinally ribbed valve gear covers. But in both models, the oil cooling serpentine located in the right-hand front wing is replaced by a more efficient proper oil cooler. Both this modification and the increased output of the cooling blower followed the opening of new stretches of German Autobahn where maximum speed can be held for periods of up to 30 minutes.

In practice, the 911 SC has proved to be significantly faster than the 911/2.7 and significantly slower than the Carrera 3.0 only in maximum speed, as illustrated by the comparison of three *Auto, Motor & Sport* road tests:

	911/2.7 **(1975)**	**911 SC** **(1978)**	**Carrera 3.0** **(1975)**
Maximum speed	138.1 mph	141.6 mph	146.2 mph
0-100 km/h	7.3 sec	6.3 sec	6.1 sec
0-160 km/h	18.7 sec	15.8 sec	15.0 sec
Standing start km	27.9 sec	26.6 sec	26.2 sec

Back to 98 Octane

When the 2.4-litre engine replaced the 2.2 in the 1972 models, the compression ratio of the 'S' version was dropped from 9.8 to 8.5:1, partly to reduce the nitrogen oxide emissions, but mainly to lower the octane requirement of the engine in view of the reduction of the lead content which, at that time, was soon to be made compulsory in Germany. It had been feared that the octane rating of 98 might be reduced so the engines were all tuned to run on Regular fuel of 91 octane rating. By 1980, however, this had become a waste of energy as well as an anachronism, as the comparatively low compression was detrimental to the engine's thermal efficiency. Consequently, for the 1981 model 911 SC, known internally as 911 SC, B-series, the compression ratio was raised back to 9.8:1 with 98 octane fuel mandatory. For better combustion efficiency, the shape of the piston top was modified to increase the squish effect, while the camshaft timing was changed back to the same as the Carrera 3.0, giving increased power at a slight expense of torque. The characteristics of the distributor of the electronic ignition system and of the K-Jetronic fuel injection plant were modified to suit, the K-Jetronic installation also benefiting from various developments, among them an improved cold start system, the nozzle of which sprayed directly into the plenum chamber feeding the six cylinders. Steel injection pipes replaced the flexible ones. The result was an increase of the power developed to 204 bhp at 5,900 rpm and an unmodified torque of 27 mkg (195.7 lb/ft) at 4,300 rpm — 200 rpm higher than before. With this engine, a reversion was made to a clutch plate incorporating coil spring damping in the hub.

Except for the improved K-Jetronic injection plant, none of these modifications apply to the engines delivered to the USA, Canada and Japan which run on a 9.3 compression ratio and are fitted with a three-way catalyst making lead-free fuel mandatory and a lambda sond.* Their specifications remain as for the 1980 models.

* A bi-metallic device which is inserted into the exhaust manifold and connected with an electronic controller. It measures the percentage of oxygen in the exhaust gases and the controller modifies the mixture to keep 'lambda' as close to 1.0 as possible. (Lambda stands for the Greek letter so-named; it is used as a technical symbol and equals 1.0 if the air/fuel mixture is such that the number of molecules of oxygen in the quantity of air aspirated by the engine is exactly twice the number of molecules of carbon contained in the fuel, so that the combustion procedures CO_2 with no residues of either carbon or oxygen.)

For 1983, the 3.3-litre Turbo engine, type 930/66, benefited from minor modifications to the K-Jetronic injection system and the vacuum control of the ignition timing was made to advance the spark under certain light load conditions. In addition, the waste gate got its own, small silencer, reducing noise without affecting the performance. The maximum torque went up from 42 to 44 mkg (303 to 318 lb/ft), still at 4,000 rpm, and the average 'standardised' fuel consumption was reduced by 15 per cent from 19.5 to 23 miles per Imperial gallon.

As the power of the standard 'Turbo' engine has not been increased since the 3.3 litre was introduced as a 1978 model, there have been requests for even more power, specially as the car has been progressively burdened with more luxury equipment which has increased its weight. This requirement has been met by Porsche's 'Special Requirement Department' (which also undertakes body modifications, such as the 935-like 'Flachbau' front end). It carries out modifications inspired by the '930 Group B' (described in Chapter 8) raising the maximum power to 330 bhp. The modifications include raising the turbocharger boost, fitting a larger intercooler and a freer flow exhaust system, deleting the recirculating valve for which there is no space left and adding an oil cooler integrated in the front air dam. Cars thus modified are claimed to have a maximum speed of 167 mph with the standard body and 170 mph if the body is modified to the more aerodynamic 'Flachbau'.

The 3.2 litre atmospheric engine

At the end of 1980, Professor Ernst Fuhrmann (who had been in charge of Porsche's activities since the beginning of 1972) resigned from his office one year before his contract expired. For some time it had been an open secret that, despite the fact that Porsche's turnover had been multiplied by four under Fuhrmann's management, there had been increasing differences of opinion between the Managing Director and the company's main shareholders, the Porsche and Piëch families.

Fuhrmann's resignation was to have a profound influence on the 911's future. He was replaced at the head of the company by Peter W. Schutz, a German-born American with a degree in engineering whose previous activities had been with large diesel engines as an engineer for the Caterpillar company, a rather far cry from the sports car business. Although he speaks perfect German, he has a distinct American accent and was completely unknown in European industrial circles. Neither did Dr Ferry Porsche and the co-owners of the company know him until a few months before his nomination, but he settled down to his new job with great enthusiasm. Obviously, the decision to put him at the head of the company was taken after prolonged talks with the company owners, led by Ferry Porsche, whose influence came to bear much more on the company's policy than it had under Schutz's predecessor.

Fuhrmann, under whose leadership the Porsche 924, 944 and 928 had been developed, was much more inclined to push these cars than the 911. This is not only humanly understandable, but also had some justification in the fact that the Porsche 944 which now replaces the 924 shares many parts of its engine with the 928, reducing the production costs, while the 911 stands completely alone. But Dr Ferry Porsche, who had been the real 'father' of the 911, had different views. The car was already a living legend with many fanatical followers, and he was convinced that it could be further developed with great success. His view was shared by the company's Chief of Development, Helmuth Bott, and by company co-owner and Ferry Porsche nephew Ferdinand Piëch who, being in charge of Audi development, had already launched the 'Quattro' operation. He was convinced of the merits of four-wheel drive and the 911 (which has exactly the same layout of its main

Above left *Peter W. Schutz, Porsche's Managing Director 1981–88.* **Above right** *The 911 can even fly! At the end of 1983, Porsche obtained the homologation of a 200 bhp light aircraft engine, developed from the 911 K-Jetronic engine. Main mechanical difference is the replacement of chains by gears to drive the camshafts. In contrast to existing small aircraft units, the Porsche is controlled by one lever only, operating the throttle valve. The correction of the fuel mixture and ignition advance in function of engine speed, load and altitude as well as the variation of the propeller pitch are all fully automatic—an enormous advance.* **Below** *Intercooler of 3.3-litre Turbo is located on top of the engine.*

At the Frankfurt motor show of 1983, Porsche showed this, as yet untried prototype of the future Group B 911 featuring a four-valve twin turbocharged 2.85-litre engine, four-wheel drive and wishbone suspension all round. Some of the body modifications may well hint possible evolutions of the production 911 in future years.

components as the Audi, only back-to-front) was the Porsche which best lent itself to a conversion. The idea to produce a convertible had also been put forward to Professor Fuhrmann, but had been rejected on the grounds that the 911 was now an obsolete model.

Professor Fuhrmann's policy had led to a considerable reduction of the 911 development programme, but as soon as Peter Schutz took his office, in January 1981, the decision was taken to reactivate the development of the model. Dipl Ing. Wolfgang Bezner was made responsible, and in 1982 the biggest share of the development budget went to the 911. Immediately, two projects which had been shelved were taken up again: the convertible and the four-wheel drive version which, at the time, had not gone beyond the 'suggestion' stage. A crash programme enabled Porsche to disclose both to the public in the shape of a 911 Turbo-based Cabriolet at the 1981 Frankfurt motor show. It was made quite clear that this was purely a show car (and in fact all the development work still had to be done), but it also demonstrated that there was no longer any foundation in the rumours that the 911 series was to be abandoned in the near future. As told in Chapter Six, the Cabriolet was eventually put into production a few months later, but as an addition to the normal 911 SC, rather than to the Turbo range.

From 3.0 to 3.2

Since August 1977, the 911 engine had been stretched to 3.3 litres in its turbocharged version, which had a good reliability record, and in the early '80s Porsche even developed and built a number of 3,164 cc, fully air-cooled racing engines of 911 configuration, developing around 700 bhp with twin turbochargers, which were sold to 935 owners. These engines use the 74.4 mm throw crankshaft of the 911 Turbo with the 95 mm bore cylinders of

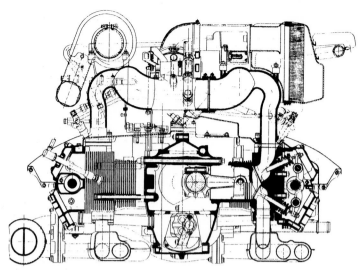

Above *Cross section of 1984 3.2-litre engine, type 930/20.*
Below *Schematic drawing of the 3.2-litre engine's fully electronic injection system.* **1** *Fuel pump;* **2** *Fuel filter;* **3** *Pressure check connection;* **4** *Injectors;* **5** *Pressure damper;* **6** *Air metering unit;* **7** *Air intake temperature sond;* **8** *Full load switch on throttle valve;* **9** *Idle micro-switch;* **10** *Idle speed regulator valve;* **11** *Cylinder head temperature sond (on head No 3);* **12** *Pressure regulator;* **13** *Ignition distributor;* **14** *Ignition coil;* **15** *Fuse box (10 fuses);* **16** *Relay for digital engine electronic;* **17** *Altitude corrector (weakens the mixture by 6 per cent over 1,000 m);* **18** *Digital engine electronic control unit;* **A** *Connection to battery +;* **B** *From fuel tank;* **C** *To fuel tank;* **D** *To throttle valve housing.*

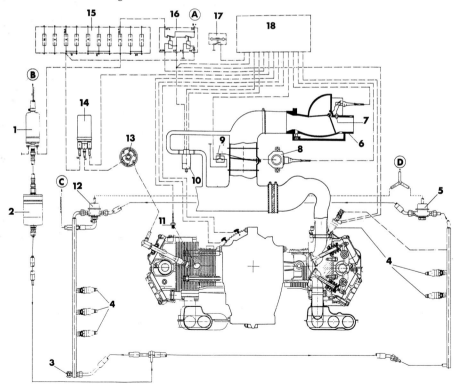

the 911 SC. There was thus no technical reason why the atmospheric 911 could not be stretched to the same capacity or to the even larger size of the Turbo, of which the bore is 2 mm larger: in fact, back in 1976, a couple of experimental engines with 100 mm bores and a capacity of 3.5 litres were successfully built, Development Chief Helmuth Bott using one for many years in his own 911. For the 3.2-litre engine, as it is known (Type No 930/21 for the USA, Canada and Japan and 930/20 for the rest of the world), only Nikasil cylinders are used.

Since the late 1970s, however, the engine development team had a new golden rule: any increase in power should only be obtained with a corresponding decrease of the fuel consumption. This is why the 911 had to wait until its 20th model year to get its bigger and more powerful 3.2-litre Carrera engine, the name 'Carrera' significantly returning where it belongs, after having adorned a short-lived version of the 924. For the 3.2-litre type 930/20 is not just a 3.0 fitted with the Turbo's 74.4 mm throw crankshaft to give it a capacity of 3,164 cc. Many other modifications contribute to raising the power from 204 to 231 bhp DIN (both at 5,900 rpm) and the maximum torque from 27 mkg at 4,300 rpm to 28.6 mkg (207 lb/ft) at 4,800 rpm, the highest figures attained by a normal production atmospheric 911/930 engine.

The major factor contributing to the 3.2-litre's improved efficiency, reflected by a full load specific consumption remaining below 200 g/hp/hour from 1,500 to 4,600 rpm and touching a record low of 187 g/hp/hour around 2,600 rpm, is the Bosch-made electronic engine management system combining the computerised ignition control with a sequential LE-Jetronic fuel injection system which also completely cuts off the fuel supply to the injectors as soon as the accelerator is released above an engine speed of about 1,080 rpm. In this system, the best combination of ignition advance and quantity of fuel injected for maximum efficiency within the frame of current exhaust emission regulations is obtained at the development stage on the bench for several hundreds of different engine speed and load conditions. These optimum settings are kept in the memory of a micro-computer which automatically reproduces them as the engine operates in similar conditions on the road, or modifies them as the result of data introduced into the computer by sensors signalling the intake air and cylinder head temperatures and the atmospheric pressure.

This system which safely keeps the engine working close to, but below the knock limit under all circumstances, taking into account such parameters as engine oil temperature and intake air temperature, has allowed an increase of the compression ratio from nominally 9.8 to nominally 10.3:1, which in itself contributes to higher engine efficiency. The installation also incorporates an idling speed regulator which has made it possible to reduce the idling speed to 800 rpm—and, consequently, the idling consumption—while retaining reliable idling. It consists of an air pipe bypassing the throttle valve, in which the air flow is controlled by an electronically operated valve, itself controlled by the computer. New, higher pistons, now forged again for greater strength*, provide the increased compression ratio and the valve timing has also been altered by advancing the existing camshafts by 3° to give the following valve timing (with the normal 0.10 mm running clearance):

Inlet opens/closes	27°btdc/73°abdc
Exhaust opens/closes	69°bbdc/23°atdc

or, as Porsche have been specifying for some time to facilitate workshop operation:

Inlet opens/closes	4°btdc/50°abdc
Exhaust opens/closes	46°bbdc/atdc

* Forged pistons had been used in 2.0-, 2.2- and 2.4-litre 'S' engines, and had last been used in normal production 911 models for the 2.7-litre Carrera. The Turbo has, of course, always had forged pistons.

Externally the 3.0-litre 911 SC and 3.2-litre Carrera engines greatly differ because of their different air intake and fuel injection systems. No air pump is required with the Carrera's 'Motronic' (above). The unit on the right is the air conditioning compressor.

with zero clearance and when the lift has reached 1 mm. The valve sizes remain unaltered at 49 and 41.5 mm for intake and exhaust respectively, but the port diameter is increased by 2 mm to 40 mm for the intake and to 38 mm for the exhaust. No cylinder head gasket is used.

Although the Porsche flat-six engine has been generally very reliable from the beginning, its timing chain tensioners have always been an Achilles heel, even though several minor modifications did improve the situation over the years. As the decision was taken to keep the 911 in production for several years to come, and to make up for its lack of development in the last years of the Fuhrmann era, this problem also received attention. Up to the 1983 models, the jockey pinion of the tensioners (one for either timing chain) was pushed against the chain by a spring enclosed in a cylinder and acting on a piston. The cylinder was filled with oil for life and the piston acted as a damper. Any leak on the piston rod seal would, however, let air penetrate into the unit and interfere with the damping, allowing the chain to oscillate and slacken at the risk of jumping a tooth or more — with expensive results. Closer tolerances and careful assembly brought considerable improvements in later years, but in an effort to brush the problem away once and for all, it was decided that the new 3.2-litre engine would have a tensioner cylinder permanently fed with oil from the engine's pressure system. The 3.3-litre Turbo engine was modified in the same way.

Despite having the same valves and a slightly more torque-oriented valve timing than its 3-litre predecessor, the 3.2-litre engine has a higher specific output of 73 bhp per litre, compared to 68 bhp/litre which the 0.5 higher compression ratio cannot alone justify. The explanation lies in the larger ports and in a freer flowing exhaust system comprising new heat exchangers (in which outside air is heated to feed the body heating system) with larger diameter exhaust gas pipes and a larger silencer. The new exchangers also have a double outside skin to reduce heat losses to the atmosphere. Other modifications are minor. They include limiting the engine speed by cutting off the fuel supply to the injection system when the revolutions exceed 6,520 per minute. The cut-off is electronically controlled and much more accurate than the centrifugal control shorting the high tension current in the distributor, as previously used. Another electrical change is a further increase of the alternator output (the third in the 911's life) to take care of the ever-increasing number of electric controls in modern cars.

These modifications raise the weight of the dry engine from 190 to 219 kg, which is 35 kg more than the original 901 engine of 1964 while the specific weight dropped from 1.41 to 0.95 kg/hp over the period. This is the lowest specific weight achieved by an atmospheric production engine of the 901/911/930 family, except for the competition-oriented 2.7 and 3.0 RS units, and it is worth mentioning that a 3.2-litre engine could still be dropped straight into the engine bay of a 20 years-older 911 . . . but a good man would be necessary to sort the electrics out!

One question remains to be answered: why has Porsche not taken the full step and used the 97 mm bore cylinders of the Turbo to give the new Carrera the same full 3.3-litre capacity? The reasons are twofold. One is probably a commercial one: as the 911 is to live on for several years, the Management thought that it would not be bad to keep something up their sleeve. The other is purely technical: the torque of the 3.2-litre engine is all that the type 915 gearbox can take while maintaining the durability and reliability standards Porsche set themselves, and even to achieve this, some modifications were necessary, as described in Chapter Four. Had the engine capacity been raised further, it would have been necessary either to fit the type 930 gearbox of the 3.3-Turbo (which is a lot heavier and has only four speeds, so was considered undesirable) or to develop a new five-speed unit, for which there was insufficient time. A new five-speed gearbox, type G.50, came with the 1987 model and is scheduled to be used, with minor differences, in the 1989 model Turbo.

In view of the increased power output, obtained at the same engine speed as in the 3-litre, the fourth and fifth gear ratios were modified. Fourth gear is now 0.966 (with 28:29 tooth pinions) instead of 1.000 and fifth is 0.763 (29:38) instead of 0.786, with the usual 8:31 final drive, giving an overall ratio in fifth of 2.96:1. Factory performance claims have always proved to be rather conservative and are regularly bettered by independent testers. This also applies to the Carrera which, in the hands of *Auto, Motor & Sport*'s star test driver, Michael Mehlin, achieved the following spectacular figures, compared with those for the 204 bhp 911 SC (in parentheses):

Maximum speed	157.5 mph	(149.1 mph)
0-100 km/h (62 mph)	5.8 sec	(5.9 sec)
0-160 km/h (99.5 mph)	13.9 sec	(14.7 sec)
Standing start km	25.6 sec	(25.9 sec)
Overall fuel consumption		
(Imperial)	20.8 mpg	(18.6 mpg)

It must, however, be said that, though other reliable testers, including the author, were always able to equal and usually exceed the 245 km/h (152 mph) claimed by the factory, a figure nearing that measured by *Auto, Motor & Sport* was never seen again and in later tests of standard Carreras, even that famous German magazine could never quite match the set of figures reproduced above.

The official fuel consumption figures are outstanding for a powerful sports car and better those of the 3-litre by no less than 7.6 per cent:

At a steady 55 mph	6.8 litres/100 km or 41.6 miles per Imperial gallon
At a steady 75 mph	9.0 litres/100 km or 31.4 miles per Imperial gallon
EEC urban cycle	13.6 litres/100 km or 20.8 miles per Imperial gallon.

For increased longevity, chrome-plated valve stems were introduced with 1986 models, but the 930/20 engine remained virtually unchanged for at least five years. The 'Club Sport' lightweight Carrera introduced in 1987 used lighter weight, hollow intake valves to extend the permissible revolution range from 6,400 to 6,700 rpm and the Motronic control unit was adjusted to cut the fuel supply at 6,840 rpm instead of 6,520 rpm. As the range extension lies beyond the power peak, maximum power and torque are not affected.

The capacity increase naturally also applies to the engines fitted to cars exported to the USA, Canada and Japan, all running on lead-free petrol, as required by the use of a lambda sond and three-way catalyser. These engines (930/21) use the same type of electronic engine management system as the European version and also have the same valve timing, but the compression ratio is 9.5:1 and they initially produced 207 bhp DIN at 5,900 rpm (200 hp SAE net) and 26.5 mkg (191.5 lb/ft) of torque at 4,800 rpm using 91 octane fuel. The overall gearing in fifth gear is 3.06:1 with the same 30:38 fifth gear as on the 1981–83 European 3-litre version. The overall gearing in 5th remained unchanged as the G.50 gearbox replaced the type 915 box in 1987 models. Simultaneously, the 930/25 engine replaced the 930/21 engine in US and Japan models. This new engine was tuned to use 95 instead of 91 octane lead-free fuel, retained the 9.5:1 compression ratio of its forerunner, but used a different Motronic unit. Power and torque are raised to 217 hp and 27 mkg respectively, at the same revolutions as before. The Swiss specification engine, type 930/26, introduced in 1985 models, differs from the 930/20 unit only by the addition of an air pump blowing into the exhaust ports, similar to the unit fitted to 911 SC models. Power and torque figures are as for the 930/20 engine.

Chapter Four

The evolution of the transmission

The Porsche synchronising system was originally developed for the 1953 model year of the 356 series of Porsche cars. Its main feature is that, instead of being a full ring, the female part of the synchronising mechanism is a split ring of which either end is free to abut against a stop. Consequently, as soon as the split ring comes into contact with the inner cone carried by the male part, it hits the stop with one of its ends (which end depends upon the relative speed of the male and female parts) and tends to open up in the same way as the leading shoe of a drum brake. The pressure between the two parts is thus considerably increased until the two parts rotate at the same speed, so that full synchronisation takes place very quickly. In 1959, the system was further developed to include a baulking system positively preventing the dog clutches from engaging to select the required gear until full synchronisation is obtained, whatever the force applied by the driver on the gear lever.

The new transmission developed for the then entirely new six-cylinder car, officially called the 901 at the time of its announcement in September 1964, incorporated this latest type of synchronising system on all its forward ratios. This transmission, designed to withstand higher loads than the gearbox of the 356 models, had a one-piece main housing made of sand-cast aluminium alloy and combining the housings for the clutch, the differential and the gearbox. It was open on the engine side, and had an opening on the left-hand side to insert the differential and one at its front

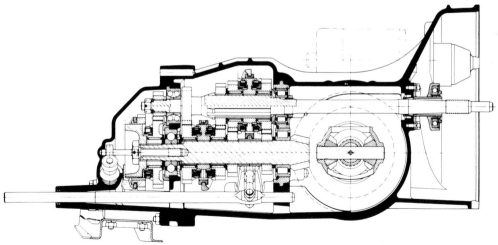

Type 901/902 transmission as fitted to all 911 models up to 2.2 litres.

end through which the gear clusters were inserted. The gearbox part of the housing had two walls carrying the bearings of the two gearbox shafts, of which the centres were 68 mm apart. Roller bearings were used at the engine end and ball bearings took the thrust at the front end. The second to fifth gear sets were located in between the bearings, whereas first and reverse gears were outrigged at the front and included in the end cover, which also carried the speedometer driving gears. All gear wheels were separate from their respective shafts, except the second speed input gear (first speed in four-speed boxes) which was cut on the input shaft itself. This permitted the selection of any pair of gears individually to suit the characteristics of the engine or any particular individual requirement, though if a non-standard second gear ratio was required the entire input shaft had to be changed. All free-running gears were on needle bearings. The selector shaft, carried in the rear wall and in the front end

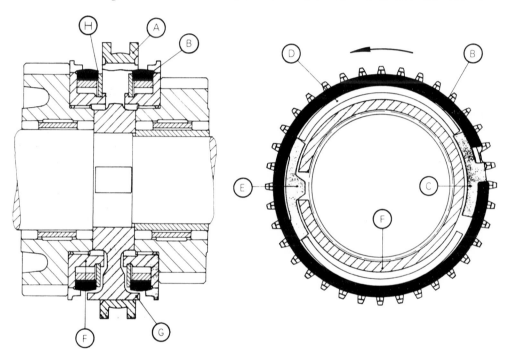

In the longitudinal sectional drawing, the selector sleeve (A) has just made contact with the synchronising ring (B) of the gear to be selected. Thanks to the friction, the ring is turned in the direction of sleeve rotation (see cross section) until it comes up against the thrust block (C) which, in turn, transmits the force to the brake band (D) and thence to the anchor block (E). The anchor block has a projection facing inwards, located in a cut-out in the clutch body (F) carried by the gear to be selected. The circumferential force transmitted by the thrust block (C) to the brake band (D) and to the anchor block (E) creates a radial component force which tends to open up the synchronising ring (B), preventing the selector sleeve (A) from moving any further. The higher the force applied by the driver to move the selector sleeve (A), the higher the force transmitted by the thrust block (C) to the brake band (D) and to the anchor block (E), and the higher the force tending to open up the synchro ring. This results in both an increased synchronising moment and a higher baulking force. As soon as the sleeve (A) and the ring (B) carried by the gear to be selected rotate at the same speed, the friction moment between them is eliminated and the force put into the synchronising mechanism is cancelled. This enables the selector sleeve (A) to compress the synchronising ring (B) and to slide over it to engage the splines of the gear to be selected. G — Synchro hub, A — Selector sleeve, H — Lock ring, E — Anchor block, D — Brake band, B — Synchronising ring, F — Gear and clutch body, C — Thrust block.

cover came out to the front where it was connected to the gear selecting rod. The selection pattern was: left plane forward for reverse, rearward for first, the upper four gears being selected on the usual H-pattern. The left plane could only be selected against a strong spring pressure.

The differential was lubricated with the same oil as the gearbox and had two star wheels. A seven-tooth pinion meshed with a 31-tooth crown wheel, giving a final drive ratio of 4.428:1. The transmission was designed for a maximum input torque of 19 mkg (138 lb/ft) and two basic versions were developed, called the 901 and the 902. The 901 series box had five speeds and the 902 box had four. They were originally destined to be fitted to the cars bearing the same type numbers, which later became the 911 and the 912. In principle, the only difference between the two boxes was that the 902 box had only four ratios, only reverse being outrigged and contained in the front cover.

The clutch disc had an outside diameter of 215 mm and pressure was provided by a diaphragm spring, with a ball release bearing. An oil seal was provided around the input shaft between the clutch housing and the differential housing.

It did not take long before a five-speed box could be specified on the Porsche 912 (virtually a 911 with the old pushrod four-cylinder engine of VW derivation). In fact, it was standard on US export models from the start, and as the transmission was virtually identical with the Type 901 box it is quite normal to find transmissions bearing the 902 type number on Porsche 911 models. This happened, for example, when the factory decided that a 902 transmission with a given set of gear ratios would be suitable for the 911 series, or when that particular set of ratios was specified for a particular export market.

Though there was a sufficient number of gear sets to allow anyone to choose his own set of ratios, every type of car was standardised with a given set which, in many cases, was different for the US and other markets. The type number of the transmission, plus its suffix number, gave a clue to the ratios it contained. As an example, 901/02 was the standard box on 1967 and 1968 911 S models. In addition to the standard sets, there were 'recommended sets' sold as special options, such as sets for hill-climb racing, for aerodrome racing, for fast tracks and a 'Nürburgring' set.

Early 911 models had a peculiar and ingenious type of universal joint at the differential ends of the half shafts. These were developed by Nadella, the needle bearing specialists. Instead of featuring a cross joining the two universal joint forks, the two forks were connected by a hinged link allowing axial movements of the half shaft without necessitating the use of splines and obviating any possibility of locking up under torque. Unfortunately, these joints did not ensure constant velocity and, though a constant velocity drive from the differential to the wheel was ensured by the universal at the other end of the shaft, the shaft itself did not run at constant velocity. Because of the shaft's inertia, this tended to create vibrations. These were increased when the suspension was deflected by a large amount from its normal static position as, due to the extension of the hinged link, the half shaft became slightly eccentric in relation to the differential output shaft. In the interest of more refined running, this type of joint was abandoned when the 911 S was introduced at the end of July 1966, all models from then on being equipped with Rzeppa-type constant velocity joints, in which the balls transmitting the drive also allow low friction axial movements of the shaft. This type of joint is still used today, though the joints themselves progressively increased in size with the rising torque produced by engines of increasing capacity.

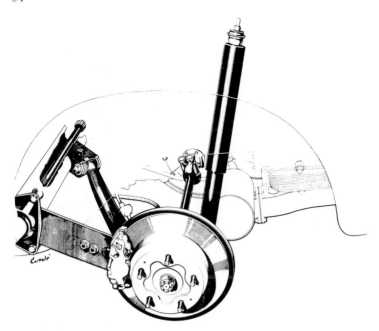

*Original 901/911 rear
suspension and drive
shaft. Note interesting
universal joint also
allowing axial move-
ments. It was later
replaced by a Rzeppa
constant velocity joint.*

During the production run of the B-series of cars (1969 models), the sand-cast aluminium transmission housing was replaced by a die-cast aluminium housing which raised the input torque capacity of the transmission to 20.5 mkg (148.5 lb/ft). This still left a good safety margin when the engine capacity was increased from 2 litres to 2.2 litres. With 2.2 litre engines, a new clutch was used, the disc diameter being increased from 215 to 225 mm. In this clutch, the pressure plate was driven by means of flexible steel straps instead of lugs, as the latter's friction in the outer clutch casing tended to reduce the effective pressure applied to the disc.

Even more important was the fact that instead of having its fulcrum points between the diaphragm spring centre and the rim, with the latter exerting the pressure on the plate, in the new clutch the diaphragm spring had the tips of its blades located in the cover. The clutch pressure plate was thus pushed by the blades along a smaller radius providing a more advantageous leverage and an increased pressure without increasing the pressure required for releasing the clutch. This also meant that the release mechanism now moved towards the engine to disengage the clutch, instead of away from it.

The Type 905 Sportomatic transmission

From the Type 901 transmission a special semi-automatic version was developed in co-operation with Fichtel & Sachs and announced in August 1967 for availability on 1968 model six-cylinder cars. This consisted of a three-element hydraulic torque converter with a maximum torque multiplication of 2.2 at stall, a vacuum operated single disc diaphragm clutch (with the release mechanism moving towards the engine) and a manually operated four-speed box. Except for the ratios, the gearbox was generally similar to four-speed versions of the 901/902 box, but a 7:27 pinion and crown wheel combination was used instead of 7:31 in order to reduce the crown wheel diameter and gain space for the incorporation of the torque converter, which also required a differently shaped one-piece housing. The housing incorporated

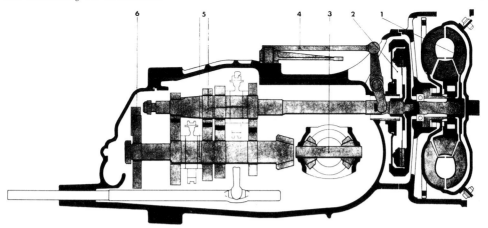

The Types 905 and 925 Sportomatic transmissions. 1 — Hydraulic torque converter, 2 — Clutch, 3 — Differential, 4 — Clutch linkage, 5 — Four-speed transmission, 6 — Locking device for parking.

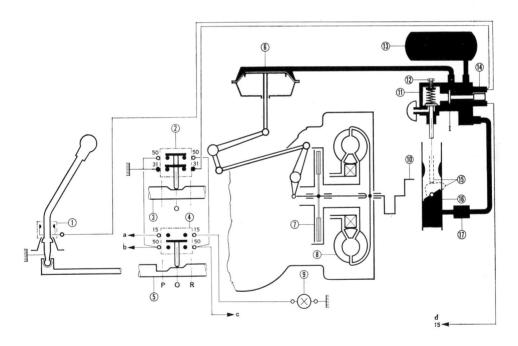

Sportomatic transmission control. The gear selector rod actuates a switch (2) controlling a solenoid operated valve (14). When neutral is selected (position illustrated), the manifold vacuum (with reservoir, 13) operates the vacuum servo (6) which disengages the clutch. When a gear is to be selected, moving the gear lever operates the lever switch (1) energising the solenoid (14) to maintain the clutch disengaged while the selection takes place. When the gear lever is released, the current supply to the solenoid is cut and air is admitted through the control valve unit (11) to reduce the vacuum in the servo and progressively re-engage the clutch. The rate of re-engagement is controlled only by the spring pressure which can be adjusted by the screw (12), but is accelerated when the driver accelerates after a change up, by a cam operated by the throttle valve and forcibly opening the control valve.

the lugs for the attachment of the automatic clutch operating servo and its linkage.

In this transmission, the only purpose of the disc clutch is to separate the engine from the transmission for gear selection, either at rest or in motion. It is not used for starting and must not be released when stopping, all those functions being taken care of by the hydraulic torque converter. Clutch operation is entirely automatic: switches incorporated at the foot of the gear lever and in the gear linkage ensure that, as soon as the driver tries to move the lever, the clutch is released. This is done by a solenoid connecting a vacuum reserve tank (maintained at a low pressure by a connection with the engine's intake system) with the vacuum chamber of a simple diaphragm servo linked to the clutch release mechanism. An additional modulating valve adjusts the speed of the clutch engagement after a change of ratio, according to the driving conditions, engagement being much quicker if full throttle is given immediately after the change than if the shift is made with the throttle shut.

The hydraulic torque converter is fed with oil from the main engine oil tank, but the circuit is entirely independent, circulation being obtained by a small gear pump driven off the front end of the left-hand engine camshaft. As the converter oil mixes with the engine oil in the tank, no provision is made for cooling the converter oil separately: this is taken care of by the engine oil cooler.

Two-pedal driving is thus obtained with a comparatively simple system providing extreme flexibility and driving ease, with no clutch wear in city driving, while on the road the gearbox can be used to obtain full performance, the driver retaining complete control over the ratios selected.

Automatic or semi-automatic transmissions are not normally very popular with sports car drivers and it was important for Porsche to find a means of fighting this prejudice when the Sportomatic transmission was announced. The occasion was provided by the 'Marathon de la Route' 84 hours trial which took place at the Nürburgring the month the new transmission was announced. This event, organised by the Belgian 'Motor Union' of Liège was not exactly a race, but rather a high-speed reliability event lasting for 3½ days and nights non-stop. A maximum lap time was assigned to the various car classes (Porsches were in the fastest class), which had to be held on *every lap*. Competitors were free to go faster, in order to turn the highest number of laps within the 84 hours, but for *every minute* above the scheduled lap time or any pit stop of more than a minute's duration (excluding refuelling) a full lap was subtracted from the total, except for a 20 minute pit stop for servicing allowed every 75th lap. The winner was, of course, the car which, at the end of the 84 hours, totalled the highest number of laps, after the penalty laps had been subtracted from the real total.

For this event, Porsche entered three different cars: a 911 R (a special racing version of the 911 S, to be described in the chapter on racing development of the 911) fitted with Sportomatic transmission; a 911 S with Sportomatic transmission; and a 911 S with normal five-speed transmission.

All cars had standard engines in 'Stage 1' (Sportkit 1) tune, each giving off approximately 170 (DIN) bhp. Some of the suspension attachment lugs had been reinforced, but except for some extra equipment such as an emergency alternator, an emergency fuel pump and extra lamps, they were very nearly standard. The 911 R had 6 inch wide wheels and racing tyres, the other two were on 5½ inch rims shod with HR or racing tyres, according to conditions. All tyres were Dunlops.

To cut a long story short (and 84 hours *do* make a long racing story!) one of these cars finished the event and won it . . . and to everyone's delight it was the Sporto-

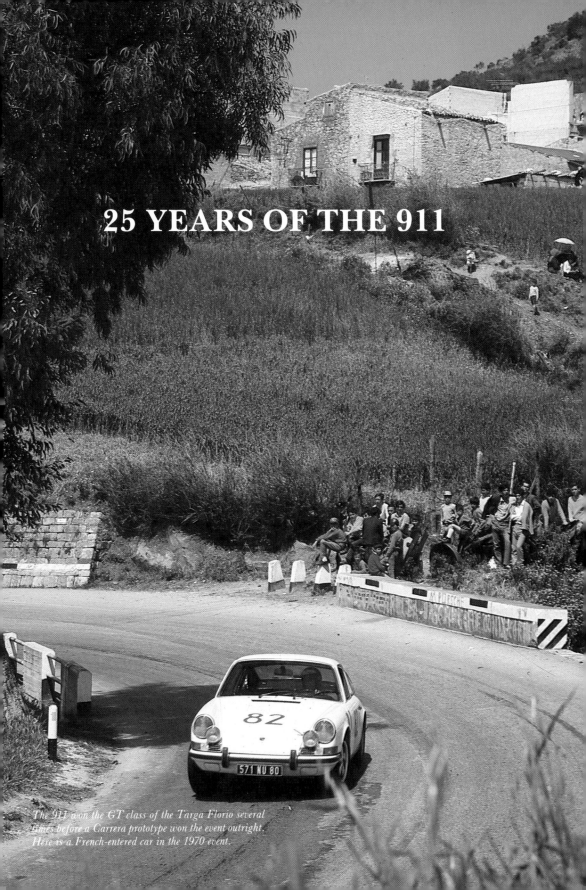

25 YEARS OF THE 911

The 911 won the GT class of the Targa Florio several times before a Carrera prototype won the event outright. Here is a French-entered car in the 1970 event.

The 911 has a glorious history in motor sport. From right to left, 1965 2 litre 911 'Monte', 1978 3.2 litre 935/78 'Moby Dick', 1987 2.85 litre 961, the race version of the 959.

Above *The 2.14 litre Turbo Carrera finished second overall in the 1974 Le Mans 24-Hours race* (M. Cotton).

Below *In the International Race of Champions in 1974 at Riverside, the drivers were each allotted a 3 litre Carrera RSR, of which it was the first public outing* (M. Cotton).

Above *Porsche 935 in its 635 hp version of 1977 (*M. Cotton*).*

Below *The 935/78 'Moby Dick' was the ultimate development of the 911 for racing. It was powered by the 24 valve 3.2 litre engine and reached 366 km/h (227 mph) on the Le Mans straight in practice for the 1978 race.*

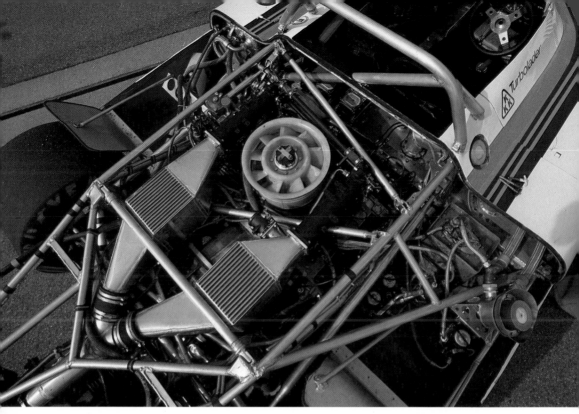

Above *The 936's engine is a development of the production 911 unit. (R. W. Schlegelmilch).*

Below *The author driving a Porsche 935 on the factory's private circuit in Weissach in 1976. The car gave Porsche the World Championship for 1976 (R. W. Schlegelmilch).*

Above *Driver's working place in the Porsche 935* (R. W. Schlegelmilch).

Below *After 1978, Porsche left it to its customers to defend its colours as here at Hockenheim in 1980. But at Weissach, development continued to keep the 935 competitive* (M. Cotton).

Above *In its type 935 racing version, the 911 even won Le Mans in 1979. The Kremer-prepared car was driven by Klaus Ludwig and the Whittington brothers.*

Below *Porsche has its own Special Equipment Department. Among its offerings is a 'Flat-nose' 911 Turbo tuned to produce 330 hp and capable of 170 mph (273.5 km/h)* (M. Cotton).

When Porsche retired from official participation in Group 5 racing, private teams continued to develop the 935 along their own lines. Two examples are shown here in 1980 at Norisring. The most successful was the Kremer K3 (below).

A prototype 911 'Speedster' based on the 911SC was built as early as Spring 1983 but was kept secret for four years. It had no weather protection.

The 911 'Speedster' was Porsche's main attraction at the 1987 Frankfurt Motor Show, one full year before it became available.

Three high ground clearance 959 prototypes were entered for the 1987 Paris-Dakar rally – 8,000 miles across the Sahara and the African forests. They took first, second and fifth places. This is the winning car of Metge-Lemoyne.

Above *In the 25 years of the 911's existence, the dashboard has retained the original shape and layout. The 260 km/h speedometer and the 3-spoke steering wheel reveal that this is a 1984 3.2 litre Carrera.*

Below *A pre-1984 911 Turbo in the old city of Munich.*

Above *The author at speed at the wheel of the 959 'Sport'. The speedometer indicates 315 km/h (196 mph)!*

Below *The author with his own 911 Carrera in 1988.*

The entire 911 range for 1988 (Auto Motor und Sport).

Above *The 911 Cabrio began its career as a 3 litre 911SC in 1982.*

Below *The aerodynamically optimized 911 Carrera 4 still retains the basic shape.*

matic 911 R which — surely not by simple chance — had been entrusted to the most outstanding crew available: Hermann-Neerpasch-Elford. It finished with a margin of 34 laps of the full Nürburgring — nearly 1,000 kilometres! — over the car placed second, a factory-prepared MG-C GT. Of the other two Porsches, the five-speed 911 S crashed on the 201st lap and the Sportomatic 911 S had to retire at about three-quarter distance due to a broken valve spring. Up to their retirement, both those cars had had a much more trouble-free run than the 911 R, which had problems first with the ignition, then with a split oil tank and finally with a front wheel bearing. But on this and the other Sportomatic car no trouble whatsoever was experienced with the transmission, and it is most interesting to note that, of the three cars entered, the two Sportomatic cars were the most economical on fuel.

This victory was, of course, a considerable asset in making the Sportomatic transmission acceptable to sporting-minded drivers.

The Type 905 Sportomatic transmission was originally designed to accept an input torque of 17.5 mkg (127 lb/ft) and was up-rated to 19.5 mkg (141 lb/ft) when sand-cast aluminium was abandoned in favour of die-cast aluminium as housing material. It remained in production until the end of the 1973 model run (F-series) when it was fitted to 911 T models with carburettor engines, all other models specified with the Sportomatic transmission already using the beefed-up 925.

The Type 925 Sportomatic

As originally designed, the Type 905 Sportomatic transmission became inadequate when the 2.4 litre engines were introduced, at the end of 1971, except in the case of the 911 T which produced a maximum torque of 20 mkg (145 lb/ft), where it could just be expected to meet Porsche's strict longevity standards. For the more powerful versions, the transmission had to be redesigned to take a larger diameter torque converter and clutch, a larger crown wheel and pinion assembly (the ratio remaining 7:27) and a stronger differential, while the housing itself was generously reinforced by additional heavy ribs. There was no fundamental change in the design, but the torque capacity was increased to 23.5 mkg (170 lb/ft). This transmission was introduced for the E-series cars in August 1971 (except for the 130 bhp 911 T) and enabled Porsche again to offer the Sportomatic transmission on 911 S models. It was just adequate for the 2.7 litre K-Jetronic engines, but further increases in engine torque made further reinforcements necessary. In view of this requirement, the Type 925 Sportomatic transmission was further developed under the project number 925/10, which has a three-speed instead of four-speed gearbox. It became available on US models as from the H-series (1975 models) but only became essential when the I-series 3 litre Carrera was introduced. The reduction of the number of ratios to three was a logical development in view of the very high torque and flat torque curve produced by the latest engines and made it possible to increase the width of the gears in order to increase their load capacity, while retaining the existing external dimensions of the transmission. This latest version of the Sportomatic uses an 8/27 crown wheel and pinion combination which is more robust than the 7/27 combination. But even so, it would not have been up to the torque of the 3.2 litre engine and the request had shrunk considerably; the Sportomatic was discontinued with the advent of that more powerful engine.

Other transmissions developed from the original Type 901

Several other transmissions were developed from the original Type 901 unit. The first was the Type 904, used in the central-engined Type 904 competition Coupé.

This was virtually identical with the 901 transmission, except for the fact that the differential was inverted in its housing (crown wheel on the other side) because of the inverted position of the engine unit in the car. From this, the Type 914 transmission (for the VW-Porsche 914) was derived, differing mainly from the 904 transmission by its rectified gears (for increased quietness) and a different gear selection mechanism. The 904 box was used practically unchanged in the Porsche 906 (Carrera-6) sports racing car, in which it was known as the Type 906 transmission and, with a different housing to relocate the differential at the end opposite the input side, as the Type 909 box in the Type 909 'Bergspyder' hill-climb racing car which had its 2 litre flat-eight engine, the clutch, the gearbox and the differential arranged in that order in the chassis.

The Type 915 transmission unit

Followers of Porsche's racing activities will remember that the Type 908, 3 litre, flat-8 sports prototype was developed in record time from the Type 907 by replacing the 2.2 litre Type 771 flat-8 by the entirely new, bigger unit. As the Type 906 box would not stand up to the torque of the larger engine, this was initially mated to a six-speed box, with the clutch located at the end opposite to the engine, which had been developed for Porsche's hill-climb cars, but had never been used because it turned out to be too heavy. In those times, under the technical direction of Ferdinand Piëch, unnecessary weight was the last thing tolerated and the transmission engineers were immediately commissioned to design a new, much lighter transmission in which five ratios were deemed sufficient. This was the Type 916 transmission which was fitted to the 908 prototypes from the beginning of the 1969 season. It was a larger transmission than the Type 901-906 series, the distance

Type 915 transmission as fitted to all 911 models from 2.4 litre onwards, five-speed version. 1 — Front cover, 2 — Reverse gear, 3 — Fifth speed fixed gear, 4 — Needle bearing, 5 — First speed fixed gear, 6 — Gearbox housing, 7 — Second speed fixed gear, 8 — Third speed idling gear, 9 — Synchronising ring, 10 — Selector guide, 11 — Fourth speed idling gear, 12 — Thrust bearing, 13 — Roller bearing, 14 — Lock nut, 15 — Input shaft, 16 — Differential and clutch housing, 17 — Breather, 18 — Seal, 19 — Speedo driving pinion, 20 — Selector, fifth and reverse gear, 21 — Lock nut, 22 — Fifth and reverse gear selector fork, 23 — Fifth speed idling gear, 24 — Roller bearing, 25 — First and second gear selector fork, 26 — Internal gear change lever, 27 — Locking plate, 28 — Spherical bush, 29 — Input shaft, 30 — Differential.

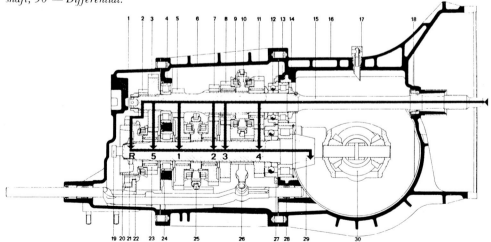

Type 915 gearbox with oil cooler, as fitted to 911 Carrera models 1984–86. The gear pump circulating the oil is included in the flange holding the serpentine and is driven by a large gear carried by the satellite housing.

between shaft centres being increased by 9 mm from 68 to 77 mm, allowing the use of larger gears. Another difference was that there were now two separate main housings bolted together, one for the clutch and differential unit and one for the gearbox itself, which allowed the gearbox to be removed for servicing or a change of ratios without disturbing the clutch. In order to prevent oil churning which, according to tests carried out by the factory, cost 7-8 bhp at 185 mph, the oil in the gearbox casing was kept below gear level and circulated by a gear pump included in the gearbox cover which fed it to jets spraying the lubricant on to the most highly stressed areas.

One important modification, compared with the earlier 901-906 design was that the first and the fifth gear sets were now inverted, fifth being outrigged and easily accessible by removing the gearbox cover, which facilitated the change of fifth gear ratio — the most commonly required change following practice for a sporting event.

This Type 916 transmission, rated at 33 mkg (239 lb/ft), is the unit from which a new transmission, Type 915, was developed for 911 production models, to be introduced with the 2.4 litre range of engines for which the Type 911 transmission had become inadequate. It generally follows the pattern set by the Type 916 box, but has a shaft centre distance of 76 instead of 77 mm, it being considered desirable to lower the differential output shafts as little as possible in relation to the wheel hubs. The differential assembly is, of course, turned through 180° in view of the overhung position of the engine and normal production models have splash lubrication, the oil pump being deleted, though it is fitted to cars modified for racing and was a standard feature on the limited production Carrera RS 3.0. When a pump is fitted, the transmission lubrication circuit includes an oil cooler.

In this transmission the clutch and differential housing is made of die-cast aluminium, while the gearbox and its cover are magnesium alloy. Compared with the Type 911 transmission, the bearings are considerably reinforced: both the input and the output shaft run on large roller bearings at either end, end thrust being, in both cases, taken by large ball bearings retained by a plate bolted into the differential housing, so that no thrust is fed into the magnesium gearbox housing and the clearance between the crown wheel and the pinion is affected only immaterially by the different heat expansion rates of the steel shaft and the alloy housing.

The production 915 transmissions exist in four- and five-speed versions. Four-speed versions have the usual H-selection pattern, as before, but reverse is obtained by pushing the lever against a spring resistance to the right and back, whereas previously it was selected by moving it to the extreme left and forward. Five-speed transmissions have the four lower gears in the same, conventional H-pattern and fifth is obtained by moving the lever against spring pressure to the extreme right and forward (opposite reverse). Not all Porsche owners welcomed this change from the accepted Porsche practice (when first gear was on its own, on the extreme left and back and the four upper ratios arranged according to the conventional H-pattern) to what used to be known as the 'Alfa'-pattern, as they (rightly) felt that they could make quicker and nicer changes between fourth and fifth and vice-versa when the two positions were in line than when they had to be selected in two different lanes. Porsche's view is that, traffic becoming increasingly heavier, even Porsche owners move the lever very much more often between first and second than between fourth and fifth and that, consequently, the former is the more important change of the two. With time, the current pattern seems to have become generally accepted, especially as detail developments have smoothed the selection process compared with early 915 boxes.

The gear cluster of the standard 915 transmission is designed to take an input torque of 25 mkg (181 lb/ft), but for racing higher torques can be transmitted using a reinforced final drive and adding a pump circulating the oil through a cooler and feeding jets spraying the most stressed gears and the crown wheel and pinion assembly. Such a transmission (type 915/50) was a standard fitment on the Carrera RS 3.0 of the 1974 model year. For racing, where long-term wear is irrelevant, input torques of up to 38 mkg (275 lb/ft) are permissible thanks to the cooling effect of the oil jets. When the H-series (1975 models) was introduced, the 7/31 crown wheel and pinion assembly was replaced with a more robust 8/31 assembly. The 1st and 2nd gears of the four-speed and the 1st, 2nd and 3rd gears of the five-speed gearbox remained unchanged, which means that these ratios were now geared 14 per cent higher than before, which helped the cars to pass German noise regulations. The other gears were adapted to leave the overall gearing in the highest ratio almost unchanged, the new ratio being 3.183 compared with the previous overall ratio of 3.206:1. In later years, the ratios of the type 915 box were adapted to the characteristics of the engines as they were developed, but with the advent of the 911 SC (model year 1978), the four-speed gearbox was phased out. Though it had never been designed for the task, the type 915 gearbox, after being given some reinforcements, was used successfully, in the racing 911 Turbo Carrera of 1974, the 2.14 litre turbocharged engine of which produced over 55 mkg (400 ft/lb) of torque. This was not without some problems, however.

From the 1976 models on (I-series), a magnetic speed sensor was included in the differential unit of all gearboxes, except Sportomatic, to monitor the newly-introduced electronic speedometer.

As time went on, reversion to cast aluminium was progressively made for most major castings which, after having originally been made of aluminium had, for some years, been cast in magnesium alloy in order to save weight. The reversion to the heavier, but more resistant aluminium was dictated by the higher stresses imposed by the ever increasing torque output of the engines. Typical examples are the engine crankcase and the housing of the type 930 gearbox specifically designed for the Turbo, and for which aluminium was chosen from the start. In 1977, the type 915 gearbox was the only major magnesium casting in the 911 and it was decided, mainly in order to rationalise production, to replace the magnesium by an aluminium casting for the 1978 model year. This step would probably have become necessary anyway as the capacity of the atmospheric 911 engine was increased from 3.0 to 3.2 litres for the 1984 models, in which the gearbox set the limit to the possible increase in performance. Even with the power and torque available from that engine, it was necessary to use fourth and fifth gear pinions with a higher modulus and to lower the oil temperature. In contrast to the racing gearboxes which have an oil pump in the front cover, the oil pump used in the revised gearbox is incorporated in the side cover through which the differential unit is inserted and driven from the left side output shaft. It circulates the oil through a cooling serpentine located on the side of the gearbox housing, which makes the whole installation a self-contained unit. If a limited slip differential is specified, the differential gear housing of this transmission is made of cast steel instead of heavier and less resistant cast iron.

The type 930 transmission

When the type 915 gearbox was originally designed, the possibility of turbocharging the flat-six engine had not been envisaged and it could not conceivably be expected reliably and durably to transmit the torque of even the 3-litre 'Turbo' (and even less the torque produced by its racing developments). Consequently, a new transmission was designed under the same project number 930 as the Porsche Turbo. This is, in fact, a development of the type 915 transmission. In standard form it has splash lubrication, but a version with an oil pump and cooler is available for competition work. In this case, both the clutch and differential housing and the gearbox itself were made in aluminium from the start and are very heavily ribbed. The clutch disc diameter is increased from 225 to 240 mm, the gearbox shafts are thicker and the gears themselves wider. This is strictly a four-speed transmission, no provision being made for a five-speed version. Small modifications were also made to the synchronising system: the split synchronising rings of the upper three ratios have a collar fitting into the internal tooth ring of the gear to be selected, limiting the amount of opening up of the split synchronising ring. In the case of first gear a full, ie, non-split synchronising cone is used in order to facilitate the selection when the car is at rest. From the K-series on, the modified synchronising rings were also used in first and second gears of the type 915 gearbox, while further to improve selection from rest the teeth of the first gear dog clutches were cut asymmetrically.

In the type 930 transmission, a four star differential (optionally of the 80 per cent limited slip type) is used. Originally, two final drive ratios were available (9/36 and 9/38) to suit different tyre diameters, but as 16 inch diameter wheels became available for the low profile (50 series) tyres, the 9/36 option was deleted. The transmission is rated at 45 mkg (326 lb/ft) for production, but did, with a reduced life expectancy, transmit the torque of the most powerful Group 5 engines.

Gearbox chatter at low engine speeds, under load, has plagued the 911 models from the start. For the L-series (1978 model) cars Porsche developed its own type of rubber-damped clutch disc hub allowing an angular movement of 34° either side of the central position (instead of only 2.5°) in the case of the 3.3-litre Turbo and 29° (instead of 14°) in the case of

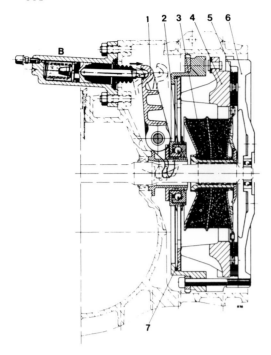

Above *Clutch disc with rubber cushioned hub for 911 Carrera 1987 and later models. A similar disc has been used in the Turbo since 1978.*

Left *Hydraulically-operated clutch of Carrera 3.2, from 1987 model on, showing rubber cushioned disc hub. 1. Release lever. 2. Release bearing. 3. Rubber cushioned hub. 4. Pressure plate. 5. Clutch disc. 6. Flywheel.*

the 911. The movement is limited by a positive abutment to prevent overstressing of the rubber under full torque. Additionally, the clutch housing material was changed from light alloy to cast steel and the weight of the pressure plate increased, to increase the polar moment of the clutch. This has effectively suppressed the low speed chatter, but the thickness of the clutch disc hub has, in the case of the Turbo, required a new gearbox casting in which the bell housing is lengthened by 30 mm, moving back the entire engine by the same amount.

Although the large-sized rubber-damped hub proved satisfactory in the Turbo, the smaller size hub would not have been able to transmit reliably the higher torque of the 204 bhp engine used in the 911 SC from 1981 on, and a reversion was made to coil springs, though the rubber-damped hub was retained for the USA, Canada and Japan models. Thanks to a better hub design and to the heavier pressure plate introduced for the 1978 models, the return to a metal-sprung disc hub did not increase the gear chatter significantly. The asbestos-free clutch linings introduced in the 1984 models are a contribution to the reduction of air pollution.

The Type G50 transmission

The gearbox oil cooler and its pump added to the type 915 gearbox were an expensive solution to the problem of adapting the transmission to the high torque of the 3.2 litre Carrera engine. Meanwhile Porsche had also realised that their own synchronising system, while being very durable and reliable required higher shifting forces than the widely-used Borg-Warner system. Porsche had an extensive experience of this system, because it was used in the Audi-based gearbox of their 924 and 944 models, and the right conclusions had already been drawn when the gearbox of the Porsche 928 was redesigned to incorporate that system. No wonder that the Borg-Warner synchronisers were chosen when a new five-speed gearbox was designed to take care of the 3.2 litre's torque without requiring a cooler as first used in 1987 Carrera models. It was designed with a sufficient development potential to transmit the torque of the 3.3 litre Turbo engine of the 1989 model.

The new gearbox, type G50, is manufactured by Getrag, as its predecessor, and, as fitted to the 3.2 litre atmospheric engine, has a torque rating of 300 Nm (30.6 mkg or 221 lb/ft). The shaft centre distance is 85 mm—9 mm more than in the 915 box—and the housing is die-cast aluminium, but so designed that a magnesium housing would also provide sufficient strength—just in case. While in previous transmissions, the springs and baulking mechanisms of the shifting system were part of the lever console, in the G50 box they are incorporated in the gearbox itself. The noise insulation of the linkage was also modified. The shift pattern comprises four planes: instead of being located in the same plane as 5th gear, the reverse position is in a plane on its own, at the extreme left and forward of the gate.

The clutch too was reinforced to match the gearbox's torque rating: the 240 mm diameter disc of the Turbo is used, complete with its large rubber cushioned hub which has all but eliminated low speed gear chatter. On the same occasion, the cable operation of the clutch was replaced with hydraulic operation which has a better mechanical efficiency and has noticeably reduced the pedal pressure.

In the case of the Turbo, the space taken by the rubber-cushioned hub made it necessary to move the engine 30 mm back, which did not make life easier for the chassis engineers. In the case of the G50 gearbox, the clutch housing was designed to make this unnecessary and the weight distribution remained unchanged. The rear crossmember carrying the rear suspension and the gearbox, however, had to be redesigned to suit the new box. The suspension pick-up points have remained unchanged, but the splines in which the torsion bars of the suspension are inserted were modified to SAE norms for more accurate ride height adjustment.

The new gearbox was designed to fit into the unmodified body shell. This is helped by using a hypoïd crown wheel and pinion assembly, reducing the overall length of the box,

Type G50 gearbox introduced in 3.2 litre 1987 models.

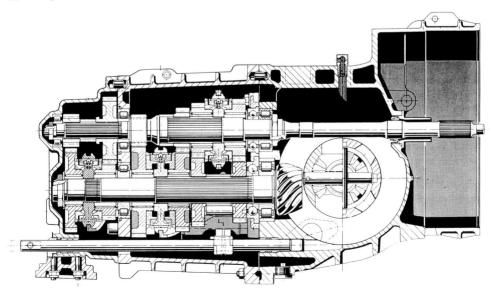

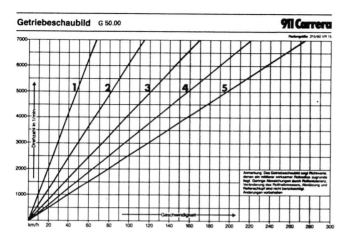

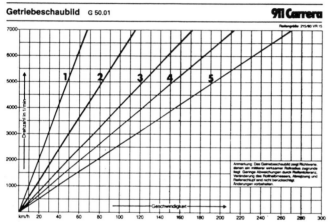

Engine speed/car speed diagrams for Carrera 3.2 litre with G50 gearbox. Below: USA, Canada, Japan and Australia models. Above: Rest of world, except Switzerland.

in place of the former spiral bevel gears. The hypoïd gears also have the advantage of leaving the differential at approximately the same level as before, in spite of the 9 mm increase in the gearbox shaft distance, so that the drive shaft universals must not operate at a larger angle than before. The ratio of the hypoïd gears is 9:31 = 3.444:1.

European specification cars (except those exported to Switzerland) have the gearbox with the type number G50/00 which has the following ratios:

1st   12:42 = 3.500:1
2nd 17:35 = 2.059:1
3rd 22:31 = 1.409:1
4th   27:29 = 1.074:1
5th   36:31 = 0.861:1
Rev 21:40 = 2.857:1

The type G50/01 gearbox for Australia, Japan, the USA and Canada has slightly lower 4th and 5th gears (36:32 = 1.125 and 32:36 = 0.889), while that for Switzerland has the G50/02 gearbox with slightly taller 1st, 2nd, 3rd and 4th gears to meet the local emission and noise regulations, which is far from ideal for an essentially mountainous country.

From 1989 models on, the 911 Turbo's 4-speed gearbox with Porsche synchromesh was replaced with a new 5-speed box of the G50 family featuring Borg-Warner synchromesh and having the following gear pairings and ratios:

1st 13:41 = 3.154:1
2nd 19:34 = 1.789:1
3rd 26:33 = 1.269:1
4th 30:29 = 0.967:1
5th 33:25 = 0.758:1

With the 9:31 = 3.444:1 final drive ratio, this results in a speed in 5th gear of 24.5 mph at 1,000 rpm.

The four-wheel drive project

Porsche's special show exhibits usually herald future evolutions of production models. For that reason, the turbocharged four-wheel drive Cabriolet disclosed at the Frankfurt motor show of 1981 was to be taken very seriously: proof is that the drophead version of the 911 was officially announced only a few months later, albeit with the atmospheric 3-litre engine and the narrower wheel arches of the normal 911 SC range. At the time, Porsche made no secret about the fact that four-wheel drive would be part of future 911 developments, and two years later, again on the occasion of the Frankfurt Motor Show, Porsche disclosed a prototype of what was to be the base for a Group B racing car, derived from the 911, but featuring permanent four-wheel drive. Meanwhile four-wheel drive development had made much progress and only a few months later three 911 Carrera-based cars with four-wheel drive had successfully competed in the 7,500 mile Paris–Dakar Rally in which they ran as part of the four-wheel drive development programme. All three cars finished the gruelling event in which they took 1st, 6th and 26th place, neither the transmission nor the engine having suffered any serious problem.

Except for a compression ratio lowered to 9.5:1 in deference to the inferior fuel available in Africa, the engines were virtually standard Carrera 3.2, but the ground clearance of the cars had been increased to 27 cm (10.6 in) and the front suspension—still using torsion bars—had been modified to twin transverse wishbones with reinforced lower wishbones and two shock absorbers per wheel. At the rear, the Turbo's beefier inner semi-trailing arms were used. The rear power unit was rigidly connected to the front differential by a thick tube through which the propeller shaft was led, a layout similar in principle to that found in the front-engined Porsche models. The manually-lockable, torque-splitting, epicyclic differential was bolted to the front end of the gearbox housing and transmitted 69 per cent of the torque to the rear and 31 per cent to the front axle. As in normal Porsche racing car practice, there was no rear axle differential, while the front differential could not be locked. Two fuel tanks, one under the front bonnet, the other in the cockpit, behind the seats, had a total capacity of 260 litres (57 gallons). The gearbox ratios had been chosen in function of the conditions prevailing in the desert and the cars had a maximum speed of 220 km/h (137 mph).

The Paris–Dakar 911s were only a first step towards more sophisticated answers to the four-wheel drive problems and the technique incorporated in the Group B project. This eventually matured to become the Porsche 959 and its competition-derivative 961 in which the variable torque split between the front and rear axles is monitored by a micro-processor, as described in Chapter 8, while a development of the transmission of the 1984 Paris–Dakar cars is used in the 911 Carrera 4 described in Chapter 9.

Chapter Five

Improving the handling and safety

According to the factory's development engineers, 901 production prototypes handled reasonably well, though some intensive development was necessary to achieve this result within the framework of the basic requirements the designer had to face, one of which was that the car should not require any routine servicing.

This meant that some sort of rubber bushes or self-lubricating units had to be used and at the time the car was under development Boge, the manufacturers of shock absorbers and various hydraulic equipment, came up with a new type of rubber bush which, instead of working in shear, as does a Silentbloc, allowed some movement between the rubber insert and the metallic cylinder in which it was enclosed, wear and friction being reduced to a minimum by a permanent lubricating fluid. The advantages claimed for these 'Fluidbloc' bushes, as they were called, was that they allowed large angular movements with only a small resisting torque which could be neglected when calculating suspension rates, whereas the spring action of a Silentbloc or Flanbloc (similar to a Silentbloc, but with abutments to limit axial movements) must be taken into account and is likely to vary with age and fatigue.

Unfortunately those Fluidblocs which had given excellent results on testing rigs did not live up to the claims made for them when on the car. There were apparently situations when the lubricating fluid was squeezed out and the bush became almost solid, completely upsetting the springing characteristics. They were also tried on the Type 904 racing coupé, which was developed at the same time as the 901 (later 911) and following a dramatic testing session at the Nürburgring, when the 904's handling was improved out of all recognition when the Fluidblocs were replaced by Flanblocs, the Fluidblocs were finally discarded for ever.

New problems cropped up when the car was put into production and tolerances could not be kept within the extremely close limits of the prototype shop. Whereas the considerable influence of the throttle opening on the car's cornering behaviour was an inherent characteristic of the design, many of the production cars behaved differently on right- and left-hand bends and in many cases the straight-line stability left very much to be desired. Investigation indicated that the erratic cornering behaviour was usually caused by unequal weight carried by two wheels of the same set, due to unequal torsion bar loading. This cannot be checked unless appropriate scales are available — which they were not on the production line — as a car can be perfectly horizontal, from a front view, with two diagonally opposed springs wound up very hard and the other two carrying only very little of the car's weight. This problem was solved when appropriate scales were installed in the production shop.

Poor straight line stability is an inherent characteristic of any car with a strong rear weight bias and a low polar moment of inertia, but in the case of the Porsche it was

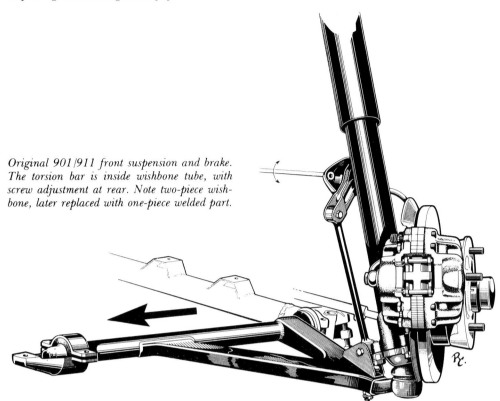

Original 901/911 front suspension and brake. The torsion bar is inside wishbone tube, with screw adjustment at rear. Note two-piece wishbone, later replaced with one-piece welded part.

made worse by excessive friction in the lower front suspension ball joints accommodating both steering and suspension movements. The early design was generally similar to the current set-up with the steel bolt peg bolted to the MacPherson strut and the two steel-backed shells (with spring loading for automatic adjustment for wear) made of a plastic material called Delrin. Unfortunately the plastics of 1965 were not those produced ten years later, and the already comparatively high friction was in many cases aggravated by the plastic of the upper shell creeping around the pivot and interfering with the self-centring action. The remedy was to separate the functions of suspension and steering: instead of being integral with the ball, the pivot was allowed to turn in a plastic bush inside the ball to accommodate steering movements, while the ball took care of the suspension movements. This considerably improved the self-centring action around the straight-ahead position, with beneficial results on the straight-line stability and made it possible to reduce the castor angle from 7°45′ to 6°45′ while steering response was improved by giving the wheels 40′ toe-in. The reduction of both friction and castor contributed to making the steering appreciably lighter. The pivoted ball system which went into production roughly one year after the first cars rolled off the production line was continued for approximately two or three more years, during which development work on fixed ball joints continued until a satisfactory plastic material combining a high load resistance with very low friction was found and approved for production, which continues practically unaltered today. Initially, the castor angle was kept unaltered at 6°45′, but from the C-series (2.2 litre) on, it was further reduced to 6°5′ as the wider tyres were found to provide sufficient additional return action, thanks to their stronger self-aligning torque. It is interesting to note that, when the pivoted ball system was developed, some experimental cars were built with the pivot mounted on a needle bearing in the ball. They are said to have been extremely good and set the standard by which the other, simpler solutions were judged.

Another reason for the 911's sometimes erratic behaviour was the lack of provision for camber and castor adjustments. Ing Tomala, who was Porsche's Technical Director when the 901 was designed and originally developed, held the opinion that no adjustment was necessary at the top end of the MacPherson struts. 'Production tolerances on the body shell are very strict,' he said, 'and by drilling the upper locating holes in accordance with measurements made after the suspension has been completely assembled, it should be possible to compensate for any small inaccuracy in the body assembly and get the castor and camber settings exactly right.' In practice this never worked out, especially as extremely strict tolerances had to be observed on the front-end geometry to achieve tolerable handling, as already mentioned in Chapter 2. An early modification was thus the provision of facilities to adjust the upper location of the MacPherson strut, making it possible to adjust both castor and camber to the very close tolerances prescribed.

Obviously, all these modifications could not be developed and put into production overnight, and that is where the weighted front bumper came in, as described in

So-called 'pot' steering of early 911 models (O- and A-series). The pinion is carried in a housing floating in the steering box and is pressed against the rack by a spring enclosed in an inverted cup plunger. Excellent, but rather complicated and expensive.

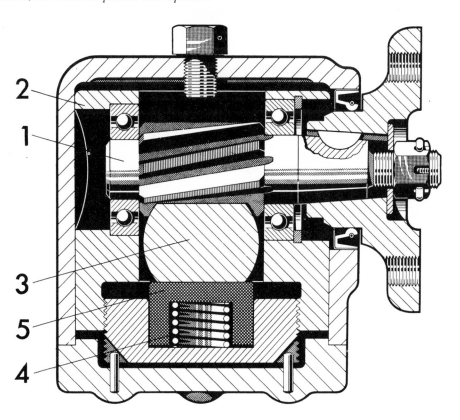

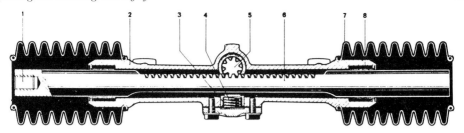

Type 914 steering used in 911 beginning with the B-series. The pinion is carried in ball bearings in the steering box. Flexion of the rack under pressure from spring and plunger suffice to ensure absence of play. 1 — Thread for track rod ball joint, 2 — Housing, 3 — Plunger, 4 — Pressure spring, 5 — Pinion, 6 — Rack, 7 — Dust cover, 8 — Bearing bush.

Chapter 2. Iron lumps, each weighing 11 kg (24.5 lb), were inserted into the extremities of the bumper, adding some weight to the light front end and increasing the car's polar moment of inertia, both around its vertical and its longitudinal axes. The improvement in straight-line stability and the reduced sensitivity to side winds were quite out of proportion to the inertia increase and to the weight transfer achieved.

This makeshift modification made it quite clear that, even if the other modifications in the course of development and the improved production methods were successful and made it possible to discard the shameful iron lumps, it must be an advantage to locate heavy components as far to the front and to the sides of the car as possible. Consequently, the single large 12V battery of 45 AH which was carried at the extreme front of the vehicle, near its centreline, was replaced, as from the B-series (1969 models) by two 36 AH batteries connected in parallel and housed in either of the front wings in a well below the headlight. There is thus a good reason why, up to F-series models, Porsche batteries are not particularly easy to get at. With the introduction of the G-series cars (1974 models) in which an 80 litre (17½ Imp gallons) fuel tank and a space-saver reserve tyre are standard, a single battery (of 66 AH capacity) is used again, located as far left as possible under the boot mat, while the spare wheel is accommodated in a well formed by the tank, at the extreme right, there being no room left in the front wings due to the reinforced bumper mountings required on several export markets.

Speaking of early developments of the front end of the 911, it may be of interest to mention that the car owes its rack-and-pinion steering only to the sheer determination of the Technical Director of the period, Ing Tomala, the experimental department being more in favour of Gemmer worm-and-roller steering, as used on the 356 series. Their opinion was that rack-and-pinion steering would wear quicker around the straight-ahead position and that subsequent adjustment might make the steering stiff on lock. Consequently a completely original design was produced. The pinion and the rack were a sub-assembly in which the rack was spring loaded against the pinion, of which the shaft, ball bearing mounted in the sub-assembly, floated in the main housing.

The design turned out to be really satisfactory, but it was rather expensive to make. Thus when Porsche designed the 914 a new rack-and-pinion steering gear was employed in which the rack had a comparatively low beam strength and was spring loaded against the pinion carried in the main housing, as is normal practice. Development testing showed the new and cheaper steering gear to be so satisfactory that it replaced the original design on the 911 when the B-series was announced, in

August 1968 (1969 models). With the new steering gear, the ratio around the central position was slightly increased from 16.5 to 17.78:1. It is interesting to note that at the time the 911 (then still known as the 901) was introduced and barrier crash tests were practically unknown, Porsche proudly pointed out that the three-piece steering column including two universal joints to meet the central steering pinion from the left- or right-hand location of the steering wheel was an important safety feature — which it indeed is. It should also be noted that the rubber coupling linking the lower part of the steering column to the pinion does not serve to accommodate any mis-alignment in the column. It is provided to damp out the reactions fed into the column by the fully reversible rack-and-pinion mechanism and its resilience has been carefully selected for this purpose: it is yet another feed-back from racing experience.

Most of the post-announcement developments were undertaken under the technical direction of Dipl-Ing Ferdinand Piëch, Dr Porsche's nephew, then only 29 years old, who had succeeded Tomala only a short time after the 911 had gone into production. Piëch, who remained in charge until the beginning of 1972, when the company was reorganised and all members of the Porsche-Piëch family resigned from key positions, is a perfectionist and, together with his development staff headed by Helmuth Bott, he was mainly responsible for turning the 911 into the outstanding car it has now become.

While obvious shortcomings at the front end of the car were being attended to, development was proceeding to improve the basic design, with the same target of providing better handling. The pivoted ball lower front suspension joints and the adjustable upper strut anchorage points were introduced, together with the reduced castor angle, with the A-series of cars (1968 models), which also had their rims widened from 4.5 to 5.5 inches to take the same 165 HR 15 tyres as before. But it was the B-series (1969 models) which really reflected the intense development which had been going on at Zuffenhausen.

In addition to the improved front end, which now included the twin batteries and the new Type 914 rack-and-pinion steering, the front/rear weight distribution was modified from approximately 41.5/58.5 to approximately 43/57 (both with a full tank), which was bound to influence the handling favourably. This was achieved by two modifications. One was to manufacture the engine's crankcase of magnesium, rather than aluminium alloy, the reliability of magnesium for this purpose having been proved by the racing versions of the Type 901 engine which had used that material from the beginning and developed up to 220 bhp. During the production run of the B-series, magnesium replaced aluminium for the transmission housing, too.

The other and probably more important contribution to the reduced rear weight bias was the increased wheelbase obtained by simply lengthening the rear suspension arms by 57 mm and moving back the wheel arches accordingly, *but without moving the power unit back in the body shell,* so that the overhung weight at the rear was correspondingly reduced. As the lengthened arms increased the leverage on the torsion bars, the diameters of the latter were increased from 22 to 23 mm. In addition, in the case of the 911 E and 911 S models, the rim width was increased again — from 5.5 to 6 inches — in order to take 70 profile tyres (185/70 VR 15) providing better grip and reduced slip angles.

Moving the rear wheels back in relation to the power unit meant that the half shafts were now permanently angled rearwards and that the Rzeppa constant velocity joints had to take care of the angularity. A larger size was thus used, in order to reduce the internal loads and keep the temperature within bounds. Before the wheelbase increase was finally adopted, a 911 S fitted with Sportomatic transmission was run for 20,000 km (12,500 miles) at its maximum speed on Volkswagen's high-speed track at Ehra, near Wolfsburg. The Sportomatic transmission was chosen on this occasion because, due to the provision of both a clutch and a torque converter, the differential housing is located farther forward in the car than with the conventional transmission. Consequently, even before the wheelbase was lengthened, the half shafts were slightly angled on Sportomatic-equipped cars, and with the wheelbase increase the angle was larger than in conventional models, imposing higher stresses on the constant velocity joints. The joints were submitted to a further severe test on three factory-prepared cars, fitted with virtually standard 911 S engines, which competed in the 'Marathon de la Route' of 1968 on the full Nürburgring and took first and second places in this gruelling 84-hour event, the third car being disqualified because a pit stop to change the injection pump exceeded the maximum time allowance of 20 minutes.

As far as handling is concerned, the B-series probably represented the largest single advance to date in the production life of the 911 and its descendants, and ever since the B-series was introduced my advice to prospective buyers of secondhand Porsches has been not to contemplate an earlier car.

How meticulously every detail that might improve the handling was investigated in that period and put into use, almost regardless of cost, if even a hardly measurable advantage could be expected, is shown by the fact that, beginning with B-series cars, light alloy brake calipers were fitted to the front wheels of 911 S models to reduce unsprung weight and that those cars also had an aluminium engine room lid and rear panel to reduce the overhung weight. A further step towards reducing the overhung weight was accomplished with the introduction of the E-series (1972 models) when the 2 gallon oil tank was moved from behind the right-hand rear wheel to a position in front of the same wheel, E-series cars being easily identifiable by the trap door covering the oil filler in the right-hand side panel of the body. With these cars, the policy of refinement regardless of cost reached its climax, and on F-series cars the oil tank was back in the rear part of the wing both for reasons of cost and convenience, as it was all too easy for filling station attendants to spill oil over the body when refilling the tank. This backward step was only taken, however, because, as a result of racing experience, it had been realised that aerodynamic factors were much more important at high speeds than moving a couple of kilograms about. This was borne out quite forcibly by the Type 917/10 turbocharged 'Can-Am' car which, in order to achieve the grip required to make full use of its over 1,000 bhp, had nearly 70 per cent of its weight carried by the rear wheels.

In fact the E-series were the first cars in which, except for the flared wings made necessary by the wider wheels and tyres when the B-series was introduced, the body contours were slightly changed from the original model. The change consisted of the provision of an 'air dam' below the front bumper to deflect the air towards the sides of the car and reduce the flow under the vehicle, which tends to create aerodynamic lift. The dam was standard on E-series 'S' models and became standard on all versions as the F-series was announced. A slightly differently shaped dam became standard on all models with the introduction of the G-series (1974 models). It was followed by various forms of rear 'spoilers', as the original body shape was found to create noticeably more lift at the rear than at the front. We shall not delve any further into these aerodynamic problems at this point, however, as we are presently more concerned with the running gear of the 911 series.

Basically, the running gear of the B-series has remained unaltered to the present day (1989 models), except for the Carrera and the Turbo. The lighter and corrosion-proof cast alloy inner rear suspension arms introduced with the G-series have not changed the geometry. It should be noted, however, that 1975 to 1982 models exported to the USA have their suspension raised by 8.5 mm to meet bumper height regulations. They can easily be lowered, but in that case it is recommended that the rubber bump stop in the shock absorbers should be exchanged for the shorter European type.

When it first appeared in 1973, the Carrera RS was the first production Porsche with a rear spoiler (the 'duck's tail' as it was called) and was a lightweight version of the F-series 911 S in which a 2.7 litre engine replaced the 2.4 litre unit. Except for the springs and dampers, tuned for competition work, its running gear differed from the 911 S only in the use of rear wheels with 7 inch wide rims and 60 profile (205/60 VR 15) tyres. In addition the rear cross-tube in which the torsion bars are housed was welded to the tunnel running along the centreline of the car in order to improve its bending stiffness. When racing tyres were fitted to 11 inch wide rims it was found that cornering forces bent this tube so much that the outside wheel assumed enough positive camber to have a perceptible detrimental effect on handling.

The main reason for producing the Carrera RS at all was to create the necessary basis further to develop the 911 within the rules of Group 4, ie, special GT cars, which stated that:

1   the engine capacity may be increased by enlarging the cylinder bore only up to the limit of the class;

2   the weight must not undercut the homologated weight of the standard model;

3   the general body contours must remain unaltered;

4   the wings (fenders) may be widened by up to 2 inches each to house wider wheels and/or tyres which they must cover over at least one third of their periphery;

5   the location of the suspension fulcrum points may not be altered.

The original F-series Carrera RS took care of the first four points:

a   its weight was lowered to 900 kg (1,989 lb) by simplifying the equipment, discarding the rear emergency seats, using lightweight plastic bucket seats and a thin-gauge Glaverbel safety windscreen, replacing the steel with plastic bumpers and lightening the body shell itself by using thin-gauge steel panels for non-stressed parts as well as aluminium or plastic for some moving parts;

b   the cylinder bores were increased from 84 to 90 mm (which was possible only by using Nikasil instead of Biral cylinders, as explained in the chapter devoted to engine developments), increasing the engine capacity to 2,687 cc, ie, above the 2,500 cc class limit and opening the way for further capacity increases up to 3 litres;

c   a special plastic engine-room lid incorporating a 'duck's tail' spoiler was a standard fitment. As we shall see in a later chapter, this did not completely eliminate rear-end lift, but reduced it by over 100 kg (220 lb) at 152 mph and created approximately equal lift force front and rear, so that the road behaviour remained consistent as the speed increased. It also reduced the drag by 3 per cent;

d   the rear wings (fenders) were widened to cover the 7 inch wide rims and fat 60 series tyres. By further widening the wings by 2 inches each, as allowed by the racing rules, 11 inch wide rims and appropriate racing tyres could be accommodated at the rear instead of the 9 inch rims which were the widest that could be fitted under legally widened 911 S rear wings.

Up to 1973 the factory had never raced the 911, except on very special occasions, and its development for racing had been limited to whatever was necessary to keep the car ahead in its class and satisfy the needs of private entrants. But with an eye on future racing formulae based on production cars, a serious programme was launched to develop the 911 specifically for racing, and in most of the long-distance races included in the World Championship of Makes series two factory-prepared and managed Carreras were entered under the Martini Racing banner in order to acquire more experience. One car was entered in the GT class and the other in the prototype class, which made it possible to try out modifications making the car ineligible for the GT class, but which might be incorporated in future production models, either because they could improve the production car, or because they made it more suitable for racing.

One such modification concerned the Carrera's rear suspension in which the pivot points of the inner suspension arms were moved 15 mm towards the car's centre line and backwards 47.5 mm by moving and extending the bracket carried by the cross tube. This had the effect of increasing the camber variations due to suspension movements, so that the very small initial negative camber angle permissible with modern, wide racing tyres would not turn into excessive positive camber when the car rolled under high cornering forces. This change, which necessitated the use of shorter inner suspension arms, was incorporated in 2.7 litre Carrera RS models after the first batch of 500 identical units required for the homologation of the model in Group 4 had been made. As the modification also slightly increases the rear wheel toe-in variations, and is thus detrimental to straight line stability, it was not applied to other models in the 911 range in which it has no justification, since with road tyres enough initial negative camber can be provided to prevent the camber from becoming positive under sharp cornering.

The experience gained by the factory in racing Carreras in GT and prototype form (an activity that was rewarded by victory in three major races) is reflected in the G-series Carrera RS 3.0 which succeeded the 2.7 litre version. As the original intention had been to make only 100 of these cars, for homologation as an 'evolution' of the 2.7 litre model, it was marketed with many components which had been fitted to Carreras modified for racing, but which were not required even for very fast road work (such as the enormously expensive Type 917 racing brakes and a transmission oil cooler, complete with circulating pump). Such equipment was, more than anything else, a matter of convenience, as the factory rightly judged that most of the RS 3.0s would be bought for racing, and had nothing to do with the modifications directly resulting from the 1973 racing season's experience which, as far as the handling department is concerned, were mainly the use of rims 2 inches wider than before (8 inch front and 9 inch rear) housed in appropriately widened wings, and a much larger rear spoiler, still part of the engine room cover. Widened within the CSI's legal limits, the wings (fenders) would now house wheels with 10.5 inch and 14 inch rims front and rear, respectively, which were found to be required to achieve fully satisfactory handling with the 330 bhp developed by the race-tuned 3 litre engine. The same goes for the large rear spoiler, which almost cancels out any lift, the 'duck's tail' having proved to be inadequate for optimum results, even though it certainly makes standard Porsches noticeably nicer (and safer) to drive through fast bends.

The next and ultimate step in running gear and suspension development is the 930 Turbo, which has largely benefited from the experience gained with the turbo-charged 2.1 litre prototypes, based on the 911 series, raced by Porsche under the Martini Racing banner throughout 1974. This car had new inner rear suspension arms, still made of cast light alloy, but stronger and featuring a larger diameter and wider rear wheel bearing housing than on other models. These arms contribute to the track increase from the production Carrera's 138 cm with 7 inch wide rims to 150 cm with 8 inch wide rims. The pivot points of the inner arms are similar to the second series of Carrera RS, except that they are raised by 10 mm, so that the arms slope more upwards from the wheel hub to counter more effectively squat under full throttle acceleration — a desirable precaution in view of the performance available.

At the front, where the track was increased by 6 cm compared with other models, partly because 7 inch instead of 6 inch rims were fitted, and partly because distance pieces were used between the hub and the wheel, most of the suspension parts are similar to those of other models. But the cross member supporting the steering rack and the rear end of the torsion bars (which are concentric with the lower wishbone axis) is made of cast alloy rather than steel (the alloy cross member became standard in all models, starting with the I-series 1976 models) and is located 13 mm higher, ie, nearer the floor pan, while the front end of the wishbone is lowered by some 6 mm. The axis of the wishbone thus drops towards the front of the vehicle, which gives rise to a component directed upwards when the car is being braked, partially counteracting nose dive.

Model differentiation

Whenever a new major development took place in the running gear, the whole 911 range benefited from it, the only exception being models specifically designed with further race tuning in mind, such as the Carrera RS and, lately, the 930 Turbo in which the running gear had to be specifically adapted to the enormous extra power available. But almost throughout the history of the 911 model range there were differences in the suspension tuning in accordance with the character of individual models, though basically the springing frequencies have remained practically unchanged since the original 911 was introduced.

At the front torsion bars of 19 mm diameter have been used on all production models, including Carrera RS and Turbo, and the length of the suspension wishbone they control has remained unaltered, though a one-piece wishbone replaced the original two-piece design as from the B-series. The only exceptions were the B-, C- and D-series (1969 to 1971 models) 911 E in which the torsion bars were replaced by self-levelling Boge hydro-pneumatic struts which remained optional until 1973.

Rear torsion bars of 22 mm diameter were used originally, but were replaced by 23 mm bars from the B-series on, when the 5.7 cm longer trailing arms applied a greater leverage to them. Up to 1979 models, heavier rear torsion bars were used only for competition work and on the Turbo which had 26 mm bars from the beginning, as also the limited production Carrera 3.0 RS, model year 1974. To take care of the increasingly extensive emission equipment, reinforcements dictated by power increases and ever more extensive options, 24 mm bars were used from 1980 to and including 1985 models. Meanwhile the suspension characteristics had been reconsidered within the frame of the 911 development programme and rear torsion bars of 25 mm diameter were used at the rear, together with noticeably stiffer anti-roll bars of 22 mm front and

21 mm rear, the front torsion bars remaining unchanged at 19 mm. On the same occasion, twin tube gas filled Boge dampers, as used since the 1985 model year in the Turbo and Turbo-look, and had been an option on the Carrera, became standard wear.

While the 25 mm rear torsion bars of the 1986 model are interchangeable with those of the previous series, those used from 1987 models on are not, as they carry different splines to SAE norm. The modification (external side of bar 47 splines instead of 44, internal side 46 instead of 40) was made to allow a finer adjustment of the ride height and goes hand in hand with the modified rear cross tube supporting the G.50 gearbox. The openings in the wheel arches through which the bars can be removed were simultaneously increased in diameter, as had been done in the Turbo body one year earlier.

If the basic suspension remained the same for all normal production models, this does not apply to anti-roll bars and dampers which varied according to the engine fitted. The original 911 had Boge dampers and a front anti-roll bar only. This was a straight bar of 13 mm diameter with serrations at both ends to take levers connected to the wishbones by rubber bushed links. Except for varying diameters, this front anti-roll bar layout remained unaltered until the advent of the G-series (1974 models) when it was replaced by a simplified design in which the anti-roll bar was cranked at both ends to meet the wishbone, to which it was connected by a rubber bushed bracket. However, the 3 litre Turbo and RS models continued to use the more elaborate design because it allows the use of harder rubber bushes, improving the anti-roll bar response, and their replacement by metallic spherical joints for racing.

Any tail-heavy car will oversteer under high lateral forces if it is not set up to understeer strongly when cornered more gently, and as, in addition, the original 911 was very sensitive to the throttle opening when cornering, it was set up to understeer very strongly under most conditions. The result was that, on all but large radius bends, its admittedly high maximum cornering speed was limited by understeer. When the 911 S was introduced in summer 1966 it was considered that drivers choosing this higher-performance model would be competent enough to manage a car which would actually slightly oversteer at the limit and be even more tricky if the accelerator had to be lifted while cornering fast, but would be faster around corners. Consequently a 16 mm diameter anti-roll bar was added to the rear suspension while the front one was increased in diameter from 13 to 15 mm. This produced the desired result, while also considerably reducing the roll angle for a given cornering speed. In addition Koni adjustable dampers were fitted, with harder settings than those of the normal 911, and forged alloy wheels replaced the stamped steel wheels, saving 2.3 kg (5.1 lb) unsprung weight per unit, though the effective gain was less, due to the use of heavier brakes.

By the time the A-series was launched (1968 models), many early problems such as bad straight-line stability, sticky lower steering ball joints, inaccuracies in the front-end geometry and some lesser ones had been at least partially solved. The rim width had also been increased from 4.5 to 5.5 inches, resulting in smaller slip angles. It was considered that the normal 911's (which had meanwhile become the 911 L) understeer could now be reduced and the diameter of the front anti-roll bar was lowered from 13 to 11 mm, while the newly introduced 911 T had no anti-roll bar at all. Purely from the comfort point of view, this is the best solution, as a high roll stiffness tends to create what Alex Moulton calls a quick 'roll-rock' movement around the car's longitudinal axis, detrimental to comfort, and it also adversely affects straight-line stability on rough road surfaces.

With the introduction of the B-series, in which the rear overhang was reduced, the

Boge hydro-pneumatic self-levelling front strut introduced on B-series 911 E and optional on all models up to F-series. A, A', B, B' — Oil chambers (Porsche version without membrane in the low-pressure chamber), A'', B'' — Gas chambers, P — Pump chamber, R — Regulator opening, D — Pressure valve, S — Suction valve, U — Overload valve.

Procedure in operating chambers A & B:

Expansion of A''
through oil flow A'→A,
Compression of B''
through oil flow B→B'

Oil transfer A→B'
as long as regulator bore R
remains open

Procedure in the pump:

Suction B→P
Suction valve S open

Suction valve S closed
Pressure valve D closed

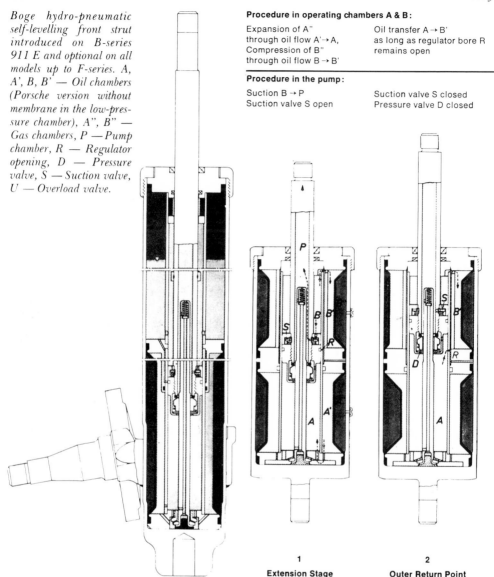

1
Extension Stage

2
Outer Return Point

batteries re-located and the engine unit lightened by the use of a magnesium crankcase, the largest single step was taken to improve the 911's handling. In the case of the E and S models this was further helped by another increase in rim width, this time from 5.5 to 6 inches to take 70 series tyres, providing a larger contact area with the road and further reduced slip angles. As any under- or oversteer is caused by the difference between front and rear slip angles, it is obvious that if the angles themselves become smaller, the difference must become smaller, too, and the attitude angle taken by the car less drastic.

The 911 T was still without anti-roll bars and with 165 HR 15 tyres on 5.5 inch wide rims, though a 'comfort equipment' version was offered with 185 HR 14 tyres on 5.5 J 14 rims, while the 911 S continued with the same dampers and anti-roll bars

Compression of A" through oil flow A → A' Expansion of B" through oil flow B' → B	All connection from A to B closed	Procedure as in position 1	Expansion of A" through oil flow A' → A Compression of B" through oil flow B → B'
Pressure P → A Pressure valve D open	Suction valve S closed Pressure valve D closed	Procedure as in position 1	Suction A → P Overload valve U open Suction valve S closed

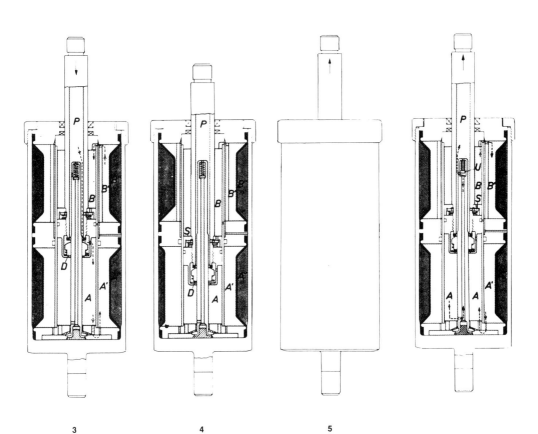

3	**4**	**5**	
Compression Stage	**Inner Return Point**	**Extension Stage**	**Extension Stage With Overload**

as before. The 911 E, however, which was supposed to be the comfort-oriented model in the range, used Boge hydro-pneumatic struts at the front instead of the torsion bars performing the duty of springs in the other models. These struts were self-levelling to compensate for any load carried in the car, pumping themselves up to a predetermined height as the wheels met road irregularities, and as they had a rising rate no front anti-roll bar was fitted.

Porsche had such confidence in those hydro-pneumatic spring units that they did not hesitate, as a final test of them, to enter three basically standard but lightened B-series 911 S models, fitted with hydro-pneumatic front struts, for the 1968 Marathon de la Route on the full Nürburgring racing circuit. The cars had a light-weight body shell with several panels made of thin gauge steel, aluminium front and rear lids and aluminium front wings and bumpers. The interior trim was much simplified and, complete with their aluminium roll bar, the cars weighed around 855 kg without fuel, but with the full complement of oil. The engines were standard fuel injection 911 S 2 litre units except for the deletion of the air filter element and for intake trumpets of 43 mm instead of 46 mm diameter at the top, the bottom diameter being 38 mm as standard. Their power output ranged from 176 to 180 bhp, which fell to 167 to 170 bhp after the 84 hours race in which more than 10,000 km (about 6,300 miles) were covered.

Being fitted with the hydro-pneumatic front struts, the cars ran without any anti-roll bar, but the Boge units were set up to provide the same roll resistance as the normal S suspension with anti-roll and torsion bars. The rear dampers were given softer than standard settings at low operating speeds, but harder for quick movements, while harder than standard bump stops were used front and rear, with reinforced damper anchorage points. Dunlop racing tyres were fitted to forged alloy wheels with 6J 15 rims at the front (standard) and 7J 15 rims at the rear. Except for 0°30' negative front camber, the suspension settings were standard.

As explained before, the event put the accent on reliability: the winner was the car that completed the highest number of laps in 84 hours, but except at intervals of 75 laps (about 1,350 miles) when a 20 minutes pit stop was allowed for servicing, any pit stop exceeding one minute cost a lap which was deducted from the total, while for any lap exceeding 24 minutes or any pit stop taking more than 20 minutes (except for the permitted stops at 75-lap intervals) the penalty was exclusion.

On this occasion, Porsches did even better than the previous year, when the Sportomatic-equipped car won: two of the team cars filled the first two places with the crews Glemser-Kauhsen-Linge and Blank-Schuller-Steckkönig, respectively, both having officially completed 356 laps, though the winner had actually covered 361 and the second place car 357 laps at an overall average speed of 76 and 75 mph, respectively. The second place car also won the regularity contest, having incurred only one penalty lap. The third car was excluded at about quarter distance when the time taken to change an injection pump exceeded the permitted allowance.

No trouble was experienced with the hydro-pneumatic struts on the winning car, but on the second place car the right-hand front strut had to be replaced twice: the first time because a weld had cracked around the stub axle mounting, the second time because of a bad oil leak.

As a matter of interest, the best lap time for the full (28.4 km) circuit achieved by the winning car was 12 min 29 sec, an average speed of 85 mph, and the first and second place cars did 11.4 and 12.9 mpg, respectively.

What happened to one car in the Marathon — oil leaking from an hydro-pneumatic strut — occasionally happened in the hands of customers, too, and though the self-levelling characteristics of the units, making up for a full complement of luggage and a full tank, allowed a slightly softer suspension to be used, the front luggage locker capacity was not such that the suspension could be made soft enough for an obvious advantage to be noticed by the occupants seated not far from the centre of gravity of the car. Furthermore, Porsche owners are a prejudiced bunch of people: if they cannot afford the top model — the S in this instance — or if they think the engine characteristics of another model are better suited to their needs, they are very anxious that the specification of the car they buy should otherwise be as near the S as possible, and there is little doubt that this is a major reason why the self-levelling struts were never very popular. In fact, there are countries where all 911 E models were imported with the 911 S running gear and the self-levelling struts were removed from the standard 911 E specification with the introduction of the 2.4 litre E-series models, which went back to their former torsion bar suspension, but without front or rear anti-roll bars. Except on hydro-pneumatic strut models, however, anti-roll bars have always been an option on any model if not provided in the standard equipment, and in many cases the choice of 15 or 16 mm rear anti-roll bars was offered while, except for early 911 and 911 L (O- and A-series) models, the front bar was always of 15 mm diameter until the front anti-roll bar design was simplified with the advent of the G-series. Of the H- and I-series models, only the 930 Turbo still uses the more elaborate design with separate arms and links, and in this case an 18 mm bar is used in conjunction with an 18 mm rear bar, which is a standard fitting on all types of Carrera from the 1974 models (G-Series) to 1985 models included but, except for RS models, with the simplified front anti-roll bar of 20 mm diameter. The same combination was used on all 911 SC models. For 1986, the suspension settings were revised and together with the 25 mm rear torsion bars, the Carrera got stiffer anti-roll bars of 22 and 20 mm front and rear respectively. The 1989 model 911 Turbo's rear torsion bars were increased in diameter from 26 to 27 mm, while the anti-roll bar's diameter was reduced from 20 to 18 mm, so as to approximately retain the former rear roll stiffness and handling characteristics. As in the Carrera two years earlier, the torsion bar splines were changed to SAE norm.

The simplified front anti-roll bar was adopted for the Turbo from the K-Series (1977 models) on and front and rear diameters became 20 and 18 mm, as for the contemporary Carrera 3.0, but were changed to 22 and 20 mm from 1985 models on. A summary of the various combinations for post-1973 (except RS) models is given below (the years are model years). It should be noted that as the leverage of the simplified front anti-roll bar is not the same as that of the link type, comparisons taking into account the diameter of the bars are inconclusive.

	Anti-roll bars Dia mm		Main torsion bars Dia mm	
911 and **911 S** 1974–77	F 16	R none	F 19	R23
	(Option F 20, R 18)			
Carrera 1976–77	F 20	R 18	F 19	R 23
Turbo 1975–76	F 18	R 18	F 19	R 26
	(link type)			
Atmospheric 911 1978–79	F 20	R 18	F 19	R 23
Atmospheric 911 1980–85	F 20	R 18	F 19	R 24
Atmospheric 911 1986–	F 22	R 21	F 19	R 25
Turbo+T-look 1977–78	F 22	R 20	F 19	R 26
Turbo+T-look 1989–	F 22	R 18	F 19	R 27

Measured results

Among small production manufacturers, Porsche are unique in having not only their own proving ground but also a proper racing circuit which was completed in 1968. These facilities allow any modifications to be tested under closely controlled conditions and exact conclusions to be drawn. The circuit was a considerable help in sorting out the 911's handling, even though it was not available at the time the car was put into production, but the circular steering pad, one of the first testing facilities built on Porsche's proving ground in Weissach, had been completed by the time the 911 was originally developed. Though it does not provide a complete picture of a

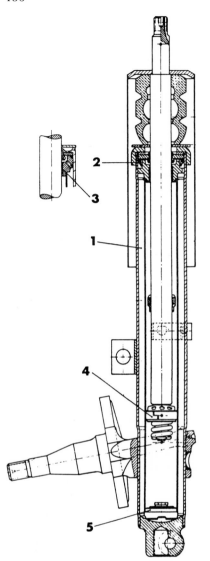

From 1986 models on, gas-filled, twin tube Boge GZ dampers became standard on Carreras. A front strut is shown here. 2 and 3 show the different design in the upper seal of the gas filled damper (2) and the previous non-pressurized damper (3).

car's handling, it does allow road holding to be translated into exact figures. It is interesting to note the effect which the various developments of the 911 series had on the centripetal acceleration the car could achieve, all figures having been obtained on a circular track of 193 m diameter. For a steering pad, this is a large diameter, but it still tends to favour slightly oversteering cars, as the driving force increases the side force acting upon the front wheels and tends to create excessive understeer.

O-series

The original O-series 911 achieved a lateral g-force of 0.774 on Dunlop 165 HR 15 CB 57 tyres fitted to the then standard 4.5 inch wide rims. It was a high figure for the period, when anything above 0.65 g was considered pretty good for a road car and 0.7 g ranked as excellent.

The O-series 911 S, running on the same sort of tyres and rims, but with a rear anti-roll bar in addition to a heavier front one, bettered the normal 911's figure only marginally to 0.78 g, according to the records of the circular track, which is rather less than the 2 per cent announced by Ing Helmuth Bott on the occasion of the new model's announcement.

A-series

The only modification introduced with the A-series models (first produced in July 1967) which might have had a serious influence on cornering speed was the one inch increase in rim width. In the case of the normal 911 (now called 911 L) the slight reduction of the front anti-roll bar diameter might also have brought a minor advantage by slightly reducing the understeer.

In fact, the advantage brought about by the 5.5 inch wide rims was less than could have been expected: it raised the lateral g-force by only 0.005 g, ie, by about 0.7 per cent, using the same type of Dunlop tyres as before. In addition, the figures show that the anti-roll bars have little effect on the steady-state behaviour of the car (which constant-speed cornering on a constant radius involves), exactly the same g-force of 0.78 g being obtained for the newly introduced 911 T with no anti-roll bars as for the 911 L which had a comparatively small one at the front only. Only the 911 S, with its two heavy anti-roll bars providing considerable roll restraint, betters this figure fractionally to 0.785 g. Comparing the results obtained for the O- and A-series, it appears that the decisive factor was the A-series' wider rims.

B-series

As already stated, the B-series for which the wheelbase was increased by 2¼ inches, reducing the rear overhang by the same amount, and for which some 22 lb were saved on the (overhung) engine crankcase by making it of magnesium instead of aluminium, marked the greatest improvement in the 911's handling history, and this is reflected by the results achieved. Using the same rims and tyres as those fitted to A-series cars, the 911 T and 911 E achieved a lateral g=0.810, improving by 0.03 g or nearly 4 per cent on the previous model's figures, while 70 series tyres 185/70 VR 15 of the same compound, which were eventually standardised on the B-series 911 E, raised the figure to 0.826 g, another 2 per cent improvement. On the same tyres and rims, the 911 S did even better, achieving a lateral acceleration of 0.841 g, an improvement of 0.056 g or 7 per cent on the A-series. But this is still a long way away from the results achieved on the then new Michelin XVR tyres of the same dimensions, on which a figure of 0.897 g was reached. This indicates that, as far as ultimate cornering speed is concerned (as opposed to handling), tyres are more important than suspension details.

In the course of three years, development on suspension, weight distribution and tyres combined to increase the maximum possible lateral acceleration from 0.774 g for the 911 and 0.78 g for the 911 S to 0.897, an improvement of 14.5 per cent. In practice this is equivalent to a 7.2 per cent increase in the maximum possible cornering speed.

The change back from hydro-pneumatic front suspension struts on the 911 E to normal torsion bars and dampers apparently did not affect the cornering ability of the car either way, and as there were no other important changes in the running gear of the cars or their tyre equipment up to and including the F-series (1973 models), their cornering ability, as measured on the steering pad where speeds are of the order of 60-65 mph and aerodynamic aids have virtually no effect, remained unchanged throughout the production period of the B-, C-, D-, E- and F-series, ie, from 1969 to 1973, typical figures being as follows:

	Acceleration	Wheels	Tyres
911 T	0.810 g	5.5 J 15	Dunlop 165 HR 15-CB 57
911 E	0.826 g	6.0 J 15	Dunlop 185/70 VR 15-CB 57
911 S	0.897 g	6.0 J 15	Michelin XVR 185/70 VR 15

Even higher cornering forces were reached with the F-series Carrera RS, thanks to a combination of lighter weight (some 140 kg or 310 lb less than a 911 S) and lower profile rear tyres mounted on 7 inch wide rims on which 0.912 g was achieved.

	Acceleration	Wheels	Tyres
911 Carrera RS	0.912 g	6J 15 (front)	Pirelli CN 36 185/70 VR 15 (front)
		7J 15 (rear)	Pirelli CN 36 215/60 VR 15 (rear)

G- and later series

The G- and following series Carreras are heavier than their predecessors, of which the lightweight version was discontinued in favour of a fully equipped model. Also starting with the G-series, the simplified front anti-roll bar was used on all models, except the RS 3.0 and the Turbo. The bar was made strong enough to increase the understeer slightly to improve the high-speed stability, but with adverse effects on the comparatively short radius circular track. Consequently the g-figure remained at its previous level only in the case of the 911 T (now re-named 911), probably thanks to the combination of the added front anti-roll bar (the first series in which the bottom car of the range had one as standard fitment) and of a change from the now dated Dunlop CB 57 to Pirelli CN 36 tyres, still mounted on 5.5 inch wide rims. This was improved from 0.810 g to 0.826 g in the H-series when 70 series tyres and 6 inch wide rims became the standard equipment of Porsche's bottom model. In fact, most of the 911 T models sold had been equipped with the optional 6 inch rims and 70 series tyres for many years.

The overwhelming influence of the tyres will again be noted in the following comparison table applying to H-series (1975) models of which, except for the tyres, the 911 and 911 S have an identical running gear, though it must be remembered that first-class grip is usually obtained at the expense of tread life:

	Acceleration	Wheels	Tyres
911	0.826 g	6J 15	Pirelli CN 36 185/70 VR 15
911 S	0.882 g	6J 15	Michelin XWX 185/70 VR 15
911 Carrera	0.882 g	6J 15 (front)	Dunlop SS 185/70 VR 15
		7J 15 (rear)	Dunlop SS 215/60 VR 15
930 Turbo	0.882 g	7J 15 (front)	Dunlop SS 185/70 VR 15
		8J 15 (rear)	Dunlop SS 215/60 VR 15
930 Turbo	0.912 g	7J 15 (front)	Pirelli P7 205/50 VR 15
		8J 15 (rear)	Pirelli P7 225/50 VR 15

Despite its considerable rear weight bias (58.5 per cent) and its noticeably greater weight (about 100 kg more than other Porsches), the 930 thus achieves the same cornering forces on the latest 50 series tyres as did the 240 kg lighter lightweight Carrera RS two years earlier, equalling the record figure achieved by the latter.

Similar skid pad tests were made with 1982 models and reflect further progress. In this case a 1981–82 model 911 SC and a 3.3-litre 930 Turbo were tried on standard size tyres and rims, which gave the following results:

	Acceleration	Wheels	Tyres
911 SC	0.877 g	6J 15 (front)	Pirelli CN 36 185/70 VR 15
		7J 15 (rear)	Pirelli CN 36 205/60 VR 15
930 Turbo	0.949 g	7J 16 (front)	Pirelli P7 205/55 VR 16
		8J 16 (rear)	Pirelli P7 225/50 VR 16

These figures indicate that the 911 SC achieved virtually the same performance (it also achieved 0.887 lateral g on the 60 m diameter circle and 0.897 g on the 40 m diameter circle) on comparatively dated CN 36 tyres as the Carrera had achieved seven years earlier on the more sophisticated Dunlop SS tyres, the running gear having remained virtually unaltered. This reflects the progress which can be obtained by meticulous development of a basic type of tyre. In the case of the Turbo, the performance was also improved in spite of the fact that moving the engine back 30 mm to make room for the new clutch raised the weight carried by the rear wheels to over 60 per cent of the total. This was compensated for by raising the rear tyre pressure from 34 to 42 psi while, from 1977 models on (K-Series), the rim diameter was increased to 16 inches, providing a slight increase in the tread contact area. The better performance of the Turbo, compared to the lighter 911 SC — which also has a less drastic weight distribution (which should both be an advantage) — is not only due to its more elaborate tyres, but also the Turbo's wider track. It should, however, be noted that the Turbo's ultra-low profile tyres on 16-inch diameter rims are an option on the 911 unsupercharged models.

Summing up the evolution, we can say that in less than ten years development work on structure, running gear and tyres has brought an increase in cornering power which raised the centripetal acceleration from 0.774 g to 0.912 g, reflecting an increase in grip of 18 per cent and allowing an increase in cornering speed of 8.5 per cent.

In the following seven years, progress has been much slower and concerns mainly the Turbo, the grip of which has been improved by a further 4 per cent to raise the cornering speed by 10.8 per cent compared with the original 911 of 1964. From the 1986 model onwards, the previously optional 8 in front and 9 in wide rear rims became standard on the Turbo and Turbo-look models, together with 245/45 VR 16 tyres which should further increase their cornering ability, though this was apparently never recorded.

Wheel and tyre sizes

As seen in today's perspective, the 911 seems to have been born with wheels and tyres too narrow. It is a fact that, even on the very successful Types 904, 906 and 910 Porsche racing cars of the 1964-67 period, the tyres used were on the narrow side compared with some contemporary competitors. This was because, where racing cars were concerned, the final development tests always took place on the Nürburgring, the bumpy surface of which required long suspension travels, and testing had indicated that, with the comparatively soft springing making use of that travel, comparatively large camber changes preventing the camber from becoming negative under cornering were beneficial to cornering speeds. As some initial camber was also required, this meant that at full bump the wheels assumed a considerable negative camber angle which could be accommodated only by tyres with a sufficiently rounded tread profile incompatible with very wide rims.

But Porsche were far from being unaware of the advantages of *comparatively* wide rims and tyres, and particularly of the higher cornering forces that could be achieved with a given tyre by mounting it on a wide rim. As far back as the early 'fifties, wider rims than specified by the tyre manufacturers had been used on Type 356s for sporting events and tests had indicated that in many cases they also reduced the tyre wear. Following this, 4.5 inch wide rims (very wide for the period) were adopted for production models at the end of 1955, a move for which the factory had to take the entire responsibility, rim and tyre manufacturers going so far as to require a signed discharge from Porsche in case any accident should happen attributable to the use of a wider than standard rim. But three years later, 4.5 inches became an officially recognised rim width for 165-15 tyres, as used by Porsche under their own responsibility.

This combination having given satisfactory results it was automatically adopted for the original 901/911, but very soon tests with wider rims were initiated, the normal method being to select the combination providing the highest cornering power on the circular steering pad and then to carry out endurance tests with the combination selected.

Such tests led to the adoption of 5.5 inch wide rims for the A-series, after the standard 165 HR 15 tyres of the period had been tried even on 6 inch rims, 1.5 inches wider than the tyre manufacturer's recommendation. The 6 inch rims required wider tyres than the standard 165 HR 15 to give the best results, however, and became common wear for the top Porsche models only after further tests had been carried out with the then new 70 series tyres in the 185/70 VR 15 size which were introduced with the B-series cars in July 1968. For reasons of cost, however, the 165 HR 15 tyres on 5.5 inch rims remained the standard wear for the 911 T up to and including the G-series 911, though the vast majority of the cars delivered were ordered with the optional equipment of 70 series tyres on 6 inch rims. Whereas in the years 1969-70 35 per cent of Porsche's production still used 5.5 inch rims, the proportion fell to 15 per cent in 1971 and to 5 per cent in 1972 and 1973.

For many years the development engineers had wanted to take care of the rear weight bias of the 911 by using wider rims and tyres on the rear wheels than on the front ones, but they were prevented from doing so by the German (and probably some foreign) authorities which required that the spare wheel could be used as a substitute for any of the road wheels, and this only became the case when the Goodrich Space Saver folding spare tyre was introduced, which was officially approved as a spare for either 185/70 VR 15 or 215/60 VR 15 tyres which have almost exactly the same rolling radius. The combination of the former on 6 inch rims at the front and the latter on 7 inch rims at the rear was first used on the Carrera RS and remained standard wear on Carreras, to be adopted for the 911 SC and on the second generation 911 Carrera, starting with 1984 models. The wider rims and tyres necessitated bulging out the rear fenders slightly, making Carreras and post-1977 911 models easily recognisable. A similar tyre combination, but on 7 and 8 inch rims, was used on early 930 Turbos, but on 1976 models (K-Series), the optional Pirelli P7 tyres of the dimensions 205/50 VR 15 (front) and 225/50 VR 15 (rear) became standard, only to be substituted by 205/55 VR 16 and 225/50 VR 16 tyres on 16 inch diameter wheels in the following year, to bring the overall diameter of the tyred wheel back to approximately its original dimensions. Rim width remained 6 in front and 7 in rear for atmospheric models and 7 in and 8 in respectively for the Turbo, with one inch wider rims all round an option for atmospheric models on 15 in diameter wheels until the 7/9 inch combination became standard on Turbo and Turbo-look in the 1986 model year. In the 1988 model year, the rim width of 911 Carrera models was increased by one inch to 7 in front and 8 in rear, for the standard 15 in diameter wheels with 6J16 front and 8J16 rear an option. In 1989 models, the latter combination became standard.

While initially only the Pirelli P.7 were approved for the 16 in wheels, other manufacturers eventually produced tyres to the required standards, which were also fitted as original equipment.

When the 70 series tyres on 6 inch rims were introduced for the 911 E and 911 S B-series cars, it was thought that some customers might not accept the slightly harsher low-speed ride caused by the lower profile tyres. An alternative was therefore offered to 911 E buyers in the form of 185 HR 14 tyres thicker than the 165 HR 15 used hitherto (which continued as the standard wear for the contemporary 911 T) and fitting a 14 inch diameter rim of 5.5 inch width. The higher and more curved sidewalls should have made the car definitely more comfortable. It was specified as standard equipment for the Sportomatic version of the 911 E which was supposed to attract buyers more interested in comfort than sheer performance. But once again it was proved that Porsche buyers of all categories are primarily interested in performance and handling and the 14 inch wheels were a commercial failure. They remained an option on the 911 T only throughout the C and D (2.2 litre) series and were then discontinued, to be revived with the same lack of success as part of the 'comfort kit' option for the 911/2.7 in 1977. As the maximum speed permissible on HR rated tyres is 130 mph—a speed the car could comfortably exceed—an ignition cut-out was fitted to prevent that speed being exceeded.

Porsche alloy wheels

Few wheels have created such a fashion as Porsche's forged aluminium type which were the standard wear for the 911 S from the day of its announcement. Within a few months of their introduction you could buy from accessory shops, at highly varying prices according to quality and resemblance, wheel covers which made any car's wheels look more or less like Porsche's. Then as today, however, fashion was one of the remotest preoccupations of Porsche designers and the purpose behind the design of these aluminium wheels was mainly to combine strength with the lowest possible weight, a further advantage being that out-of-roundness can be controlled much more accurately on forged (or cast) wheels than on stamped steel ones.

Low unsprung weight has always been a major preoccupation at Porsche, this being particularly important to combine good roadholding and comfort in a car of low total weight, and it had been Ing Tomala's intention to specify cast magnesium wheels for the 911 at the time of its introduction, though last-minute development difficulties made this impossible. It is not generally known, however, that in order to reduce the unsprung weight Porsche have been using aluminium wheel securing nuts ever since the alloy wheels were introduced and that few — if any — other production cars use aluminium calipers (which are, of course, standard practice on racing cars) of the type that Porsche fit to the front brakes of their top models.

The Porsche alloy wheel story begins with the development, in collaboration with the German firm VDM, of a cast magnesium wheel intended as original equipment for the 911. It took a long time, and a lot of money was spent on it by the manufacturers, but it was finally abandoned because cracks could not be avoided under Porsche's very severe testing conditions. The idea was not given up, however, and thoughts turned towards forged aluminium as a supplier called Fuchs made excellent forged aluminium rollers for roller track vehicles manufactured by Porsche for the NATO forces, and they would probably be able to solve the problem.

Development started in 1964 and the wheels, which had a forged aluminium centre and rolled aluminium rim, were ready for production when the 911 S was announced in July 1966. Originally the alloy wheel was 2.3 kg (5.1 lb) lighter than the equivalent pressed steel wheel, but by the time the rim widths had increased to 5.5 inches for the steel wheel and 6 inches for the forged aluminium wheel, the difference became as much as 3.5 kg (7.7 lb), the respective weights being 9.3 kg and 5.8 kg (20.5 and 12.8 lb). Unfortunately the cost of the forged aluminium wheel, polished and finished as normally fitted to the car, is over five times that of the painted steel wheel and still twice as much as that of a chromium plated steel wheel. Unpolished and painted, it would still be over three and a half times as expensive as a painted steel wheel.

Though the forged aluminium wheel became the standard equipment for the 911 S and a very popular option on other models — quite apart from becoming a sort of unregistered Porsche trade mark — its cost prompted further research into the possibilities of light alloys and led to the development of a die-cast magnesium wheel which was ready for production by Mahle (the piston specialists) in 1968. Wheel centre and rim were cast in one piece but unfortunately the dies had been made for the manufacture of 5.5 inch wide rims, and by the time the wheel was fully developed 6 inch rims were required for the upper 911 range. So the wheel could be offered as an option only on the 911 T on which 5.5 inch rims remained standard until 1974, and on the VW-Porsche 914. Compared with the polished forged aluminium wheels, they were only about 20 per cent cheaper anyway, as magnesium alloys must be treated against corrosion and there were more rejects due to crack formations during the casting process which had to be checked by X-raying and crack testing every single wheel. It was the lightest wheel produced for a production Porsche, however, weighing only 4.5 kg (10 lb), which is 1 kg less than the corresponding forged aluminium wheel and less than half as much as a steel wheel of the same size.

The cost of the magnesium wheel meant that it wasn't worth developing a new version with a wider rim. Another solution was sought, eventually materialising as a low-pressure aluminium alloy casting with a high silicon content which was introduced with the F-series (1973 models) where it was the standard equipment of the 911 E and later became the standard wear of G- and H-series 911 and 911 S models. This wheel, which is painted on its outer face only, costs less than twice the price of a steel wheel, even though every single wheel must be X-rayed, and weighs only 0.2 kg more than the 5.8 kg forged aluminium wheel of the same size. Because of the lower elasticity of the cast material, it is less shock resistant than the forged aluminium wheel, and is also less distinctive.

Originally, the cast wheels were made in only one size: 6J 15, so that the forged aluminium Fuchs wheels were mandatory on cars requiring 7-inch wide rear rims, such as the Carrera 3.0. But when the range was reduced to the single 911 SC model for 1978, the standard fitting was cast alloy wheels all round, the rear ones being 7J 15. Those wheels were never made in 16-inch diameter size, so that the optional ultra-low profile tyres could only be fitted to the classic forged wheels. And though they were the standard wear for most of the Porsche models for 11 years, the five-spoke cast wheels never made a real impact. For 1984 they were replaced by holed cast aluminium wheels reminiscent of those which had become a hallmark of the Porsche 928 models and soon became known as 'telephone disc' wheels. They were abandoned from the 1988 models on, when the much lighter forged aluminium 'Fuchs' wheels became standard again, now in the sizes 7J15 front and 8J15 rear, 6J16 front and 8J16 rear being an option. The weight difference between a 1988 forged Fuchs wheel and a cast 'telephone disc' wheel of identical size exceeds 2 kg, as exemplified by 7x15 wheels which weigh 5.72 and 7.85 kg respectively.

Brake developments

The 911 was originally equipped with a single circuit service brake operating on four discs and a cable-operated handbrake operating on small drums surrounded by the rear discs. The discs were plain and the calipers — of ATE manufacture — were of the fixed type with two pistons each and provision for changing the pads quickly without dismantling the caliper. The mean swept disc diameter was 235 mm at the front and 243 mm at the rear,

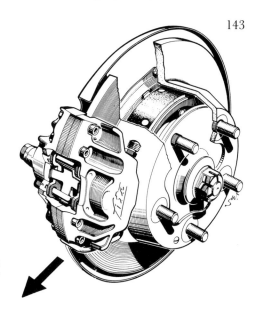

All 911 models have a duo-servo handbrake operating on the rear wheels. The drum is in one piece with the disc which, in later cars, is radially ventilated.

overall disc diameters being 282 and 290 mm, respectively. The cast iron calipers used were ATE's M-type with 48 mm piston diameter at the front, providing a pad area of 52.5 sq cm (8.14 sq in) per wheel and L-type with 35 mm pistons at the rear, providing a pad area of 40 sq cm (6.2 sq in) per wheel.* The mechanically operated rear drum parking brakes worked on the Bendix duo servo system, providing a two leading shoe self energising effect in either direction of rotation. The reason for the expensive luxury of having separate drum brakes for parking or emergency hand operation was that it is extremely difficult to obtain a reasonably good braking effect with a mechanical linkage operating the service disc brakes.

When the 911 S was introduced in July 1966 radially ventilated discs were used in order to take care of its higher performance, and the calipers were widened accordingly by the insertion of a distance piece between the two halves. Their dimensions were otherwise unchanged, except that the rear calipers now had 38 mm instead of 35 mm diameter pistons in order to increase the rear wheel braking, a modification which was soon extended to the normal 911. The decision to fit ventilated discs all round was taken following tests carried out descending the Stelvio, which has 52 consecutive hairpin bends. With ventilated discs, the pass was descended in less than 18 minutes to Gomagoi without fade being experienced. With plain discs, the brakes faded completely at the 33rd hairpin, the fluid starting to boil and the discs reaching a temperature of 650°C — 150°C more than the ventilated discs. In both cases Ferodo DS 11 linings were used. The cooler running ventilated discs also had the effect of dramatically increasing the life of the brake pads. Comparative tests carried out on the southern part of the Nürburgring indicated that a standard 911 lapping in an average time of 2 min 55 sec per lap wore its pads at the rate of 5 mm per 1,000 km, whereas a 911 S lapping in 2 min 40 sec — which is a lot faster — had an average pad wear of 2.5 mm per 1,000 km.

With the introduction of the A-series in July 1967, when the 911 T was launched, all models appeared with a twin braking circuit, the diameter of the master cylinder remaining unchanged at 19.05 mm (¾ inch), and ventilated discs replacing the plain discs on the 911 L (the successor to the 'normal' 911), the brakes of which were now identical with those of the S model. Except for its plain discs, the 911 T had the same brakes as the other two models and, even on this bottom model, ventilated discs were fitted all round if the Sportomatic

* ATE calipers are designated by the letters 'L' for 'light', 'M' for 'medium' and 'S' for 'schwer' (heavy).

transmission was specified, in order to compensate for the reduced engine braking obtained with this transmission and in view of the increased use of the brakes it imposes in city driving.

With the introduction of the B-series — the real breakthrough in the 911 development history — came two further improvements: at the rear the small L caliper was replaced by the M caliper as used on the front brakes since the beginning of the 911 production, but with 38 instead of 48 mm diameter pistons, increasing the brake pad area per wheel from 40 sq cm to 52.5 sq cm (from 6.2 to 8.14 sq in), while a special aluminium version of their S caliper was developed by ATE specially for the 911 S. This new caliper, with 48 mm pistons, made in one piece for better rigidity, not only reduced the unsprung weight, but also increased the brake pad area per wheel from 52.5 to 78 sq cm (from 8.14 to 12.1 sq in), considerably increasing the pad life.

The engine capacity increase from 2 to 2.2 litres, which coincided with the introduction of the C-series in July 1969, raised the power of the T engine to within 5 bhp of the 2 litre L engine of the A-series of two years earlier, and logically it had to inherit its ventilated discs, too, so that from that series onward all Porsches were fitted with ventilated discs all round.

No further changes were introduced until the G-series was announced and for four years the 911 T and 911 E had identical brakes with cast iron M calipers on the four wheels, while the 911 S had aluminium S calipers at the front and cast iron M calipers on the rear wheels. All cars had ventilated discs, and when the Carrera was introduced it had the same brakes as the 911 S. These were retained for the Carrera in the G- and H-series and they have such a margin that they were adopted with only a change in brake pad specification for the 930 Turbo, up to 1977 models.

With the G-series cars, the 911 S not being the top model any more, and having had its power cut down, it had its front aluminium S calipers changed to the smaller cast iron M calipers, only the Carrera keeping the aluminium calipers through the H-series, when they were also adopted for the Turbo. With the I-series 1976 models, when the range was reduced to three models again, a new front caliper was introduced for both the bottom and middle range models, the 165 bhp 911 and the 200 bhp 3 litre Carrera. This is the A caliper*, made of cast iron, which takes 10 mm thick linings of the same area as those used in the S calipers. Aluminium S calipers with 13 mm thick linings were retained on the Turbo. The A caliper, which provides a pad area of 12.1 sq in, upgrades the brakes, compared with the G- and H-series 911 and 911 S and makes it possible to use the same front struts for all models, whereas the M caliper requires different attachment lugs from the S and A calipers. The decision to use the cast iron A caliper on the I-series Carrera, instead of the aluminium S caliper, mainly for reasons of cost but at the expense of 1.56 kg (3.44 lb) extra unsprung weight, was taken after weighing the four different kinds of tyres approved for the car. Only when it was discovered that the difference between the lightest and the heaviest was 4.5 kg (10 lb) — three times the weight penalty of the cast iron caliper — was the iron caliper adopted.

For the sake of accuracy it should be added that the limited production Carrera RS 3.0 made at the beginning of 1974 inherited the entire braking system of the Type 917 flat-12 sports racing car, featuring liberally finned aluminium four-piston calipers of Porsche design and manufacture and ventilated discs. These were extremely expensive racing brakes, however, and were used on that particular model only because it was specifically designed for racing.

---

* The A caliper is similar to the cast iron S caliper, but narrower. It was developed originally for Alfa-Romeo, hence the A designation.

Wind tunnel testing. At maximum speed, total lift is reduced from 397 lb for the car without aerodynamic aids **(above)** *to a mere 38 lb with the front air dam and rear 'tray' spoiler* **(bottom)** *which also reduce the drag by 2 per cent. Rear lift is reduced from 276 lb to 68 lb by the 'duck's tail'* **(right)** *and to 29 lb with the 'tray'. The car is a G-series Carrera 2.7.*

Above and below *In addition to reducing rear end lift by over 70 per cent, the 'duck's tail' improves the flow of air into the engine compartment and over the tail lights, keeping the latter cleaner in bad weather. These properties were further developed by the 'tray' spoiler.*

Top *If a 'tray' spoiler is fitted at the rear of G or later series models, an additional hard rubber front air dam is mandatory to balance front and rear lift forces. Both are standard on the Turbo seen here on 50-series Pirelli P7 tyres and 15 in diameter rims.* **Above** *The 3.3 litre Turbo (right) is easily recognised by its raised rear spoiler, clearing the intercooler. On the left is a 911 SC. Both are 1980 models.*

Below *I-series body shells are fully corrosion-proofed by the use of zinc-coated steel for the entire structure, which additionally gets the full anti-corrosive treatment of earlier models. Further protection results from the use of corrosion-proof light alloys for such major components as the external parts of the entire engine and transmission, the steering box, the rear suspension arms, the front suspension cross member, the wheels and even the wheel securing nuts, while the entire exhaust system is made of stainless steel, also used for the Targa's roll arch. The cast aluminium wheels were introduced on F-series 911 E models, and later became the standard wear for all 911 and Carrera 3.0 models.*

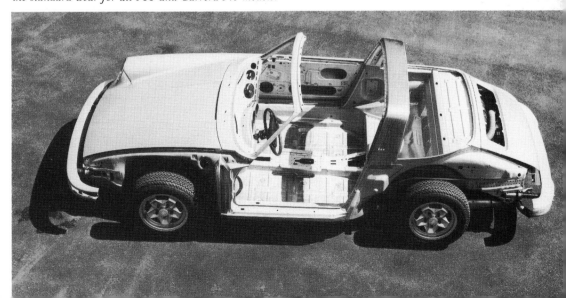

Above *First factory entry in a major event, this 911 driven by development engineers Herbert Linge and Peter Falk came fifth overall in the 1965 Monte Carlo Rally.*

Below *Vic Elford (right) and David Stone, 3rd in the 1967 Tour of Corsica with this 911 R. A similar car won in 1969 and, that year, also won the Tour de France, both times crewed by Larrousse/Gelin.*

Above *Functional beauty: the 911 R, of which only 20 were made in 1967. The doors, lids, front wings and bumper assemblies were of glass fibre and most transparent surfaces were perspex. The wings were flared and allowed the use of 6 and 7 inch rims, as on the current Carrera. The oil tank was located in front of the right rear wheel, as in E-series models five years later.*

Below *Early 911 models were raced on the standard 4.5 inch wide rims. This picture shows the car driven by Gaban and 'Pedro' winning the 1967 Spa 24 hours race at an average of 104.94 mph.*

Above *This was a frequent attitude of early 911s on racing circuits. Here Vic Elford, with David Stone as co-driver, is winning the 1967 Lyon-Charbonnière rally.*

Below *What **not** to do to a Porsche! Burdened as it was, this car did no good in the 1968 London-Sydney rally.*

Above *The B-series had a good start in life, finishing first and second in the 1968 Marathon de la Route — 84 hours on the Nürburgring. These works cars were fitted with the Boge self-levelling hydro-pneumatic struts.*

Below *This picture of Elford/Stone in the 1969 Monte Carlo Rally (they finished second behind Walde-gaard/Elmer's similar 911 S) shows the rally exhaust system.*

Above *The 911 R during its world record breaking run at Monza in 1967. Note how the air pressure deforms the light glass fibre front lid.*

Below *Conditions encountered in the East African Safari are illustrated by this picture of the Herrman-Schuller car in 1968.*

Above *Compared with the 3-litre Turbo, the 3.3 has a raised spoiler to clear the intercooler. Twin exhaust pipes came with the 1980 model (new A-series) illustrated.*

Below *For the 1981 model year (new B-series), directional lights were added in the side of front fenders. They identify high compression, 204 bhp 911 SC models.*

The optional rear spoiler (to be fitted only in connection with the additional front air dam) of the 1984 Carrera has the same air intake area as the Turbo's, but lower side 'fences'.

At the time, however, the racing discs that were both ventilated *and* transversely drilled were not fitted to the road version of the 3.0 RS as their proneness to cracking required careful, expert watching. But development continued, as these drilled discs ran cooler, were noticeably lighter and provided better wet weather response, as any water was forced into the holes at the first application of the pads. By 1978, their development had proceeded so far that they were used on the 750 bhp 935/78 (the Group 5 version of the Porsche Turbo) at Le Mans and could safely be fitted to the production Turbo 3.3, complete with the full 917 brake assembly: when pushed hard, the 3 litre Turbo had proved to be a lot of car for its brakes and the racing-type units were a must for the even more powerful and heavier 3.3. Their light alloy, quick-change calipers have four pistons each, front 38 mm, rear 30 mm, while the pad area is increased from 78 to 94 sq cm and from 52.5 to 94 sq cm, respectively, providing much longer pad life than with the old brakes. The discs themselves are much more massive, being increased in diameter by approximately 20 mm to 304 mm front and 309 mm rear and in thickness from 20.5 to 32 mm and from 20 to 28 mm, respectively. The rear drum parking brake is retained. At the same time, the diameter of the Hydrovac was increased from 7 to 8 inches in the Turbo only. From then on, the braking system of the Turbo has remained almost unchanged. Only the internal leverage of the servo unit was increased from 2.25 to 3.0 to reduce the pedal pressure, beginning with the 1985 model year and the manufacturing process of the holed discs was modified in the 1987 models. Instead of being part of the disc casting, the holes were drilled and their extremities recessed for better evacuation of brake pad dust which was prone to be baked and to clog the holes.

For 12 years, thanks to the use of high quality materials of great rigidity, which allowed a high multiplication ratio between the pedal and the brakes, Porsche had got away without using a servo, where much lighter and slower cars use one, thus providing an excellent 'feel'. In fact, the mechanical advantage used far exceeded the brake manufacturers' recommendations and when Porsche decided to make use of it, they had to take full responsibility for their choice, made possibly only by extremely strict quality control.

But since the 911 was put into production, considerable progress was made both in the running gear and the tyre departments. Earlier in this chapter, we emphasised that the Turbo achieves cornering forces up to 22.6 per cent higher than early 911 models were able to record. Retardation forces have risen in approximately the same proportion, implying a 15 to 20 per cent higher pedal load to achieve the maximum retardation. Some customers, specially ladies, found the push to be exerted too heavy for their convenience and even safety, and consequently, from the K-series on, all cars were fitted with a vacuum servo, except the basic manual 911/2.7, though it was part of the 'comfort kit' available for it. It is located in the left side corner of the luggage locker, carries the twin master cylinder and is rod-operated from the brake pedal. It took another year (1978 models) before it was fitted to right-hand drive cars.

For seven years, the brakes of the atmospheric 911 were left unchanged but, as late as 1983, Ferdinand Piëch, Chief of Development at Audi, told me: 'For us, the 911 brakes still set the standards. They are the target we try to achieve at Audi'. But with 3.2 litres and 231 bhp in a narrower car, the 1984 model 911 is very nearly as fast as the original 3-litre Turbo, the brakes of which, similar in size and design to the normal 911 brakes, were considered by the Porsche engineers to be only just adequate. Consequently a lot of attention was devoted to providing the 3.2-litre Carrera with brakes well up to its performance. Almost every component of the braking system was reconsidered:

— The thickness of the front and rear ventilated brake discs was increased to 24 mm (from 20.5 mm front and 20 mm rear), involving a corresponding widening of the calipers.

— The rear brake cylinder bore was increased from 38 mm to 42 mm (same as the front calipers) to spread the work equally between the front and rear brakes in normal retardations.

— A brake pressure limiter was added in the rear braking circuit to prevent premature rear wheel locking under panic braking (which would inevitably occur with equal size brake cylinders front and rear).

— The diameter of the brake servo was increased from 7 to 8 inches (same as the Turbo).

— An engine-driven vacuum pump was added in view of the low vacuum in the intake system at full throttle, which could create a response problem in a sudden and hard application of the brakes after a full throttle spell.

— All brakes were connected to a warning light on the dashboard. The light is incorporated into the bezel of the seat belt and hand brake warning lights.

This should ensure that the 911 brakes live up to their reputation even in the fastest and heaviest production atmospheric 911 made so far.

From the 1988 model year on, asbestos-free brake pads were fitted to all 911 models exported to countries in which they are required by legislation. The modification was extended to all 911 models for 1989.

Chapter Six

Body developments

The body structure and shape

As far back as the time of the 356, Porsche publicity stressed the 'ageless shape' of Zuffenhausen's cars, and they must be right, since for more than 35 years the general outline of a Porsche has remained the same, and few cars underwent so few styling changes in their long production life as did the 356 and the 911. The reason is that their styling is dictated mainly by function, with the main object of achieving the best possible performance from as compact and light a package as possible. Fashion played a negligible part in the design of either car.

There is very little to report on the evolution of the 911's body structure, which was mainly the work of Ing Erwin Komenda who translated Butzi Porsche's styling projects into solid metal. Except for moving the rear wheel arches back 2¼ inches when the B-series was launched, and modifying the front skirt under the bumper to create an air dam, beginning with the E-series 911 S, the side view of the car remained unaltered until American legislation forced the adoption of a new type of bumper, nine years after the original 901/911 was launched. Up to the adoption of the new bumpers, characteristic of the G and following series, the only other significant modifications were related to the adoption of wheels and tyres of increasing width. The original O-series cars had unbeaded wheel openings which accommodated the 5.5 inch wide wheels of the A-series in July 1967 without requiring a modification. The openings had to be beaten out to make room for the 6 inch rims

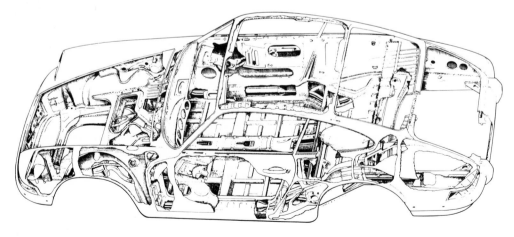

Body structure of early 911. It has remained virtually unchanged.

and fat 70 series tyres of the B-series 911 E and 911 S models. More flaring was required at the rear to accommodate the 7 inch rims and 60 series tyres of the F-series Carrera 2.7 and the wider rear wheel openings have remained a good identification mark for Carreras ever since. Much wider lateral extensions are, of course, required to accommodate the wider wheels and wider track of the 930 Turbo: added to the deep front air dam and the large rear spoiler, they provide a distinctive touch which is not only technically functional but helps to distinguish a Turbo from 'lesser' Porsches.

Except for the move rearward of the wheel arches in the B-series, the only modification which involved any significant sheet metal changes was the adoption of the larger and higher bumpers required to meet American regulations. The internal sheet metal had to be modified and the body structure locally reinforced to accommodate the hydraulic shock-absorbing struts and resist the forces generated by the 5 mph impact test. In cars exported to America, a reinforcement rail was also incorporated in the doors to meet the side impact test. As nothing has proved these two items of the American specification to be really worth while, they were not part of the European specification until February 1985 when the door rail was fitted to all cars (but not the heavy bumper struts). Since the local reinforcements to the body have added some weight, the big bumpers are made of aluminium to compensate for some of this, while additional weight is saved by the use of a plastic (rather than steel) fuel tank, of a single instead of twin batteries and by replacing the F-series seats by the notably lighter G-series seats with integral headrests. The result of this is that the weight of G-series cars, which also have lighter cast alloy rear inner suspension arms than their predecessors which had fabricated steel arms, shows practically no increase, compared with the 2.4 litre models which preceded them.

Weight and noise

It is in fact quite remarkable that, in strong contrast to the usual course of events, Porsche have for a long time succeeded in keeping the weight of the 911 down, despite the inevitable sophistications required by ever-increasing demands for comfort, despite all safety and emission laws and, above all, despite engine capacity increases of up to 50 per cent which were achieved without increasing the weight of the unit itself, but made it necessary to reinforce the entire transmission and to use bigger brakes. Taking the road tests by *Auto, Motor & Sport* as a basis of reference, the lightest Porsche (excluding lightweight models) they tested was the original A-series 911 T which weighed 1,075 kg (2,373 lb) with its 62 litre (13.7 Imp gall) fuel tank full, while the heaviest was the G-series Carrera which weighed 1,180 kg (2,605 lb) with its bigger, 80 litre (17.6 Imp gall) tank full. But if we consider equivalent models, the difference is much less still, for the original O-series 911 S weighed 1,090 kg in 1966 and its 1974 G-series equivalent weighed 1,110 kg — only 7 kg (15.6 lb) more if its larger tank is taken into account. Unfortunately, from the second half of the '70s on, the car put on weight at a quicker rate, first as a switch back from magnesium to aluminium was made for the gearbox housing and the engine's crankcase, then as cost was saved on certain items (as when the cast alloy brake calipers were discarded in favour of cast iron ones), as higher performance demanded general reinforcements of transmission and brakes (brake disc thickness was increased with the advent of the 3.2 litre engine), as emission, noise and safety legislation required more sophisticated equipment and sound shielding, and, last but not least as ever more luxury was required by a large number of customers: such facilities as electric window operation, electric seat adjustments, centralised door locking system, electrically-operated mirrors are now all standard equipment to which most customers add an electric sliding roof, air conditioning, a radio and, in many cases, leather upholstery. So even if the factory still quotes an honest 1,210 kg, few Carreras leave the factory weighing less than 1300 kg. While most customers are happy with this, there is a minority which mourns such cars as the 1973 lightweight Carrera RS 2.7, and from 1987 on, the factory has been sympathetic to their demands and offers the Carrera 'Club Sport' which officially weighs only 40 kg less than the standard model, but in fact weighs 100–110 kg less than most normal Carreras leaving the factory, which has a very perceptible influence on performance and handling agility. As the body structure remains completely unchanged, including the movable parts such as doors and bonnets which are made of zinc coated steel as the rest of the car, the weight saving has been achieved exclusively by deleting every non-essential part of equipment, including a large part of the sound-proofing material. The attention to weight saving goes as far as the deletion of the coat hooks and passenger side sun visor, but the major deleted items are the rear emergency seats, the fog lights, the automatic heater control and defrosting boosters, the electric window lifters, the radio pre-equipment and the rear compartment trim. The car comes with stiffer shock absorbers, more rigid engine rubber mountings and an aluminium emergency spare wheel. The engine has hollow intake valves for lighter weight, which in connection with a modified Motronic unit pushes the revolution limit from 6,400 to 6,700 rpm, without any power or torque benefit.

A full road test by *Auto, Motor & Sport* has revealed the following performance data for a Club Sport weighing 1,179 kg, compared with a fully-equipped Carrera weighing exactly 99 kg more (parentheses):

Max speed:	154.1 mph (153.5 mph)
0–100 km/h (62 mph):	5.9 s. (6.4 s.)
0–160 km/h (99.5 mph):	14.1 s. (15.2 s.)
Standing start km:	25.7 s. (26.4 s.)

What the figures do not reflect, however, is the enormous fun to be derived from the combination of the light car and the more sporting suspension.

With most of its sound-proofing material discarded, the Carrera 'Club Sport' is by no means a quiet car, though it is not overly noisy by enthusiastic owners' standards or even compared with a 328 Ferrari. The Club Sport's noise levels are still probably below those of early 911 models. Neither are later 911 models, such as the Carrera 3.2 quiet cars, but the table below, summing up some data extracted from *Auto, Motor & Sport* road tests shows that considerable progress was made as development proceeded, especially in the first ten years of the car's life, the biggest step having been achieved with the introduction of the G-Series (1974 models). It is, however, interesting to note that there is virtually no difference between the G-Series 2.7 litre 911 S and Carrera models, except at the highest speeds, indicating that the 'softer' valve timing of the K-Jetronic models (represented by the 911 S) has little to do with the much quieter running achieved. This appears to be mainly a result of better sound-proofing, better intake and exhaust silencing and higher gearing: at 125 mph, the first 911 S 2 litre engine was running at 6,000 rpm while both versions of the 2.7 litre G-Series were geared to run at 5,500 rpm at the same speed. As the engine capacity and power increased, gearing was further raised and the 3.2 Carrera's engine is down to 5,000 rpm at 125 mph, but this seems to have made little difference to the noise level.

Noise measurements in top gear also make an interesting comparison:

	O-series 911 (2 litre)	E-series 911 S (2.4 litre)	G-series 911 S (2.7 litre)	G-series Carrera (2.7 litre)	1978 mod. Turbo (3.3 litre)	1979 mod. 911 SC (3.0 litre)
At 100 kph	78 dBA	76 dBA	73 dBA	72 dBA	73 dBA	73 dBA
At 140 kph	82 dBA	81 dBA	76 dBA	75 dBA	78 dBA	79 dBA
At 180 kph	89 dBA	88 dBA	80 dBA	81 dBA	81 dBA	83 dBA
At 200 kph	—	91 dBA	82 dBA	85 dBA	84 dBA	85 dBA

Defeating corrosion

For the first six years of production, the 911 was rustproofed by the best of the then conventional methods, including bonderising and electrophoretic painting, but with the enormous amount of chemicals sprayed on German roads during the winter this did not prove entirely satisfactory, and rust attacks were not at all in keeping with the image of quality Porsche wanted to establish and maintain. As far back as 1967 three special experimental cars were built with a body shell entirely made of polished and unpainted stainless steel. All three covered large mileages without suffering in the least from corrosive attacks. Two of them were eventually destroyed in crashes, but one of them has been preserved. Unfortunately, these cars could only be part of an experiment carried out in co-operation with the German steel industry, as the cost would obviously have been prohibitive for a production car. A more realistic approach was to galvanise the most exposed parts of the underbody sheet metal and the wheel arches. The process proved very satisfactory and although it added DM 70 to the cost price of the vehicle, it was adopted for production, starting with the D-series (2.2 litre models) in summer 1970. The only other car I know of which was treated similarly at the time is the Rolls-Royce Silver Shadow. Further progress in the battle against corrosion was made when stainless steel was adopted for the entire exhaust system and for the engine oil tank, which made it possible to increase the service intervals from 10,000 to 20,000 km (6,300 to 12,600 miles). With the G-series came the use of rustproof cast light alloy rear suspension arms.

For 1976, however, Porsche went the whole way, and following up the project for a 'long life' car they had exhibited at the Frankfurt Motor Show of 1973, they extended the use of zinc-coated sheet metal to the entire body shell of the I-series except, for a few months, the Coupé's roof. This was not only to greatly simplify maintenance, especially in winter when tons of chemicals are poured on the roads to combat the formation of ice, but also help to preserve the structural strength as well as the appearance of the car over a long period. It will certainly extend its useful life, as it is quite common today for mechanical components to outlive the car's structure, particularly when the car is built to such high engineering standards as a Porsche.

The zinc-coated steel sheet used is supplied by the Thyssen steel works. The zinc layer is not applied by an electrolytic process, but rather by immersion of the steel sheet in a zinc bath at a temperature of 500°C. The sheet is then laminated to reduce the coat to the required thickness, which is 20μ for the most severely exposed parts and 10μ for the others — in either case much more than the layers usually obtained by an electrolytic process. The thickness of the layer is very important as an electric tension builds up between the zinc and the steel, which makes the zinc creep and cover any nearby part of the steel which damage to the zinc layer may have left unprotected, but this happens only as long as there is enough zinc in the vicinity for efficient covering. Thanks to this creep, which is a galvanic action activated by humidity, any cracks in the zinc surface which may develop during the stamping process, as well as the welds which cause the zinc to evaporate locally, are soon covered by the protective layer, while accidental damage is of little consequence.

In addition to the protective zinc coat, applied to both sides of the sheet steel, the full anti-corrosive protection previously applied is maintained and the tests carried out have been so conclusive that Porsche immediately gave a six years' warranty against rust damage on the entire floor panel, and this was extended to a period of seven years on the entire body structure from the 1981 model year on and to 10 years from 1987 models on without any intermediate treatment. Though the structure is otherwise unchanged, the use of zinc-coated sheet material has entailed many assembly line modifications, such as different welding electrodes, higher welding voltage and protection of workers against zinc vapour.

The Targa

So far, we have always mentioned the 911 as if it were produced in only one body style: the Coupé, which in fact remained the only body style available in the first three years of Porsche 911 production. Compared with the old 356 model range, this was a retrograde step and there were many requests for an open model, especially as — let's face it — hot weather ventilation has never been one of the 911's strong points. This request raised two main problems: the inherent lack of rigidity of an open car and the tooling costs. Normally an open car requires a considerably reinforced floor structure to compensate for the inherent rigidity of a properly designed all-steel body. This involves a weight penalty (medium sized open cars are usually around 50 kg heavier than corresponding closed models) which Porsche were loath to accept, and some additional tooling. And, also to save tooling costs, it was essential that the greatest possible part of the body panels used for the Coupé should remain unaltered. There were also indications that the ever more safety conscious American legislation might ban conventional open cars altogether. It was with all these considerations in mind that Porsche created a completely new body style incorporating a stainless steel 'rollover hoop' which was eventually destined to set a fashion. Practically all the sheet metal of the Coupé located below the waist line remained unchanged and the stylish, polished, stainless steel rollover protection (which later became black eloxided) hopefully took care of an American legislation which never actually materialised. The floorpan required only a few local reinforcements to achieve an adequate rigidity and the lighter soft top almost exactly made up for their additional weight.

This completely new body style was given the name 'Targa', recalling the victories of Porsche racing cars in the famous Sicilian 'Targa Florio', and the car made such an impact that to-day 'Targa' has become the regular word to describe an open car with a rollover hoop. Of course increased safety was claimed in the case of an accident, which was certainly justified if the occupants were properly restrained. It also permits the use of a removable roof panel, doing away with the complicated and heavy folding roof mechanism normally used in drop-heads and which would have taken up a lot of room in the back of the car, possibly requiring higher body side and rear panels to make it disappear when folded, which, in fact, did not prove necessary when 17 years later, the 911 Cabriolet was developed. Instead of this, the removable roof panel can be easily folded to be stowed away in the luggage locker, where it takes up little space, while the original flexible PVC rear panel could be opened by just pulling a zip-fastener. With the top removed and the rear panel folded, full fresh air motoring could thus be enjoyed with the extra safety of the roll arch.

In fact, four different combinations were possible:
car totally closed,
car totally open,
roof removed, rear panel in place, and

roof panel in place, rear panel open.

Owners quickly found out, however, that the most pleasant way to enjoy open air motoring was to remove the roof panel while the rear panel remained in place. In this condition, the car could be driven fairly fast without disturbing draughts being created around the passengers. The logical conclusion of this, quickly reached by Porsche, was to offer buyers the choice of the soft rear panel or an enveloping rigid glass panel providing perfect air- and water-tightness and having less tendency to flap. It was also more robust, more elegant and completely thief-proof. Another, unpublicised advantage of the rigid rear enveloping window was that it materially contributed to the torsional rigidity of the Targa which, despite the roll arch, was still not quite equal to that of the Coupé and still does not quite match it with the rigid rear window, for which the demand soon became so overwhelming that the soft rear panel was discontinued.

Close observation of the Targa also indicates that it required no change in any of the body pressings: even the rear wings and the entire rear part of the car, including the engine room cover, are identical to those of the Coupé.

This novel form of convertible was introduced with the A-series and was available in both the 912 and 911 series, the weight being identical with the Coupé's. The cockpit ventilation was even worse than in the Coupé and even when, from the B-series on, air extractors were added in the sides of the roll arch, the pivoting front quarter lights were retained until the face-level ventilation was added in the K-series. Main reason for the deletion of the pivoting lights was to make the car more thief-proof, following an episode when three 911s were stolen in four days from members of the factory team racing at Monza! For the same reason the knob-operated inside door locks were introduced (K-series), and the following year the rear quarter lights became fixed on all models.

The Cabriolet

For many years, the entire motor industry had been led to believe that open cars without a roll-over bar of the kind featured in the Targa would soon be ruled out by the ever-increasing safety requirements of the American legislation. Even American manufacturers stopped making their popular 'convertibles', but the threat eventually failed to materialise and, although the 911 Targa had always been a popular model, accounting for roughly 40 per cent of 911 sales, it did not satisfy the most convinced among the addicts of open air motoring. Consequently, the marketing people came up with a request for a car which could be fully opened, but they came too late, at a time when Professor Fuhrmann had decided to phase out the 911 as soon as possible and did not want to invest in any project of the sort. With the reversal of the policy regarding the 911 that came with the new management, the project was immediately revived and a very small group of men in the experimental shop was given a few guidelines and asked to build what was called the 911 Cabriolet. It didn't take them long to saw off the roll-over bar of a Targa and to install a complete soft top which, when folded, protruded only a fraction over the body sides and behind the rear seats, and at very little cost of interior space: the width of the rear compartment remained unchanged, but the squabs of the occasional rear seats had to be made slightly more upright when used. The soft top can be raised and dropped single handed and in a single movement, without fastening or releasing any buttons. In order to avoid tedious buffeting noises when the car is driven fast, the cloth is backed by two large pieces of aluminium extending rearwards from the leading edge of the folding top and forward from its rear arch. Another feature is that the entire rear panel carrying the transparent vinyl window can not only be opened by pulling a zip fastener, but is entirely detachable and can be replaced in its entirety if the vinyl becomes damaged or excessively scratched. As only very little rigidity is added by the 'Targa bar', its deletion in the Cabriolet caused no problem and the reinforcements required were of very minor nature. In practice, the Cabriolet has proved to be as rigid as the Targa and certainly no more noisy at speed. The interior equipment is the same as the Targa's, except that the automatic control of the heater output, which is standard on the later Coupés and Targas (except for USA, Canada and Japan models) is replaced by a manual control. From Carrera 3.2 models on, the emergency seats can be replaced by optional lockable lockers, and electric operation of the soft top is an option. From 1986 models on, both the Targa and Cabrio became available as 'Turbo' and 'Turbo-look'.

The 911 Speedster

As the price and sophistication of the 911 rose, an even stronger demand came up, specially from America, for a simpler and lighter open model, on the lines of the 356 Speedster, built in the years 1954 to 1957. That had been a fairly basic car with rather primitive weather protection, poor visibility when closed and fixed, pin-down, removable side windows. Porsche was willing to respond to the demand, and hardly had the first Cabriolet left the assembly line, work started on a simplified model. The idea was to produce a car for fine weather countries only, with no top at all, which much simplifies matters. The prototype was readied in less than six weeks and featured a very low, unframed windscreen, so low that the driver could look over its top, so that no wiper was required. The windscreen itself was more inclined than the normal 911 screen and the removable side windows were pinned into the doors. Based on a 911 SC and finished in red with forged alloy wheels, it looked very exciting, but it was decided to postpone its production until the revised 911, based on a new floorpan suitable for the intended optional four-wheel drive was put into production. As there had been leaks before the introduction of the Cabriolet, with the result that some body specialists actually produced a 911 cabriolet before the factory offered its own, it was decided that the car should be hidden in a closed garage under the responsibility of Prof Helmuth Bott, and it soon became known as the 'Bott Speedster'.

Unfortunately, the 911 programme fell behind schedule because of delays in the construction of the new body factory where the revised version was to be built, and as the Dollar crisis of 1987 resulted in a slump of Porsche's sales in the USA, it was finally decided to add the Speedster to the current programme. When reconsidering the problem, it was found that in many countries, the 'Bott Speedster' would not be legal and several details had to be reconsidered. The height of the windscreen had to be increased so that a wiper could be installed. This in turn provided a possibility to provide the car with a simple soft top of which the interior padding provided in the Cabrio was deleted. Then it was thought that the car could be made attractive for a larger number of users if the simple, but rather impractical removable door windows were replaced with wind-up windows. They in fact require a more complicated mechanism than used in other 911 models, because the full open air motoring sensation would be lost if the fixed door quarter lights used in other 911s were retained: in the Speedster, the front edge of the door window directly meets the windscreen pillar when the window is up.

The Speedster has no emergency seats, and for appearance as well as aerodynamic reasons, it was thought desirable to cover the rear compartment into which the soft top disappears completely. The rigid cover is hinged at its forward end, just behind the door openings, to give access to the top and remains in place when the latter is up, which again

Above *928-style 15-in diameter cast aluminium wheels are standard on the 1984 model (new E-Series) Carrera, but the forged 'Fuchs' wheels remain optional in both 15- and 16-in diameter sizes, the latter with ultra-low profile tyres. Improved sealing of the detachable Targa top was introduced with E-Series.*

Right *The Cabriolet was first shown as a 'study' with a 3.3-litre Turbo engine and four-wheel drive at the Frankfurt motor show of 1981.*

Below *The production Cabriolet started in 1982 as a 911 SC and continued as a Carrera for 1984. From 1986 models on, the Cabrio was also offered as a Turbo and 'Turbo-look'.*

requires a rather ingenious mechanism, as when up the rear part of the top must be wider than the recess into which it disappears. It has nevertheless been possible to devise a system which can easily be erected and folded single handed in a very short time. When the car is open, the high tail line helps reduce both air drag and draughts inside the car.

A hard top which can be screwed in place of the rigid rear cover was also designed and provision was made for transforming the Speedster into an 'offset single seater' for Club racing. In this case, the standard windscreen, which is inclined 5° more than the normal 911 screen and is screwed to the scuttle structure (this being the only difference between the structure of the Speedster and that of the Cabrio) is removed and the entire cockpit is closed with a cover, made of plastic material, leaving only an opening above the driver's seat and carrying its own wrap round windscreen, much as in a single seater racing car.

The first prototype of the Speedster's final version was exhibited in the Frankfurt Motor Show of 1987, with attendants demonstrating the various configurations, and it created great interest. Production is scheduled for the 1989 model year, though the hard top and 'Club Sport' accessories will only become available at a later date.

Heating and ventilating system

In a car powered by an air-cooled engine the output of warm air into the cockpit is dependent upon the speed of the engine cooling blower, while the heat produced is a function of engine load, making the heater output very dependent on the operating conditions. For this reason, the 911 was originally equipped with an independent Eberspächer petrol/electric heating system, supplementing the engine heater. It became available only as an option from the A-series on.

Left *The central console and automatic heater control (nearest the camera) were standard on the Turbo from the beginning and were adopted for all models from the 1979 model year on. Only the Cabriolet has manual heater controls. The console carries the loudspeaker balance switch and the air conditioner controls (as seen here), if fitted.*

Below *The instrument panel has remained substantially unchanged over the years. This is the 1984 Carrera's.*

From 1986 models, ventilation was vastly improved by the large air grilles on either side of the dash structure.

The main heating system is based on the circulation of air, derived from the engine cooling blower, in two heat exchangers surrounding the exhaust manifolds. From these, the hot air is led to two cylindrical distributors — one on either side — actuated by a control set between the seats. These distributors direct the hot air via silencers included in the box-section door sills into the car or vent it to the atmosphere. Additionally, 'fresh air admitted in front of the windscreen and activated at will by a variable speed electric blower can be mixed with the warm air. The cockpit temperature could thus be controlled by either adjusting the output of hot air, or mixing it with cold air.

Though the system has remained basically unaltered, it has been developed over the years. Introduced in July 1966, the 911 S had modified manifolding in the heat exchangers to provide a freer exhaust flow. This was standardised from the A-series and stainless steel exchangers came with the F-series. O- and A-series cars had the lower hot air outlets at the forward end of the door sills (fed with hot air only), and the upper ones at the base of the windscreen, where hot and fresh air could be mixed. Additionally there was a duct (with silencer) to demist the rear window.

From the B-series on, the lower outlets were moved to a position under the dash. Hot and fresh air could now be mixed at will and separately for the face and floor levels, while the duct to the rear window was deleted in favour of electrical heating. Small adjustable air outlets were added at either side of the dashboard to help demist the side windows from the G-series on.

Two further improvements were introduced with the H-series which features larger capacity heat exchangers. One of them is the provision of two control levers operating the two hot air distribution boxes separately so as to provide individual temperature controls for the driver and passenger sides. The other is the addition of a permanently running electric fan, upstream of enlarged heat exchangers, to activate the heated air circulation when the engine operates at low load or idles. At high engine speeds, a flap valve directs any excess air delivered by the engine blower into the atmosphere to avoid over-heating the cockpit. With the introduction of this further sophistication, the petrol/electric heater option was deleted.

The 930 Turbo and I-series 3 litre Carrera had an even more sophisticated installation incorporating an automatic temperature control. In this, the single temperature control lever is operated automatically by an electric motor energised by an electronic control unit. This in turn receives signals from two temperature sensors, one located downstream of the left-hand hot air distributor box, the other sensing the cockpit temperature above the windscreen. With this system, separate temperature control for the driver and passenger side is not possible. It was quite efficient however in maintaining the cockpit temperature fairly constant when heating was required, but still did not solve the ever-present problem of summer time ventilation, to which the solution at last came with the K-series when two adjustable cold air outlets were provided near the centre of the dash panel. This involved replacing the single loud speaker by two door-mounted speakers. Two further minute outlets were added to the sides of the dash panel, which were supposed to keep the side windows from misting up.

Prior to this addition, the only way to keep the car reasonably cool in warm weather without having to put up with the noise and draughts created by opening a window was to opt for the air conditioning plant which became optional from the B-series on. This not only added a lot of weight, but most of it is overhung at the extreme rear of the car, the compressor being belt driven off the rear end of the crankshaft and the condenser split between the rear air intake grille and the front of the car. From 1985 automatic air conditioning became available.

The automatic temperature control was continued in the 911 SC models, but was only optional in the 1978 model, becoming standard in later cars.

Further attention was given to the heating and ventilation system when the 3.2-litre atmospheric engine was introduced for the 1984 Carrera range. The improved system comprises:
— improved heat exchangers (as mentioned in connection with engine developments);
— improved efficiency of the under-bonnet fan through re-location of the pipes;
— an additional fan at the bottom of either door hinge pillar (A-pillar) (a feature already incorporated in 1983 model Turbos); and
— incorporation of the three-speed fan switch in the temperature selector knob (except Cabriolet, which has manual control only).

In addition, a tinted glass rear window became standard to reduce heating up of the interior by the sun when the car is parked, while two-stage heating of the rear window was introduced to accelerate demisting or defrosting and to reduce current consumption when the use of the window heater is only preventive.

A further serious advance towards better ventilation was made when in 1986 models larger outlet grills were adopted, both for the centre and the side outlets on the dash panel. Simultaneously, the cockpit temperature sensor of the automatic heating system was moved from above the internal rear view mirror to the dashboard.

Passive safety

In previous chapters we have dealt with many developments that have increased the active safety of the 911: ventilated brake discs, introduced for the O-series 911 S in 1966 and progressively adopted for all models; the twin circuit braking system introduced with the A-series in 1967; better handling obtained by improved weight distribution (increased

Above *In 1987 models, the 'afterthought' rear fog light was at last replaced with twin built-in lights on either side of the Porsche script, reduced in size.* **Below** *For 1988 models, the standard rim width was increased in Carrera models to 7 in front and 8 in rear and the Fuchs wheels became standard again, diameter being 15 in. From 1989 on, 16 in diameter wheels became standard.*

Above *The 911, with its functional, timelessly classical shape, has been the central model in Porsche's high performance road car range for 25 years. From right to left, 1965 2 litre 911 Coupe, 1975 3 litre 911 Turbo, and 1988 2.85 litre 959.* **Below** *Removing the standard windscreen and replacing the rear deck with a rigid tonneau cover with an opening for the driver only, the Speedster can be converted to an 'offset single seater' for club events.*

wheelbase as from the B-series in 1968, magnesium engine and gearbox casings), reduced unsprung weight (alloy wheels, alloy front brake calipers on some models) and wider rims and tyres; aerodynamic aids (front air dam and, in some cases, rear spoiler) which will be discussed in more detail in the following sub-section; and some other improvements which have up to now remained unmentioned, such as the introduction of quartz-halogen headlights and the electrically heated rear window with the B-series in 1968, headlight washers (standard or optional according to the models) with the G-series in July 1973 and the electrically controlled and heated external mirror of the I-series in 1975.

For all these improvements in active safety, passive safety was never neglected and in fact ranked very high when the 911 was originally designed. The best proof of this is that, though designed when barrier impact and other destruction tests were almost unheard of and had not been made compulsory in any part of the world, the 911 passed with flying colours any official test to which it was submitted, the only significant modification required being to reshape the spare wheel housing in the front-mounted tank in order to allow the wheel to jump out of its recess without bursting the tank. Only when 5 mph bumpers were required in the United States was any structural modification necessary, and in this context it should be remembered that this requirement was introduced for economic and convenience reasons: it has very little bearing on the car's safety as such.

However, as development went on, additional passive safety features were added to the original design, which it is as well to recapitulate.

Original 911 passive safety features:
Crash-proof body shell,
Three-piece, Z-shaped steering column,
Laminated glass windscreen.

Passive safety features added in the course of development:
Reshaped spare wheel recess in fuel tank, to permit exit of wheel in case of crash (B-series, summer 1968),
External door handles with trigger on the inside (C-series, summer 1969),
Inertia reel seat belts (US models Jan 1972, other models Feb 1973),
Doors with side impact protection rails (US models only, Jan 1973),
Impact absorbing steering wheel boss (G-series, summer 1973),
Seats with integral headrest (G-series, summer 1973),
Reinforced (US energy absorbing) bumpers (G-series, summer 1973),
Zinc-coated, fully rustproofed body structure (I-series, Sept 1975).
Electrically-operated, heated external mirror (I-Series, Sept. 1975).
Brake pad wear and fluid level warning light (Sept. 1983).
Intensive windscreen washer with heated jets (Sept. 1985).
Remote headlight beam adjustment (option, Sept. 1986).

Aerodynamic developments

The shape of the 911 was evolved with the importance of low aerodynamic drag very much in the designer's mind. The original Porsche 356 had a very efficient aerodynamic shape, its drag coefficient C_d being 0.36 according to recent tests in the VW wind tunnel, but rising to 0.40-0.41 with the introduction of the high bumpers used from the 356 B-series onwards.

The original design of the 911 aimed at a figure of the same order as early 356 models, and indeed a figure of $C_d = 0.381$ was achieved. At the time when the 911 was developed, little attention was paid to the aerodynamic lifting forces, the importance of which was only realised as a result of racing car developments, when the suspicion cropped up that some of the 911's high-speed stability problems, such as poor straight line running and sensitivity to side winds, might well have their origin in unwanted aerodynamic effects rather than in the running gear and weight distribution.

Consequently a B-series 911 S was investigated for drag, lift and side wind behaviour in September 1968, in the Stuttgart University's wind tunnel. Compared with the A-series car previously tested, the B-series had a slightly increased frontal area, due to its wider 70 series tyres and to the flared wheel openings required to accommodate them, and also a slightly higher drag coefficient, probably caused by the slight disturbance resulting from the flared wings. Taking into account corrections which had to be made following a retuning of the wind tunnel installations at a later date, the figures obtained were as follows:

A-series: $C_d=0.381$ $S=1.6853$ m^2 $C_dS=0.642$
B-series: $C_d=0.408$ $S=1.71$ m^2 $C_dS=0.697$

in both cases with the car blocked at the designed ride height and completely equipped with vertical number plates, outside rear-view mirror and twin screen wipers.

The test on the B-series car indicated that despite the car's drooping nose, there was some lift over the front axle and that the tapering rear part of the body created considerable lift over the rear axle. It further indicated that the lift increased considerably if the air stream, instead of being parallel to the car's longitudinal axis, hit the car at an angle.

Following these first tests for lift, further tests were carried out on a C-series 911 S after retuning of the wind tunnel's instrumentation, in April 1970. Except for the door handles with a hidden trigger, the C car was externally identical with the B car previously tested, and the figures obtained were as follows:

Drag coefficient $C_d=0.408$
Front lift coefficient $C_{Lf}=0.190$
Rear lift coefficient $C_{Lr}=0.264$

At 230 kph (143 mph), the resulting actual lifting forces are:

Front $L_f=83$ kg (183 lb)
Rear $L_r=115.5$ kg (255 lb)

A side wind, represented by an air flow hitting the car at an angle in relation to its longitudinal axis, confirmed the previous findings: it increased the front lift much more than the rear lift, both rising to $C_{Lf}=C_{Lr}=0.43$ for an air flow angle of 22.5° and C_{Lf} becoming greater than C_{Lr} for larger angles. And as the aerodynamic centre of pressure is about 80 cm (about 31.5 in) ahead of the wheelbase centre, this results in high side-wind sensitivity.

The tests carried out on this occasion involved trying out palliatives already applied to Porsche racing cars. They consisted mainly of adding front air dams of various depths, modifying the shape of the rear part of the body from the bottom of the rear window by making it flatter and cutting it off with a more or less vertical panel, and adding a 1,000 x 140 mm aerofoil supported by the engine compartment lid.

The best results were obtained with a front air dam and a flatter, cut-off tail terminated by a 50 mm high vertical spoiler. This gave the following figures:

$C_d=0.363$ $C_{Lf}=0.09$ $C_{Lr}=0.168$

giving a calculated front lift of 39.5 kg (87 lb) and a rear lift of 73.5 kg (161 lb) at a speed of 143 mph.

With the same front air dam and an aerofoil at the rear of the standard body angled at 16.5°, the following figures were obtained:

$C_d=0.390$ $C_{Lf}=0.106$ $C_{Lr}=0.183$

resulting in a front lift of 46.5 kg (102.5) and a rear lift of 80.5 kg (178 lb) at 143 mph.

In a side wind the front lift unfortunately increased much faster than the rear lift when the angle of the air stream was increased, which was also the case for the standard car. It is probable that the tendency for the front lift to increase very rapidly with increasing air stream angle is due to the partial blanking off of the sloping front lid by the front wings.

It was also noted that, as could be expected, making the rear part of the body taller had the effect of moving the centre of air pressure back, which should reduce the car's sensitivity to side winds.

The first result of these tests on a production car was the modified skirt under the front bumper which first appeared on the E-series 911 S, taking the form of an air dam which became standard on all models of the F-series. Due to the requirements of ground clearance, the dam could not be made nearly as effective as on a racing car, but its effect was quite noticeable on wet roads, where it reduced the tendency to aquaplane by decreasing the front-end lift by some 40 per cent, as a comparison of the wind tunnel figures with those obtained for the C-series indicate:

C-series: $C_d=0.408$ $C_{Lf}=0.190$ $C_{Lr}=0.264$
E-series: $C_d=0.408$ $C_{Lf}=0.107$ $C_{Lr}=0.261$

At 143 mph, the front lift was thus reduced from 83 to 46.5 kg (from 183 to 102.5 lb).

These figures indicate that it had now become urgent to reduce the rear end lift (still 114 kg or 252 lb at 143 mph), as the considerably greater rear lift created a tendency for the car to oversteer in high speed bends, especially if lifting off became necessary, which is just the opposite of what is required. Tests on the C-series car had indicated that a notable reduction in rear end lift could be obtained by using a cut-off tail with a flatter engine compartment top, but such a drastic body modification was not considered either practical or desirable. Consequently, further tests were made with spoilers and aerofoils, leading to the glass fibre rear lid incorporating the now well-known Carrera 'duck's tail' spoiler which proved extremely efficient in balancing front and rear end lift, and also proved beneficial in reducing the car's overall drag. It was used in connection with a slightly different front air dam with a more prominent central part in which a large oil cooler could be housed for racing, and this was apparently even more effective in reducing front end lift than the standard F-series air dam.

	Carrera RS with standard front air dam and rear 'duck's tail' spoiler	Carrera RS with standard front air dam and normal 911 rear lid
C_d	0.397	0.409
C_{Lf}	0.070	0.064
C_{Lr}	0.084	0.290
Front lift at 245 kph (152 mph)	35 kg=77.3 lb	32 kg=70.6 lb
Rear lift at 245 kph (152 mph)	42 kg=93 lb	145 kg=320 lb

The rear spoiler, which increases the rear wheel grip by no less than 20 per cent at the car's maximum speed, has the additional advantage that, combined with the front dam, it moves the centre of air pressure back from a position 10 inches behind the front wheel axis to a position 16 inches behind, with a resultant noticeable decrease in the car's sensitivity to side winds. This is further decreased by the fact that the dam and rear spoiler combination also reduces the tendency for the lift to increase in side winds. It is also noteworthy that the aerodynamic aids result in a front/rear lift ratio of 45/55, almost exactly matching the car's weight distribution — an ideal state of affairs.

Extending the front air dam downward, which reduced the ground clearance to 190 mm (7.5 inches) actually created some front down-thrust and further reduced the drag, but due to the pitching effect over the front axle, it increased the rear lift:

$$C_d = 0.375 \qquad C_{Lf} = -0.055 \qquad C_{Lr} = 0.113$$

The pitching movement created by the front down-thrust and the increased rear-end lift was undesirable, but the lesson was not lost: the deeper front dam was later used on the Carrera RS 3.0 and on the 930 Turbo, as well as for racing, in all cases in connection with a larger rear spoiler.

Investigating the possibilities of larger rear spoilers, Porsche tried to devise a shape which encompassed the entire car's width, rather similar to the spoiler experimentally developed during tests carried out on the Paul Ricard track in France during the winter 1972–73, but featuring side openings through which a high speed air jet was directed towards the tail-light area with the object of deflecting dirt from them. Unfortunately the tests led to the conclusion that a worthwhile cleaning effect led to reduced spoiler efficiency.

Though it considerably improved the car's high-speed roadworthiness, the 'duck's tail' spoiler was not accepted by the German and some other traffic authorities who considered it was too sharp-edged. Consequently development continued to find a replacement that would both satisfy the bureaucrats and achieve even better results than the 'duck's tail' which some of the larger spoilers used for racing on Carreras running in the prototype class had considerably improved upon. The development work eventually matured into the flat 'tray' spoiler moulded in one piece with the engine cover, but wider than the cover itself and framed in Pu-foam-rubber to be less aggressive to outsiders. Except for some markets where it was not officially accepted, this new spoiler became standard on G-series and later Carreras which, due to their higher and bigger bumpers, have slightly different air flow characteristics from the previous models. When the tray type rear spoiler is fitted, the skirt below the front bumper is extended downwards by a proper air dam, so as to get proper aerodynamic balance at speed. This supplementary dam is made of strong rubber in order to avoid damage when parking against kerbs. It makes an enormous difference to the front lift, as will be gathered from the following comparison:

	H-series Carrera with front air dam and rear spoiler	H-series Carrera without front air dam and spoiler	H-series Carrera without front air dam and with rear 'duck's tail'
C_d	0.414	0.423	0.414
C_{Lf}	0.010	0.112	0.113
C_{Lr}	0.025	0.246	0.062

These figures reflect the respective efficiencies of the various possible trims and make it quite clear why the front air dam is deleted on cars delivered without the rear spoiler, as is the case on certain markets: the pitching moment created at high speed would completely upset the car's balance and cause it to oversteer grossly in high speed bends. Similarly, the rear tray spoiler cannot be ordered without the supplementary front dam. Perhaps the people who have decided that Porsche's rear spoiler was dangerous would change their minds if they realised the difference it can make to the active safety of the car. With the air dam and spoiler, the total lift at 152 mph is a mere 17 kg (37.5 lb) while without them the total lift is 180 kg (397 lb). If we assume that, in the first case, the possible braking

Right *Speedster 'road version' in open, closed and hard top form.*

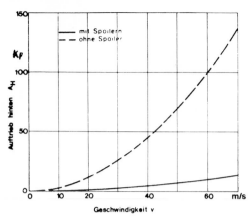

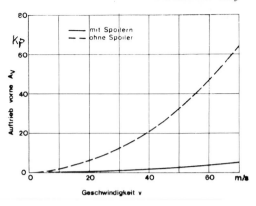

Lift over rear axle with front dam and rear 'tray' spoiler, and without spoilers (G/H/I-series).

Lift over front axle with front dam and rear 'tray' spoiler, and without spoilers (G/H/I-series).

retardation is 0.7 g, it drops to less than 0.6 g without the aerodynamic aids. It also means that the risk of aquaplaning is quite considerably increased and it should be noted that the tray was additionally shaped to smooth the flow of air over the tail-lights to combat dirt deposits.

The same front dam and rear spoiler are integral parts of the 3 litre Turbo, but a higher mounted rear spoiler, even more effective and clearing the intercooler, is fitted to the Turbo 3.3.

When the 3.3 Turbo was marketed, its new rear spoiler was also offered as an optional fitting on the 911 SC, replacing the previous model. There is, however, no doubt that the 3.3 Turbo's spoiler is less elegant than its predecessor, and a new model, fitting the standard steel engine cover, was developed for 1984 to go on the 911 Carrera when so ordered.

'Turbo-Look' Models

Ever since the Turbo was marketed, its aggressive appearance, mainly created by its widened wheel arches and wide tyres, has exerted a particular fascination on many people, including 911 owners who paid a lot of money to have their cars modified to look like Turbos, even if the increased frontal area actually made the car slower. But the demand was such that, with the introduction of the 1984, 3.2-litre 911 Carrera, the factory decided to respond, dropping the atmospheric engine with its 5-speed transmission (slightly lower geared to make up for the increased drag and weight) into a Turbo body, complete with its spoilers and its entire running gear, type 917 brakes and ultra-wide tyres included, the price being appropriately increased as is the weight—by some 50 kg, compared with the corresponding normal Carrera. How foolish some people are is indicated by the fact that there was a bigger demand for a normal 911 looking like a Turbo, even at the expense of performance and economy, than for a 3.3 turbocharged engine in a normal 911 body.

Chapter Seven

The 911 in motoring sport

In the history of motoring sport probably no other car has ever been as versatile as the 911. At one time or another, it won most major European rallies, including four victories (1968, '69, '70 and '79) in the Monte Carlo Rally and winning the Tour of Corsica. It also won the European Rally Championship and at one time it was almost unbeatable in touring car races (which perhaps reflects the stupidity of the rules, rather than the excellence of the 911 as a touring car!) until the rules were changed to ban it from such events. Even though its engine capacity remained at 2 litres until the end of 1969, it soon became the foremost car in GT racing, irrespective of the capacity class and has won the European GT Championship ever since it was created, as well as the American IMSA Championship, and the same year (1973) it won three major long-distance races, two of them of World Championship status, while in 1974 it finished second in such incredibly diverse events as the Le Mans 24-hours race and the East African Safari which it had led up to a few hundred miles from the finish. But perhaps its greatest merit is that for many years — and probably many years to come yet — it has provided thousands of private entrants with a still comparatively realistically priced, competitive and reliable tool for whatever sort of motoring sport they wished to specialise in. One such car won the Le Mans race in 1979.

The 911's racing record is not so surprising, after all, when it is remembered that its 6-cylinder engine was designed from the start with its adaptability for competitive use in mind. In fact, it was developed simultaneously for production and for racing, and this gave the production version a very large safety margin right from the start.

The first time the six-cylinder engine appeared in a racing version (engine Type 901/20) was in the Targa Florio of 1965. Fitted to a Type 904 sports racing coupé, this 210 bhp unit was immediately successful, being driven into second place by Umberto Maglioli and Herbert Linge, headed only by another Porsche using an 8-cylinder engine (Type 771) derived from Porsche's Grand Prix car unit. The main differences between the 6-cylinder racing engine and the production 911 S engine which appeared in July 1966 were its magnesium crankcase and various covers, larger ports and valves operated by steel rockers without an adjusting screw, clearance being adjusted by using caps of selected thickness over the valve stem, larger intake manifolds and carburettors (Weber 46 IDA 3), higher compression ratio, racing camshafts, twin ignition and titanium connecting rods. The cooling fan wheel was also of a slightly smaller diameter (225 instead of 245 mm) to reduce the blade tip speed and prevent cavitation at the higher rotating speeds reached. The racing engine was fully interchangeable with the standard 911 engine, however, and in 1967 such an engine was experimentally dropped into a special lightweight 911 shell with plastic doors, lids and bumpers and perspex side and rear windows standing on a standard but lowered suspension, 6 inch wide rims at the front and 7 inch at the rear with racing tyres all round. The car, called a 911 R, which weighed only just over 800 kg, was produced in limited numbers, but as only about 20 were made it was never homologated as a GT car. It could race only in the prototype group, but it was an interesting development exercise and served as a very useful model to aim at when modifying production 911s for rallying or racing.

Originally it had been intended to use a much modified engine in the 911 R, known as the Type 916, which had twin overhead camshafts for each bank of cylinders and developed 230 bhp, ie 20 bhp more than the 901/20 engine. A prototype was even used for practice in the Circuito del Mugello race in Italy, but the drivers found the engine much too inflexible and preferred the older single cam unit. This 916 engine eventually became the base for the development of the Type 908 3 litre flat-8 which earned Porsche its first World Championship title in 1969.

The 911 R was a very fast and reliable car which quite unexpectedly took a whole series of international and world records in 1967. The two very successful Swiss private drivers Rico Steinemann (later to become Porsche's Public Relations and Sports Manager) and the late Dieter Spoerry, backed by BP, had planned to attack a series of world records, sharing their Carrera-6 racing car with fellow Swiss drivers Jo Siffert and Charles Vögele, using the Monza banked track. Unfortunately the shock absorber rods did not resist the bashing they took from the abominable Monza banking and when all the spares carried in the car (as the rules require) had been used up, the party phoned the factory for help. Ing Helmuth Bott, who was then chassis development chief, offered them a 911 R which could be readied at short notice. Before final confirmation was given, however, the calculating department had to confirm that, taking into account the safety margin to be observed in a record attempt going over 20,000 km (12,400 miles), the car would be fast enough for the job. They came to the conclusion that it wasn't, but Bott was convinced to the contrary and finally accepted the challenge after he had been assured by the engine people that a proper race-prepared unit was available. This was hurriedly dropped into the car, and as some fears were expressed that the fifth gear pair might not resist running at maximum speed for 20,000 kilometres with an engine developing over 200 bhp, someone had the brilliant idea of using identical pairs of pinions for fourth and fifth gears, thus providing two 'fifth gears'. The drivers were instructed, as they took their stint, which to use, so that each set of pinions was, in fact, used for only 10,000 km. Only when the engine — the only one available — was in the car did the engine development chief, Ing Paul Hensler, realise that this was far from being a raceworthy engine: it had previously been used for a 100 hours endurance test on the bench, dismantled for inspection and hastily put back together as it was — not even with care, as it was not supposed to be used for racing at all! But time for the availability of the track was running very short and the car was nevertheless driven to Monza overnight, heavily laden with spares which had to be carried in the car during the record attempt. On the next day the run started and the car, eventually bettered five world records and 14 international 2 litre class records up to 20,000 kilometres, with an engine that had already done the equivalent on the test bed before! The chap who deserved the biggest bottle of champagne was surely the one who suggested using two 'fifth gears', as when the transmission was later dismantled it was found that both pairs of pinions were severely scuffed. The mechanics also deserved high praise for changing two front suspension struts in record time, after they had given up the severe struggle with the abominable Monza banking.

The full list of world records beaten is as follows:

15,000 km	Average speed 210.02 kph (130.50 mph)
10,000 miles	Average speed 210.29 kph (130.67 mph)
20,000 km	Average speed 209.24 kph (130.02 mph)
72 hours	Average speed 209.95 kph (130.46 mph)
96 hours	Average speed 209.23 kph (130.01 mph)

Modified production models

Before 1970, it was permissible under the existing sporting regulations to homologate in different groups models sharing the same body shell, but using different engines. Consequently the 911 and 911 L were homologated in Group 2 (modified touring cars) and the 911 T and 911 S were homologated in Group 3 (GT cars), a clever move being that the 911 T was also homologated with the 911 S engine in a special lightweight version with simplified interior trim, no sound proofing material, sports seats and lightened front bumper (without the stabilising iron lumps!), which brought down the homologation weight (without fuel) to 923 kg (2,038 lb). As anti-roll bars could be added without homologation, this was obviously the best base for a competitive GT car.

For the 911/911 L, a 'Rally' engine was offered, called the 2000 R, based on the standard (small valve) 130 bhp 911 engine, but modified within the framework of the sporting regulations, mainly by the use of the following items:

911 S camshafts,
40 IDS Weber carburettors, as in the 911 S,
911 S forged and higher compression pistons,
lightened flywheel and reinforced clutch assembly,
rally exhaust system.

This gave a power output of 150 bhp with the street exhaust system and carburettor settings and 160 bhp in competition trim.

In addition, the suspension was brought up to 911 S standards by the use of Koni dampers and front and rear anti-roll bars, each of 15 mm diameter.

For the 911 T and 911 S, a racing engine was available, differing only in detail from the full racing engine used in the Carrera-6 sports-racing car. The main differences were that the standard ignition system was retained and that the valve sizes remained standard, as required by the rules: inlet 42 mm (Carrera-6 45 mm), exhaust 38 mm (Carrera-6 39 mm). Carrera-6 camshafts were used with the following timing:

Inlet opens/closes	104°btdc/104°abdc
Exhaust opens/closes	100°bbdc/80°atdc

as well as the Carrera-6's Weber 46 IDA 3 carburettors and appropriate larger diameter inlet manifolds, Carrera-6 pistons with larger valve pockets were fitted and the compression ratio was raised to 10.4:1 by machining either the cylinders themselves or the heads. The cylinder head ports were, of course, bored out to match the larger intake manifolds and the racing exhaust system which was part of the modification. A lightened flywheel and reinforced clutch assembly were also fitted and titanium connecting rods were available but not mandatory. They were homologated for the 911 T only. Except for sprint racing, an oil cooler was added in the scavenging circuit and located in the right-hand front wing; it later became standard in production 911 S models.

Rally kits were also offered for the 2000 S engine as fitted to the 911 S and also homologated on the 911 T. 'Sportkit I' included 36 mm diameter carburettor choke tubes, larger main jets and harder plugs in addition to sundry minor equipment, while 'Sportkit II' additionally included parts to modify the exhaust system to reduce the back pressure. Sportkit I raised the output from 160 to 170 bhp and Sportkit II added another 5 bhp, though in that case the car became illegally noisy. Sportkit I was used in the works cars which ran in the 1967 Marathon de la Route, which was won by one of them.

Right from the beginning, an enormous choice of gearbox ratios was offered. In the Type 901/902 transmission used on all 911 models up to and including the D-series, all gear pairs can be chosen individually, which makes it very easy to select exactly the right ratios for a given circuit or event. In the standard box, however, the second gear pinion is cut on the gearbox mainshaft and changing it involves changing the shaft. To avoid this, a special shaft with separate gear was offered for cars used in competitions. A limited slip differential was also offered, which had a 50 per cent locking factor, later increased to 80 per cent.

In those early years, very little was done to adapt the running gear to the requirements of competition work. The production torsion bar springs (front 19 mm diameter, rear 22 mm on those early 221 cm wheelbase cars) were retained, though the ride height was reduced, which only requires a different torsion bar setting. It was recommended that the ride height should be chosen according to the type of event and the circuit on which the car was to run. Adjustable Koni dampers (standard on the 911 S) were fitted and a choice of anti-roll bars was available.

The following combinations were suggested:

Circuit racing:	16 mm Ø front and rear
Hill-climb racing:	14 mm Ø front
	16 mm Ø rear
Rallies:	15 mm Ø front
	16 mm Ø rear

By 1968, when the A-series was being produced with 5.5 inch wide rims all round, a choice of forged alloy wheels, all of 15 inch diameter, but the rim width of which varied from 4.5 to 7 inches, was offered. The factory's recommendation was to use 5.50 L-15 racing tyres on 5.5 or 6 inch rims at the front and 5.50 M-15 racing tyres on 6 or 7 inch rims at the rear.

It was also suggested that racing brake pads be used: Ferodo DS 11 for plain discs and Textar 1431 G for ventilated discs.

From 2.0 to 2.4 litres

With the introduction of the B-series, the 911 became a much better proposition for competition tuning. Handling was improved by the better weight distribution and the longer wheelbase while the flared wings used in conjunction with the now-standard 6 inch wide rims could house wider racing tyres than before, after they had been further extended by 2 inches on either side, as allowed by the regulations. Unfortunately, as long as the production cars had an engine capacity of 1,991 cc, the sporting regulations forbade any boring out above the class limit (2,000 cc in this case) and nothing could be done in the way of increasing the engine size, except if the car was entered in the prototype group. When, beginning with the C-series cars, the bore was increased to 84 mm, lifting the engine capacity to 2,195 cc, the 911

Above *After having been driven by Waldegaard in the 1969 RAC Rally and by Larrousse into second place in the 1970 Monte Carlo Rally (behind Waldegaard's similar 911 S), this 789 kg car became the lightest road going 911 ever to be built. Still driven by Larrousse, it took third place in the 1970 Tour de France, behind two Matra V-12 prototypes.*

The following seven pages *All members of a single family. The following series of seven pictures (taken in 1974) showing the cars' main components, clearly illustrates the close relationship between all members of the 911 family, from the basic production model to the 500 hp turbocharged racing Carrera and the Safari car. It illustrates the extraordinary versatility of the basic design. This close parentage also benefits the production models, as any development based on competition experience is immediately fed back into them.*

Below *Frenchman Raymond Touroul and 'Anselme' won the GT class at Le Mans in 1971 with this 2.35 litre-engined 911. It ran on 7 and 9 inch wide rims front and rear, respectively.*

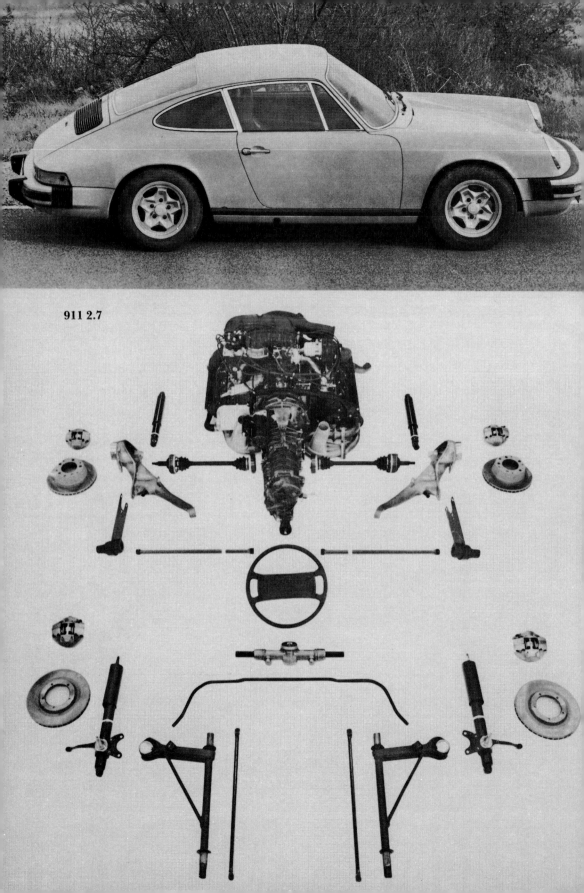

911 2.7

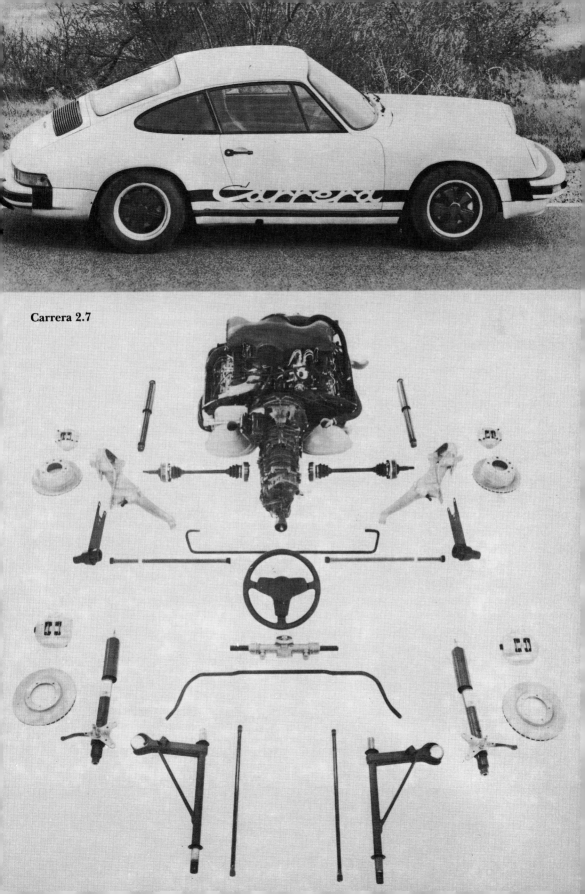

Carrera 2.7

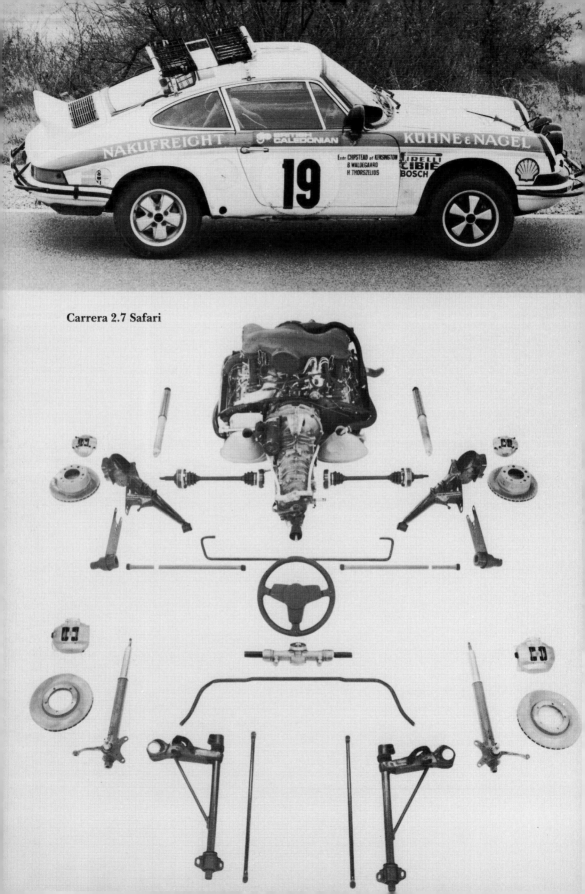

Carrera 2.7 Safari

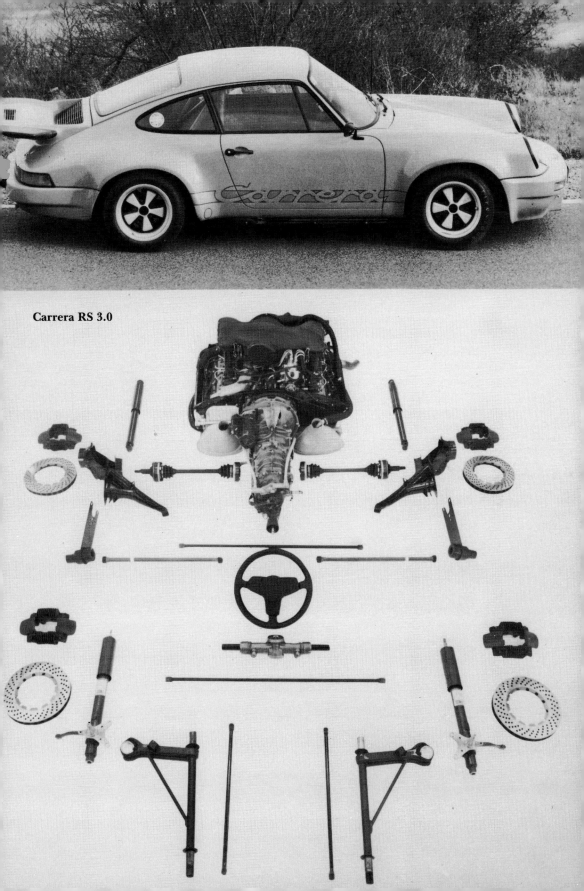

Carrera RS 3.0

Carrera RSR 3.0

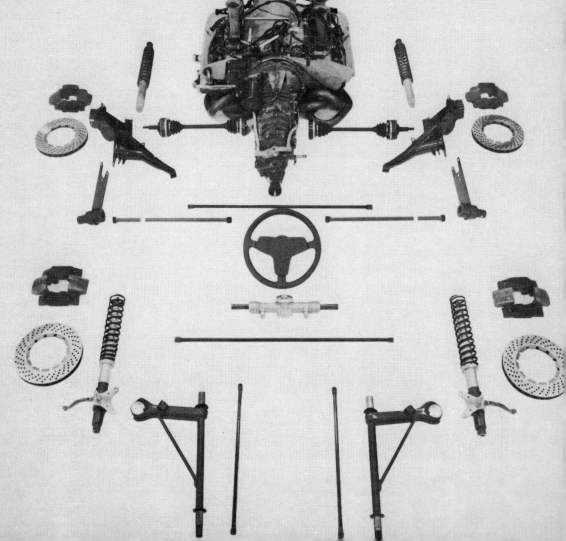

Carrera RSR Turbo 2.14

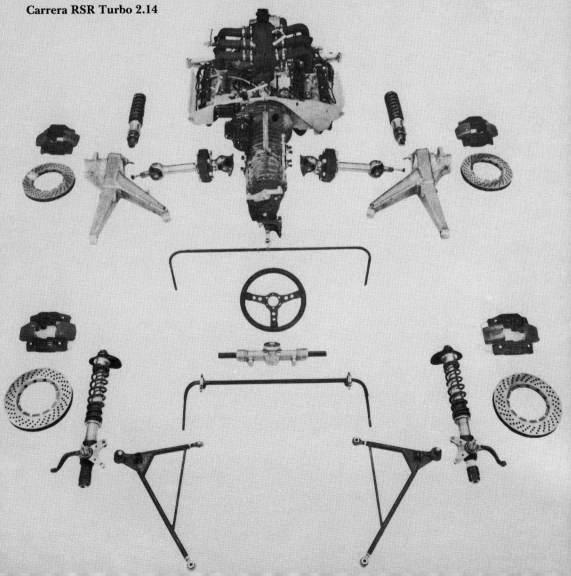

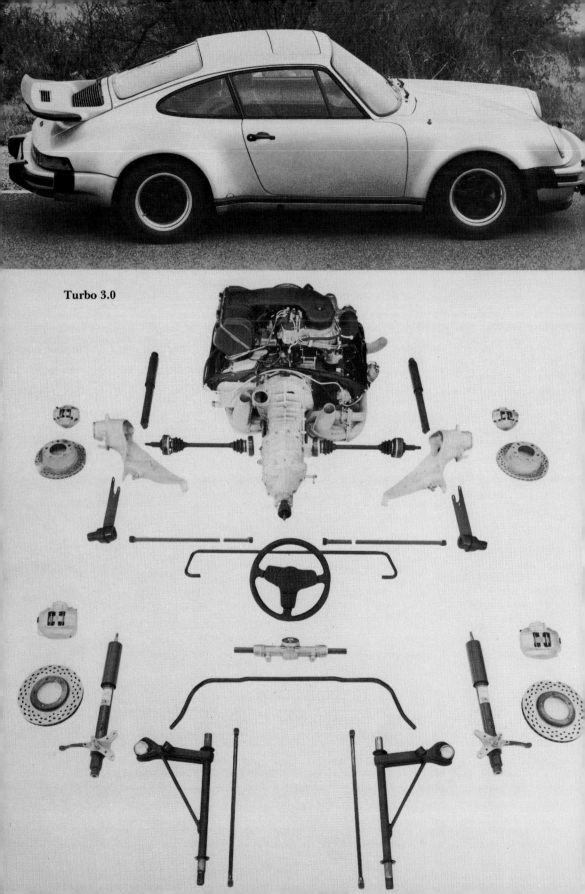

Turbo 3.0

moved into the 2,001 to 2,500 cc class, which made it legal to increase the capacity to the latter figure — if this could be done by increasing the bore only. As from 1970 all competition cars were built on the basis of the 911 S, homologated in Group 3, Porsches now having been disqualified from Group 2 and not being eligible any more for touring car events.

For the 2.2 litre cars, titanium connecting rods which weighed 450 g were never homologated, and polished and crack-tested production rods were used. They weighed 727 grams, a tolerance of only 3 grams being allowed on the rods of any given engine. On the other hand, twin ignition with conventional contact breakers and coils, as on the Carrera-6 engine, was now homologated. This did not involve any major change in the cylinder head since with air cooling this only requires boring and threading a second plug hole. As before, the Carrera-6's slightly smaller diameter cooling fan and racing camshafts were used for full racing engines, together with the standard valves, these being of 46 mm diameter on the inlet side and 40 mm diameter on the exhaust side. These diameters are both one millimetre larger than for the 2 litre Carrera-6 engine, so that very nearly the same breathing capacity could be expected. The B- and C-series 911 E and S engines had Bosch plunger pump fuel injection and a similar installation was used on the racing version of the engine, but different, tuned induction pipes without air filter were used and so was a plunger pump with settings and a space cam matching the characteristics of the racing engine. As, however, in Group 4 the intake system is free, the racing engine could also be had with two triple choke Weber 46 IDA 3 carburettors, with 42 mm diameter choke tubes, the power output quoted being the same in either case.

The racing pistons providing a 10.3:1 compression ratio could be obtained only with matching cylinders. These were Biral (cast iron cylinder with bonded alloy fin assembly), similar to the production cylinders, but obtainable in two bore sizes: 85 mm, increasing the engine capacity to 2,247 cc and, as from March 1971, 87.5 mm which gave a capacity of 2,380 cc. Engines of that size were made with fuel injection only. The power and torque figures quoted were:

2,247 cc: 230 (DIN) bhp at 7,800 rpm and 23.5 mkg (170.3 lb/ft) at 6,200 rpm.
2,380 cc: 250 (DIN) bhp at 7,800 rpm and 26 mkg (188.4 lb/ft) at 6,200 rpm.

It is interesting to note that, in either case, the standard crankshaft and bearings were used. No additional oil cooler was required for the 2,247 cc engine, a cooler in the right-hand front wing being a standard fitting in the 911 S, beginning with the B-series. For the 2,380 cc engine, however, the crankcase-mounted cooler (standard in all Porsches) was replaced by a second front wing mounted cooler, on the left-hand side.

No rally engine kits were offered for the fuel injection S engines, the only rally modifications suggested by the factory being to fit a reinforced clutch, increase the compression ratio by lowering the heads or cylinders by 0.5 mm, remove the air filter, enrichen the injection pump setting and fit a rally exhaust system, apart from the usual polishing, matching and careful assembly. This raised the power output of the 2.2 litre from 180 to slightly over 190 bhp. The factory, however, did not hesitate to use 2.25 litre 230 bhp full racing engines to power Waldegaard-Helmer and Larrousse-Gelin to the first two places in the 1970 Monte Carlo Rally, both crews driving a specially lightened model with plastic doors, lids and front wings entered in Group 4.

Together with the 2.2 litre engines, the Type 911 transmission was introduced in production, replacing the Type 901/902 transmission of which it was a reinforced development with a pressure cast magnesium housing. The same wide choice of ratios was offered, including alternative crown wheel and pinion assemblies with ratios of 7:31 and 6:32. As before, a special gearbox main shaft with interchangeable second gear pinion was available, so that any of the five gearbox ratios could be altered by merely changing the appropriate pair of gears. The half shafts remained standard.

As we have said before, the B-series of cars brought considerable improvements in the handling characteristics of the 911, and this applies to the competition versions as well as to the standard cars. Better weight distribution and a longer wheelbase played their part, but particularly in the racing version the wider wheels allowed by the flared wheel openings played a decisive role, as it became possible to use 9J 15 rims at the rear after further widening the wings by the 'legal' 2 inches each.

This now made it possible to use 7 inch wide rims on the front wheels and 9 inch wide rims on the rear wheels, with 4.75/10.00-15 and 4.75/11.30-15 racing tyres, respectively. This proved to be the best combination, though for rallying standard 6 inch rims and 185/70 VR 15 tyres were the normal wear.

With the introduction of the B-series, the 911 S brakes had been further improved by the use of M calipers on the rear wheels (which became standard on all models) and aluminium S calipers on the front wheels, and with the standard ventilated discs this proved to be quite good enough for any type of competition, provided Textar 1431 G racing linings were used.

In fact, apart from the use of wider wheels and racing tyres, the only modification made to the running gear for racing was to lower it by modifying the front and rear torsion bar adjustments. Even the shock absorbers remained the (on the 911 S) standard adjustable Konis for which a harder setting was usually adopted. How much the car was lowered — the main object being to lower the centre of gravity — depended on the sort of event or on the track on which it was to compete. On its own cars which ran in the 1968 Marathon de la Route, in which they finished first and second, the factory adopted a setting only 21 mm lower than standard, in view of the bumpy surface of the Nürburgring. For the Monte Carlo Rally-winning cars of 1970, the setting was approximately 30 mm lower than standard. The front and rear end geometry data remained practically the same as that for the standard B- to D-series cars.

Even the non-adjustable anti-roll bars recommended for competition work were those standardised on the C- and D-series 911 S. Other anti-roll bar diameters were, of course, available and for rallying the factory cars were set up to oversteer more, as exemplified by those on the 1970 Monte Carlo rally. These used 24 mm diameter rear torsion bars instead of the normal 23 mm bars with a 16 mm anti-roll bar in conjunction with a front anti-roll bar of only 15 mm diameter.

The E/F-series and the 2.5 litre racing engines

The largest bore that could be achieved with Biral cylinders was 87.5 mm, due to their comparatively thick walls, which with a 66 mm stroke limited the engine capacity to 2,380 cc — 120 cc short of the 2,500 cc class limit — as the stroke could not be increased within the framework of the rules governing GT cars. Only when, with the introduction of the 2.4 litre E-series cars, the piston stroke was increased from 66 to

70.4 mm, did it become possible to raise the racing engine's capacity up to the class limit. This was achieved by using cylinders with an 86.7 mm bore. The engine, which was made only with Bosch plunger pump fuel injection, was otherwise similar to the 2,380 cc unit, but the power output was raised to 275 bhp at 7,900 rpm and the torque to 27 mkg (196 lb/ft) at 6,200 rpm.

Unfortunately this engine was rather troublesome: crankshaft vibrations tended to loosen the flywheel securing bolts whatever was done to lock them efficiently, and in several instances the crank itself broke. As this sort of problem had never cropped up with the 66 mm stroke crankshaft, a few examples of the 2.5 litre engine were made using a 66 mm stroke with cylinders of 89 mm bore, implying that Nikasil cylinders as used in the Type 917 flat-12, which can be manufactured with thinner walls than the Biral cylinders, had to be used. Power and torque were similar to those of the long-stroke engine. The fragility of the latter must be attributed to the combination of the weaker longer-throw crankshaft and distortion of the magnesium crankcase when submitted to the high forces generated in the 275 bhp engine. Obviously, however, a solution had to be found if the engine was to be further enlarged in future years.

For racing, a considerable advantage of the E- and F-series cars was the introduction of the Type 915 transmission, with a distance between shaft centres of 76 instead of 68 mm, which had a torque rating 22.5 per cent higher than the Type 911 transmission: 30 mkg (217 lb/ft) when used for racing. With the 2,380 cc racing unit, the Type 911 transmission had become a weak point. As before, all five gear ratios could be chosen individually, but no special version of this box was made in which first gear (of which the small pinion was cut on the main shaft itself) could be changed without changing the complete main shaft. As before, two sets of crown wheel and pinion were offered, 7:31 or 7:37.

This Type 915 transmission was a development of the Type 916 transmission (with 77 mm between shaft centres) used on the Type 908/02 sports prototype. Racing versions had a front end cover incorporating an oil pump feeding jets directing the lubricant to the most highly stressed parts of the gearbox. This made it possible to maintain the oil level low enough to prevent splash, which was found to absorb as much as 7 bhp at maximum speed, and also to circulate the oil through a cooler located in the left front wing, where it took the place formerly occupied by one of the engine oil coolers. These were now replaced by one single, larger oil radiator housed in an opening below the front bumper, in the air dam which had become a standard feature of E-series 911 S models.

The running gear remained much as before, but as Bilstein non-adjustable dampers were now used in production 2.4 911 S models, they had to be replaced for racing by dampers of the same make, but with different settings.

The Carrera RS and RSR models

In 1972 the CSI banned cars of more than 3 litres capacity from the World Championship of Makes, ruling out the all-conquering Porsche 917. Porsche decided to concentrate on the American Can-Am races for which the now-famous turbocharged version of the 917 was developed and it was considered desirable to retain some sort of involvement in European motoring sport. Designing a new racing car to conform with the new Group 5 (sports-prototypes) rules was out of the question for reasons of time and money, and also because the future of sports car racing looked very uncertain. So the best choice seemed to be to further develop the 911 to run in the European GT Championship, which was to be first organised in 1973. But with such large-engined competitors as the Ferrari 365 GTB/4 and the De Tomaso Pantera looming up, it seemed desirable to extract some additional power from the engine. Furthermore, wind tunnel tests carried out on the 911 had shown that it could well benefit from the experience gained with the aerodynamic aids used by Porsche on its proper racing cars to combat lift at speed and consequently improve stability, braking and cornering.

It was also felt that wider racing tyres would be desirable to make the best use of the increased performance and also in order to benefit from the latest advances in racing tyre development. Finally the development of rally cars entered in the proto-type group had indicated that a lot of weight could be saved on the homologation weight of the 911 S — which was 995 kg. One drastically lightened 2.4 litre car, incorporating many glass fibre components, with which Gérard Larrousse finished third in the Tour de France of 1970, behind two V-12 Matras weighed only 789 kg. This had been a costly experiment, not only because a lot of exotic materials — mainly titanium — were used in the construction of the car, but also because the crew responsible for its construction had been promised a box of champagne for each kilogram of weight saved under the 800 kg limit! Nevertheless, it was considered that about 100 kg could easily be saved on the 911 S homologation weight.

To achieve the set targets, a new model had to be introduced in the 911 pro-gramme and at least 500 examples built to obtain its homologation as a Group 4 Special GT car. It had to differ from the 911 S in the following main points:

The engine had to be of over 2,500 cc capacity, to put the car in the 3 litre class and provide the opportunity to increase the actual engine capacity up to the class limit;

The body of the standard car had to be equipped with the aerodynamic aids required for racing, as the Group 4 rules required its contours to remain unaltered;

It was to have wings sufficiently wide to house 9 inch wide wheels at the front and 11 inch wide wheels at the rear, after further widening of the wings by the maximum legal amount of 2 inches each;

Its equipment was to be simplified and the car generally lightened to get its weight down to 900 kg.

This is how the Carrera RS 2.7 came into being and was marketed at the end of 1972. Its engine differed from the then current 911 S 2.4 litre only by its cylinders of 90 mm bore. But to achieve that bore size, the cylinders had to be changed from Biral to Nikasil (alloy cylinder and fins with an electrolytically deposited layer of nickel and silicon carbide forming the working surface) because only the thinner walls of the Nikasil cylinders made it possible to get a 90 mm bore within the maximum possible lower flange diameter. The engine had the same compression ratio of 8.5:1 as the 2.4 unit and developed 210 bhp at 6,300 rpm.

It was the first production Porsche with wider wheels at the back than at the front, a combination the development people had wanted to introduce for a long time, but which proved difficult to get accepted by the German traffic authorities. The wider rear wheels and tyres required wider rear wings which were designed to be just wide enough to house 11 inch wide racing wheels and appropriate tyres after further legal widening.

The glass fibre engine room cover incorporated the now well known 'duck's tail' spoiler which reduced the aerodynamic lift over the rear wheels by 75 per cent.

The weight was reduced to 900 kg, mainly by simplifying the interior and exterior trim, deleting the rear emergency seats, using light gauge panels for unstressed body parts, using glass fibre bumpers and making the windscreen of Glaverbel thin gauge laminated glass.

A detailed but important point was that there was an additional bracket by which the centre of the rear suspension cross tube was welded to the floor tunnel to avoid bending of the tube under the forces put into it by racing tyres.

For rallying, it was recommended to fit 24 mm diameter rear torsion bars and a 16 mm diameter anti-roll bar as well as sports brake linings, all eligible under Group 3 rules.

The Carrera RS 2.7 became the base for a racing version which immediately outclassed everything that had been developed before. The weight was lower than it had ever been for a Porsche running as a Group 4 GT car, handling and cornering were better than they had ever been in a 911 and full throttle let more than 300 bhp loose. In racing engines, 92 mm bore cylinders replaced the standard 90 mm bore ones, increasing the capacity to 2,808 cc. The valve sizes went up to 49 mm (inlet) and 41.5 mm (exhaust) and the ports were opened up, inlet and exhaust diameter being 43 mm, respectively, instead of 41 mm. Valve timing and lift were as before in racing engines, but the camshaft now ran in four bearings to reduce bending vibrations. A remedy for the crankshaft breakages was found in the use of a damper at the rear end, but there still were some difficulties with the flywheel occasionally coming loose.

230/600-15 and 260/600-15 racing tyres were used on the front 9 inch and rear 11 inch rims, respectively, a 110 litre glass fibre tank was fitted and Type 917 racing brakes were used, complete with twin master cylinders operated by a balance bar permitting variations in front/rear braking distribution. The discs were both radially ventilated and transversely perforated for lightness, cooling and better response in wet weather, while the Porsche-developed, liberally finned alloy calipers each had four 42 mm diameter pistons. A deeper than standard front air dam was also fitted, wind tunnel tests having indicated that at 152 mph it turned the 35 kg (77 lb) front lift into a 27 kg (60 lb) down-force, though due to the pitching effect over the front axle rear-end lift was increased from 42 to 57 kg (92 to 126 lb) at the same speed, despite the 'duck's tail' spoiler. (Without the spoiler, the tail lift increased to 145 kg or 320 lb.)

Even before it was homologated in Group 4, the Carrera RSR, as the racing version was known, managed to win the Daytona 24 hours race, at the beginning of 1973, beating opposition that consisted mainly of 7 and 7.4 litre Chevrolet Corvettes and the 4.4 litre Ferrari 365 GTB4, after the two Matra prototypes, which had looked invincible, had run into trouble. The Carrera was an entirely private entry driven by Peter Gregg and Hurley Haywood. A few weeks later, the same drivers and car proceeded to win the Sebring 12 hours race outright, too, with the car now duly homologated as a Group 4 GT car. Later in the year, a factory-entered Carrera, running as a prototype because of its oversize rear spoiler and a slightly modified rear suspension geometry, won the Sicilian Targa Florio. Again what was basically a normal production car, differing very little from those anyone could buy from the showroom, had beaten all comers, including the full team of Alfa Romeo works prototypes.

Formerly it had been quite exceptional for the factory to race its own production racing cars, as it was considered unfair to customers who had bought similar cars to race them privately. But in 1973 it became the rule to run two factory-prepared Carreras, sponsored by the Martini Racing Team, in all long-distance races counting towards the World Championship of Makes. One was entered in the sports proto-type class, which allowed any modification to be experimented with, and the other was entered in the GT class to allow comparisons.

Right from the beginning of the 1973 racing season, the factory-entered proto-type, first seen in the Monza 1,000 km race, differed externally from the GT version in having a full-width rear spoiler enveloping the rear part of the body. It was lighter, too, plastic panels being used for the doors and lids and perspex replacing most glass areas. The enveloping rear spoiler was a result of tests carried out in January at the Paul Ricard Circuit in the South of France where the 'duck's tail' (which was a great improvement on the flat rear lid for normal road work, used in conjunction with the standard front skirt) proved to be insufficient for optimum results on the track. This was especially the case when a deep front air dam was used, resulting in front wheel adhesion increasing and rear wheel adhesion decreasing as the speed built up — exactly the reverse of what is normally desirable.

As the track tests had given satisfactory results, the full-width rear spoiler was adopted without any preliminary wind tunnel tests, and only after it had run in the Targa Florio, which the car won, driven by Herbert Müller and Gijs van Lennep, did the Carrera prototype go into the wind tunnel to check how well the empirical methods (rather unusual for Porsche) had worked and if there were any means of improving on their results. The rather surprising fact is that the car, as it stood after the Sicilian race, represented about the best compromise that could be devised between drag, front downforce and rear down-force, the results being:
$$C_d = 0.413 \qquad C_{Lf} = -0.019 \qquad C_{Lr} = -0.065$$
with a frontal area $S = 1.7966$, the car being on slicks mounted on 10.5 and 14 inch wide rims front and rear, respectively. Corresponding front and rear down-forces at 250 kph (155 mph) are 10 kg (22 lb) front and 35 kg (77 lb) rear.

As a result of the development work carried out on the factory's prototypes, some suspension modifications strictly aimed at racing were introduced and either applied to the production cars or made available from the factory's Sports Department as soon as the number of cars required for homologation in Group 4 had been pro-duced.

The inner rear suspension arms were shortened and the brackets on which they pivot were moved 15 mm towards the car's centre line on the rear cross tube and extended 47.5 mm rearwards. This increased the camber variations due to suspension movements and helped to keep the flat-treaded racing tyres taking the greatest part of the cornering forces (those on the outside of the bend) in a more nearly vertical position. This modification was applied to the F-series Carrera RS after the first batch of 500 had been made and was maintained on the G-series Carrera RS 3.0, but was not extended to other production cars (except the 930 Turbo, with some varia-tions), as it is unnecessary with normal road radial tyres and tends to be detrimental to the straight line stability due to increased toe-in variations.

Special front suspension struts were offered in which the stub axle was located higher than in the standard car (126 mm instead of 108 mm above the lower ball joint centre). This had the effect of lowering the front of the car without excessively lowering the roll centre, which would be the case if the car were lowered by merely altering the torsion bar settings. The modification also preserves the full suspension travel towards the bump stop, which otherwise would not be the case.

Needle roller bearings and appropriate brackets were made available to replace the Delrin hard plastic bushes normally used on competition cars in the front wishbone pivots and as bearings for the outer (longitudinal) rear suspension arms. (Production cars have rubber bushes.) The aim was to reduce uncontrolled friction.

Racing type front struts and rear damper units with concentric coil springs — steel or titanium — of variable rate characteristics were offered. Thanks to the threaded spring abutment ring, they facilitated the adjustment of the car's ride height and they also stiffened up the suspension. This latter effect could also be obtained by fitting thicker torsion bars available from the factory.

Centre-lock titanium hubs fitting Porsche magnesium racing wheels were made available.

The modifications affecting the geometry of the front and rear suspensions were introduced early enough in the 1973 season to be used by many competitors, but most of the others came rather late and were used on few cars other than those run by the factory.

The 3 litre racing engine

If the racing engine was not immediately brought up to the 3 litre capacity limit, there had been good reasons for it. The 92 mm bore, giving a total capacity of 2,808 cc, required larger ports and valves. It was chosen because the development people knew that, using Nikasil cylinders and with a crankshaft damper fitted, there would be no major problems up to that bore size. That they were right is proved by the fact that the 2.8 litre engine was fairly reliable and achieved an output of 308 bhp at 8,000 rpm, corresponding to 110 bhp/litre, the same as for all Porsche racing engines of 911 derivation since the 2 litre Carrera-6 days. To achieve this, the port diameter was increased by 2 mm to 43 mm for both inlet and exhaust, while the valve head diameter went up to 49 and 41.5 mm for inlet and exhaust, respectively. But increasing the bore to 95 mm, which was necessary to achieve the full 3 litre capacity (actually 2,994 cc) created some problems. The biggest was that with such large cylinders the bores in the crankcase to which the cylinders were spigoted became so large that the metal separating them was too thin and tended to crack under the stresses it had to resist. Fatigue was the main problem, for the engine would resist about six hours' racing, but cracks were likely to develop after that period. Neither had the crankshaft damper completely solved the problems created by crankshaft vibrations.

These problems were solved by taking a step which, at first sight, might seem retrograde: with the introduction of the B-series, in summer 1968, the crankcase material was changed from aluminium to AZ 91 magnesium alloy. Now the magnesium alloy had to give way to aluminium again, heavier but more rigid and better able to resist high local stresses.

A new cylinder head was developed to suit the larger bore, retaining the same port and valve sizes as in the 2.8 litre engine, but the distance between the studs holding down both the heads and the cylinders to the crankcase had to be increased to clear the bores. As before, twin ignition was used and for the first time it was of the contact breaker-less type. Also for the first time a departure was made from the old Carrera-6 cams. The timing remained unaltered, but the valve lift was increased from 12.1 to 12.2 mm on the inlet side and from 10.6 to 11.5 mm on the exhaust side.

Compared with the 2.5 and 2.8 litre engines, the 3 litre was slightly disappointing, for the increase of nearly 200 cc in capacity yielded no more than 7-10 bhp, the official figure being 315 bhp at 8,000 rpm. It was not before a throttle slide was used in place of the butterfly throttles that the customary 110 bhp per litre was achieved, 330 bhp at 8,000 rpm and a maximum torque of 32 mkg (232 lb/ft) being obtained. In order to transmit the high torque, sintered metal linings were used on the single plate clutch.

The 3 litre engine was first used in the factory's sports prototype Carreras, but was also used in some GT models before the end of the season. As this got nearer its end, the differences between the GT and the sports prototype were becoming more obvious, both optically and in performance. The prototype eventually ended up with 10.5J 15 rims at the front and 14J 15 at the rear and with a weight of around 890 kg, thanks to the use of plastic doors and front lid in addition to the plastic engine cover and bumper assemblies, standard on the Carrera RS 2.7, of perspex for all the side and rear glass areas, of titanium as a replacement for many standard steel parts and to drastic reductions of interior trim. It was thus some 50 kg lighter than the GT version which, equipped for racing, never got down to its homologated weight though, as Ing Bott said, 'we could have done it if we had had enough time'.

Instead of the 500 units originally planned, some 1,600 Carrera RSs were built and this made it possible to homologate it as a Group 3 Production GT Car and run it, unmodified, in that class, in which it was highly competitive. To make it even more competitive, especially in circuit racing where racing tyres are used, alloy wheels with 7 and 8 inch wide rims were offered as an option at the front and rear, respectively. They just fitted within the body dimensions.

The Carrera 3.0 litre RS and RSR

With the first of the official European GT Championships won — rivals Frenchman Claude Ballot-Léna and German Clemens Schickentanz finishing equal first with the same number of points — Porsche were determined to remain competitive among the GT cars, irrespective of engine size. The Ferrari 365 GTB/4 with its beautiful 4.4 litre V12 engine had proved to be very quick and very reliable on fast circuits — a hard nut to crack for Porsches at Le Mans — and factory prepared de Tomaso Panteras, helped by their huge (5.7 litre) tuned Ford V8 engine, were faster around almost any track. True, they badly lacked stamina, but that could have been improved and Porsche had to be prepared for it. At the end of the 1973 season, thanks to the development of the Carrera prototype, they knew exactly what to do to make the Carrera go even faster in GT racing form. All they needed to do was to put a basic car with the required modifications into production, but the problem was that they did not want to make the 500 units required for homologation in Group 4, the proposed basic car being a lot starker and also more expensive than the original Carrera RS 2.7.

That is where they were very clever. They stopped making the Carrera RS 2.7 and, the new model called the Carrera RS 3.0 being its logical successor, they obtained its homologation in *Group 3*, ie, as a normal production car of which at least 1,000 a year must be made for homologation, as an *evolution* of the RS 2.7 (which in fact it was) after only 100 units had been completed, which is strictly in accordance with the CSI rules. That they never made many more than 109 units is, of course, nobody's business! But in addition, some 50 cars were built up in racing trim from scratch, this being the first time that racing 911s were produced from scratch rather than by modifying a catalogued model.

Externally, the Carrera RS 3.0 differs from the 2.7 not only by its G-series appearance evidenced by its larger and higher bumpers (made of glass fibre reinforced plastic, as in the RS 2.7), but by two other very important points: considerably widened wings to house 60 series tyres on 8 inch wide front and 9 inch wide rear forged alloy rims, and a large, flat rear spoiler. In fact, two rear spoilers came with the car, one for road use, accepted by the German registration office and another, even larger one, slightly overhanging the rear bumper, for use on closed circuits.

In normal road trim, the standard front air dam and the rear spoiler must have produced lift figures very similar to those obtained for a fully equipped H-series Carrera 2.7 which were:

Front $C_{Lf}=0.010$ equivalent to 5 kg (11 lb) lift at 152 mph;

Rear $C_{Lr}=0.025$ equivalent to 13 kg (28.5 lb) lift at 152 mph,

which is negligible.

In racing trim, with the car lowered and widened, and with the larger rear spoiler, the drag and lift figures were not quite as good as for the standard RS 3.0:

$C_d=0.421$ $C_{Lf}=+0.094$ $C_{Lr}=+0.073$

with a frontal area $S=1.911$ m^2.

Corresponding lift forces at 152 mph were 47 kg (103 lb) at the front and 38 kg (83 lb) at the rear. The flat spoiler has the additional advantages that it looks much better than the full-width spoiler used on the prototype and that it does not require any sheet metal modifications or additional manufacturing costs, the wing being part of the engine cover, as was the 'duck's tail'.

The wider wings were, needless to say, calculated to be wide enough to cover the 10.5 inch wide front and 14 inch wide rear wheels which had been found to give optimum results on the prototype, after the further 'legal' 2 inch extension on either side.

The rear suspension fulcrum points were, of course, the modified ones, providing more camber variations, as the rules state that the fulcrum points must remain unaltered when preparing the car for racing, and the rear wheel bearings were of larger diameter than in the production cars. The front and rear Bilstein dampers were set harder than on the normal production cars and stiffer, 26 (instead of 23) mm diameter rear torsion bars were fitted, the front ones remaining the production 19 mm bars. As the basic model was designed as a road car, it had the standard height front struts which had to be replaced by similar struts, but with the stub axle raised 18 mm for racing. Front torsion bars of 22 mm were optional, but for both road use and normal racing conditions the factory recommended the use of the softer front torsion bars together with the standard 18 mm diameter anti-roll bars front and rear, even for the car in racing trim.

Another very important point was that the die-cast aluminium (rather than magnesium) crankcase, essential for long-term reliability in the 3 litre engine, was now part of the homologation. The engine also had the new cylinder heads with the stud holes further apart to clear the larger bore cylinders and larger valves, (49 and 41.5 mm diameter for inlet and exhaust, respectively) the port sizes (43/43 mm) being the same as for the 2.8 litre racing head. For this model, it was decided that the engine should run on premium grade (97 octane rating) fuel only and the compression ratio was raised to 9.8:1. In this tune, the engine produced 230 (DIN) bhp at 6,200 rpm and a maximum torque of 28 mkg (203 lb/ft) at 5,000 rpm, still using the same valve timing and lift as all previous 911 S and Carrera models.

But as it was originally planned to produce a batch of little over 100 cars, the great majority of which would obviously be used for racing and modified accordingly, the standard car came equipped with a large quantity of mechanical units previously fitted only when the car was modified for racing. Noteworthy among them are the racing crankshaft (a standard production part, but specially crack tested), racing con-rods (standard but crack tested and polished) and bearings with a larger clearance, and the lightened engine flywheel (2.8 kg instead of 3.6 kg, reducing the total clutch weight to 7.5 kg). The enormously expensive Type 917 brakes with four-piston calipers and 300 mm diameter perforated and ventilated discs were fitted increasing the pad area from 78 to 118 sq cm at the front and from 52 to 118 sq cm at the rear, complete with twin master cylinders, 17 mm diameter for the front brakes and 22 mm for the rear ones,* providing an adjustment for front/rear pressure ratio. The transmission had an 80 per cent limited slip differential and an oil pump, complete with cooling serpentine in the right front wing and there was a large, front-mounted engine oil cooler.

The weight of the additional racing equipment and of the heavier aluminium crankcase was saved in further details, such as a plastic front lid, while the Type 917 racing brakes are actually lighter than the production ones, so that the weight remained unaltered at 900 kg (1,989 lb). But the full racing versions never got down to the limit: they usually weighed in at anything between 925 and 950 kg, not being allowed to use non-standard plastic panels and exotic materials, as used on the 1973 works prototypes.

The homologation of all these racing components on the basic road car served two extremely useful purposes. One — which is particularly clever — is that being officially recognised as an *evolution* of the RS 2.7, homologated in Group 3 as a standard production GT car, the RS 3.0 with all its racing attributes automatically falls into the same Group where it has, of course, proved virtually unbeatable. The other is that, despite the very high price asked for the RS 3.0, customers who have it modified to RSR racing specifications save a lot of money, most of the essential racing equipment being already on their car. Bringing it up to racing standard mainly involves further engine modifications, fitting a sintered metal linered clutch disc, widening the front and rear wings to fit the wide magnesium racing wheels and changing the front suspension struts for those providing a lower ride height.

When modified to RSR specifications, the engine is exactly as the unit used by the factory at the end of 1973 in prototype form, featuring the higher lift camshafts, the throttle slides and the breaker-less capacity discharge twin ignition system.

It is worthy of note that, when tested — both by myself and *Auto, Motor & Sport* — the Carrera RS 3.0 did not appreciably better the performance figures obtained for the RS 2.7, neither for acceleration, nor for maximum speed, despite its 10 per cent increase in capacity and power. This is certainly due to the increased frontal area, and the fact that the press car had some accessories and full undercoating which made it heavier than it should have been. But there is no doubt that the handling and cornering power were even better than the extremely high standards set by the 2.7, though a track test I did on the little Casale-Monferrato circuit in Italy indicated that at high cornering speeds there is still quite an abrupt change from understeer to oversteer if the throttle pedal is lifted in a corner.

* As the service instructions recommended that the balance lever should normally be centred, this implies a front/rear pressure ratio of 56.4/43.6.

The evolution of the recommended running gear settings for an early 911 S, a G-series production model, the Carrera RS 3.0 and its racing equivalent, the RSR 3.0, make an interesting comparison, showing how such settings are influenced by the evolution of tyre design.

	O-series ('66)	G-series ('74) Carrera	3.0 RS	3.0 RSR
	165 HR 15 tyres on 4.5J 15 rim all-round	185/70 VR 15 on 6J 15 rims front, 215/60 VR 15 on 7J 15 rims rear	215/60 VR 15 on 8J 15 rims front, 235/60 VR 15 on 9J 15 rims rear	245/575-15 slicks on 10.5J 15 rims front, 305/575-15 slicks on 14J 15 rims rear. (9J 15 rims front and 12J 15 rims rear for rain tyres)
Front				
Camber	0°	0°	30' neg	1°20' neg
Castor	6°45'	6°5'	6°30'	6°30'
Toe-in	40' per wheel	0°	0°	0°
Rear				
Camber	1°15' neg	1° neg	30' neg	25' neg
Toe-in	0°	0° to 0°20' per wheel	20' to 25' per wheel	25' per wheel

These 3 litre Carrera RSR cars were immensely successful and remained virtually unchanged throughout the 1974 and 1975 racing seasons. Though they were never run by the factory, they remained supreme both in the European GT Championship and in the American IMSA championships of 1974 and 1975. Their performance in America was particularly creditable in view of the strong opposition they had to face from the full force of the BMW works team of 430 bhp 3.5 litre Coupés and some extremely well prepared Chevrolet Corvettes of up to 8 litres capacity.

The 2.7 Safari Carrera

After 1971, when they prepared a team of VW-Porsche 914-6s for the Monte Carlo Rally, in which one of them finished third with Björn Waldegaard at the wheel, Porsche had virtually ceased all rally activities at a factory level. But there was one Rally — the East African Safari — which, after a gallant effort in 1971 and 1972, they really hoped to win in 1974, though it was not economic for them to invest the astronomical sums that some of the large manufacturers spend in the hope of achieving victory. The Safari is an event in which sheer structural strength counts for more than speed and power and in which any sort of repair, bar replacing the entire car, is allowed provided that it is done within the scheduled time allowance. This means that the larger the service organisation, the better the chances of a good result and most competitors use several planes with radio liaison with the cars, in addition to a fleet of service vans and cars.

In 1972, the then semi-retired Polish rally driver and former European Champion Sobieslav Zasada, who had finished fifth with a 911 the year before, asked Porsche for a car to drive in the event and Dr Fuhrmann was interested enough to provide one, sending sports assistance man Jürgen Barth along with two mechanics and a service car to help. Despite this, by modern rally standards, ridiculously small service organisation, Zasada finished second, the car being the same he had used the year before. This really whetted Porsche's appetite and during the winter of 1973-74 a new Safari car was built.

The body structure remained practically unaltered from standard, only some local reinforcements being necessary. The reinforced front wishbones were fitted with special resilient bump stops to reduce the strain on the strut mountings and the stub axles were mounted lower on the struts in order to increase the ride height. This was matched by adjusting the rear torsion bars to raise the back of the car, too, where reinforced fabricated steel inner suspension arms were used. The shock absorbers were standard Bilstein, as were the front 19 mm torsion bars, 24 mm diameter (1 mm more than standard) torsion bars being used at the rear. Naturally underbody shields were fitted to protect the front suspension, the engine and the transmission.

The engine used was a perfectly standard Carrera 2.7 driving through a clutch which was standard except for the spring pressure and the use of sintered metal linings which resist more abuse in case the car gets stuck in mud. Low gear ratios were, of course, used, limiting the maximum speed to 130 mph in fifth, and the gearbox was fitted with the racing front cover incorporating an oil pump circulating the oil through a serpentine cooler in the left front wing. Wheels were standard forged alloy 6J 15 all round and how little reinforcement the car needed for this toughest of all World Championship Rallies is shown by the fact that, with all its extra equipment, including the (aluminium) roll bar, the average speed indicator, five extra lights, a 100 litre steel tank, a duplicated ignition system, the underbody protection and so forth, the complete car weighed no more than 1,000 kg (a ton) with an empty tank, barely 100 kg more than the standard lightweight Carrera and still 30-40 kg lighter than a basic G-series 911. The body itself, with all its equipment, weighed 538 kg (1,188 lb), compared with 443 kg (978 lb) for the standard Carrera RS and 589 kg (1,300 lb) for the standard G-series 911.

This time, Björn Waldegaard was signed up, but when leading with 35 minutes in hand a drive shaft broke within 400 miles of the finish in Nairobi, and again the Porsche finished second. This is a defeat the men in Weissach never accepted and after further intensive development and testing they entered two cars for the 1978 event. They were basically 911 SCs, prepared in much the same way as the 1974 car, but Turbo semi-trailing arms and separate bump and rebound stops were fitted. The engine was a 3 litre to racing specification, with a Bosch plunger-type injection pump, but detuned for flexibility and reliability, developing 250 bhp at 6,800 rpm with a 9.1:1 compression ratio. Six inch wide alloy wheels were used and the cars were geared for a maximum speed of 142 mph, using a 40 per cent limited slip differential. They weighed 1,180 kg (2,605 lb) and their 28 cm (11 in) ground clearance surely did not help their high-speed handling. Driven by Waldegaard and Vic Preston Jr, the cars just ran away from the opposition, but suspension problems eventually delayed them and, once again, Porsche had to be content with Vic Preston's second place, while Waldegaard finished fourth. So the Safari will probably remain the only event of world-wide fame a Porsche 911 or derivative never won.

The 2.14 litre racing Turbo-Carrera

When, in 1973, they progressively developed the Carrera RSR beyond the frame of GT specifications, Porsche had set themselves more ambitious targets than just to produce a more potent car than ever for GT racing in the following years. In 1973 it was already strongly rumoured that, as from 1975 or 1976, the World Championship of Makes would be contended on the basis of a new formula which would require that the competing cars should be derived from homologated production cars. In that case, the 911 would be an excellent development basis, and a good way of obtaining sufficient power to compete successfully against larger-capacity machinery would be to turbocharge the engine. Porsche had gained a lot of experience of turbocharging from the development of the 917/10 and 917/30 cars used in the Can-Am and Interserie Championships, which they won both in 1972 and 1973, and the experience gained with the flat-12 engine could easily be transferred to the flat-6.

Obviously, a turbocharged Carrera would have to run as a sports prototype against full-blooded contenders in that group, such as the 12 cylinder Matras and Alfas and V8 Gulf-Fords, which meant that it would be severely handicapped by its weight and its much larger frontal area. As the CSI rules stated that supercharged engines of any kind were considered to have a capacity 1.4 times their actual swept volume, it also meant that the engine capacity had to be reduced to no more than 2,142 cc in order not to exceed the 3 litre capacity limit imposed for sports prototypes in world championship races.

Everyone at Porsche was well aware of the fact that, whatever they did, their production-derived car could not be competitive against the full racing machinery, but they considered that running one or two cars in a number of selected races would be the best development exercise in view of the new formula planned, even if the full details of the rules were still unknown. It was also considered beneficial to the firm's image to show plainly that they had not by any means lost interest in racing, and probably some of the more optimistic executives even hoped that, given some luck, the Turbo might win the odd race. After all, normal Carreras had won three major races outright in 1973, and the Turbo would be a lot faster. But that inevitably implied some luck and, as it turned out, the more potent opposition never fell by the wayside in the right races, as had happened in 1973 and the best the Turbo-Carrera did achieve were two very creditable second places, one in the Watkins Glen 6 hours race and one at Le Mans, in either case headed only by one of the World Championship-winning, all conquering Matra-Simca V12s.

If the Turbo was to be anything like competitive, it was essential to reduce its weight below the figure of 890 kg achieved by the 1973 Carrera prototype. In spite of this requirement, the basic steel body shell was retained but, as in the 1973 prototype and earlier 911 which had run in the prototype group, the lids, doors, front wings and front and rear shields (no bumpers in this case, not even token ones!) were made of thin glass fibre. But the front and rear parts of the structure, which had remained untouched up to now, were extensively modified: the front because the fuel tank was moved from the front of the car to a position occupied, in normal production Porsches, by the right-hand rear emergency seat which, in a side view, is just about where the centre of gravity is located. This change made the car much less sensitive to the weight of fuel carried though, in fact, it implied a slight weight penalty, as for safety reasons and in accordance with the CSI rules, the tank had to be completely shielded from the inside of the cockpit by a sheet steel hull welded to the body. But the relocation of the tank, and the fact that sports prototypes must not carry a spare wheel, made it possible to redesign completely the front end structure to duct more air to the brakes and to reduce its weight.

At the rear, the comparatively heavy cross tube carrying the suspension was deleted as well as the cross member at the extreme rear, carrying the engine, which also made redundant the box section rear side members. Instead, an aluminium tube sub-frame was inserted into the engine bay and securely bolted to the body structure to carry both the rear suspension and the engine and transmission unit. The dashboard structure was also lightened and simplified, as its important contribution to torsional rigidity was largely assumed by the strong aluminium roll-over cage fitted inside the car. These combined modifications saved 71 kg (159 lb), reducing the weight of the complete body from 480 kg (1,060 lb) for the RSR 3.0 in GT trim to 409 kg (901 lb) for the racing Turbo.

The suspension remained unchanged in principle, with MacPherson struts at the front and semi-trailing arms at the rear. But what in certain versions of the Carrera RSR had been auxiliary coil springs now became the only springing element. They were, of course, stronger than the RSR's auxiliary springs and were made of conically extruded titanium wire to combine progressive rate with extreme lightness. The only reason for dispensing with the torsion bars was to save weight. Torsion bars had been chosen for the production 911 in order to save space, as coil springs would have increased the strut's overall diameter and taken up more front boot and rear passenger space. In a racing car, this is of no importance, and by using coil springs, the front wishbones could be relieved of bending stresses and made much lighter, while at the rear it made it possible to delete the cross tube and the steel outer (trailing) suspension arm. Consequently, in the racing Turbo, very light tubular steel front wishbones, hinged in Unibal bearings are used, while at the rear the semi-trailing arms are welded up from aluminium alloy sheet metal and carry the aluminium hub housing. With identical brakes and wheels (cast magnesium), the entire front axle of the racing Turbo weighs 84 kg (185.5 lb), compared with 103 kg (227 lb) for the Carrera RSR, while the complete rear axle, also with identical brakes, but wider, 17 inch magnesium wheels, weighs 101 kg (222.5 lb) compared with 112 kg (247 lb) for the RSR. Eventually, an overall weight of 825 kg (1,819 lb) was achieved.

The front suspension geometry provides for a slightly higher roll centre while anti-dive is built into it by making the wishbone pivot axis slope down towards the front. At the rear, the semi-trailing arm angle is similar to the RS and RSR models, but the pivot points are raised to reduce squat under acceleration. Reducing dive and squat is quite important in a car in which these movements tend to assume quite large proportions due to the (by racing car standards) comparatively high centre of gravity, short wheelbase and very high performance, and in which the suspension geometry provides for comparatively large camber changes: dive increases the front negative camber and can make it become positive at the rear, generating unstable conditions under heavy braking, while the reversed conditions created by squat make the car very throttle sensitive when cornering. Drag and lift are also strongly affected by such attitude changes. The anti-dive and anti-squat geometries adopted have made the racing Turbo very well behaved under both these conditions, as personal track acquaintance with the car revealed. Similar geometries were adopted for the 930 Turbo production car.

Whereas up to then engine development had always been orientated towards increasing the capacity, this had to be brought down to the 2,142 cc limit imposed on supercharged engines. This was achieved by using a crankshaft from the old 2 litre production engine, suitably crack tested, which provides a stroke of 66 mm and, quite amazingly, this production crankshaft has proved to be fully reliable in an engine developing some 500 bhp and 50 mkg (362 lb/ft) of torque. The connecting rods are similar to those of the 2 litre engine, but are made of titanium. They are in fact those of the Carrera-6. Nikasil cylinders of 83 mm bore are used and, except for Le Mans where a die-cast aluminium crankcase was used, all turbo engines were built with the lighter, production magnesium crankcase which proved fully reliable in races of up to six hours duration. The cylinder heads were from the old racing 2.34 and 2.5 litre engines with very slightly enlarged valves (inlet 47 mm, exhaust 40.5 mm) and very similar to the production 2.2 and 2.4 litre units, except for the provision of twin ignition. Sodium cooled valves were used on the inlet as well as on the exhaust side, their material being titanium for the inlet and Nimonic for the exhaust. The four-bearing camshafts and valve clearance adjustment by caps of appropriate thickness were, of course, used. Ignition was by the breaker-less capacity discharge system first used on racing Carreras in 1973.

The development time was comparatively short, thanks to the experience gained with the turbocharged Type 912 engine in the Type 917/10 and 917/30 cars, particularly as the six-cylinder turbocharged engine is almost exactly half the size of the 4.5 litre version of the flat-12. Consequently, a turbocharging installation almost identical to that employed for one bank of the flat-12 was used.

The turbocharger adopted — with some slight variations according to the characteristics required by the circuit on which the car was to race — is of KKK manufacture and is governed to produce a maximum boost of 1.3 to 1.4 bars (18.5 to 20 psi). Its turbine is fed by the exhaust gases from all six cylinders, the maximum boost pressure being governed by a boost pressure sensitive by-pass valve of Garrett manufacture. This valve is opened by a membrane, against spring pressure, to let part of the exhaust gases escape directly into the atmosphere, by-passing the turbine, when the boost reaches the maximum governed pressure. A supplementary dashboard control enables the driver to modify the maximum boost by admitting pressure to the other side of the membrane, which raises the pressure at which the valve opens.

The centrifugal blower, which is co-axial with the turbine, feeds its output of air into a plenum chamber from which six pipes, each with its own butterfly throttle valve, lead it into the inlet ports where the fuel is injected by the usual Bosch six-plunger pump system. In order to improve the throttle response after the accelerator has been momentarily released by the driver, a flap valve actuated by the accelerator linkage is opened when the throttles are shut. This allows the blower output to escape into the atmosphere and prevents sudden back pressure from building up against the blower, and possibly damaging it. It was also thought that the absence of back pressure on the compressor would reduce its rate of deceleration on a closed throttle, thus improving the turbo's response when accelerating again, but further experience has proved this to be doubtful. The turbocharger itself runs in plain bearings lubricated by oil from the engine's main pressure system.

A new development, compared with the Type 917, is the inclusion of an air-cooled intercooler between the blower and the plenum chamber. At racing speeds, this intercooler, which takes the form of an ordinary radiator, reduces the temperature of the air pushed out by the blower by approximately 100°C. The temperature drop is beneficial in two ways: it improves the adiabatic efficiency of the blower (which means that the turbocharger absorbs less power and the exhaust back pressure it creates is reduced with beneficial results to the engine's power output), and it reduces the thermal stresses on the engine. Heat is the most important factor limiting the possible output in a turbocharged engine, and great care was devoted to its dissipation. One aspect of this care is the use of an extra large oil cooler — that used in the 917 racing cars — as it also has to dissipate the heat carried away by the oil lubricating the turbocharger. To take care of the increased volume of oil in circulation, an oil pump from the Type 908 flat-8 racing engine is fitted.

A further improvement in cooling which made it possible to raise the boost pressure from the 1.35 bar (19.3 psi) used at the beginning of the season to 1.4 bar (20 psi), with a resultant gain of some 12-15 bhp, yet a further increase in the safety margin, was reached by mounting the cooling blower flat over the engine, as it is on the flat-12. The blower itself is the same as before, but both the air flow and air distribution over the cylinders and heads are improved by the fact that the cooling air flow does not have to be deflected through a 90 degree angle before reaching its destination. The blower is belt-driven through a pair of bevel gears. The alternator, which is coaxial with the blower in the normal arrangement, is moved to a separate bracket and driven by its own belt.

In accordance with the latest flat-12 engine developments, the compression ratio is drastically reduced to 6.5:1 and in order to improve the flexibility in circumstances when the turbocharger does not produce its full output (below 5,000-5,500 engine rpm and during the short throttle response lag) a slightly softer valve timing is used than for unsupercharged racing engines. The inlet valve lift is reduced from 12.2 to 10.5 mm and is back to 10.5 mm (as for pre-3 litre RSR engines) on the exhaust side too, the timing being as follows:

Inlet opens/closes   80°btdc/100°abdc
Exhaust opens/closes   105°bbdc/75°atdc

The cam profiles are such that the maximum valve acceleration is practically the same for the 12.2 and the 10.5 mm lifts, which means that the cams for 10.5 mm lift have a steeper ramp than those for 12.2 mm lift.

Whereas, in a normally aspirated engine, the lesser overlap and lower inlet valve lift would result in notably lower volumetric efficiency at high crankshaft speeds, this is of less importance in a turbocharged engine in which the boost is a much more important factor in obtaining high power outputs than crankshaft speed, and it is worthy of note that peak power in the turbocharged engine is obtained at only 7,600 rpm — 400 rpm less than in the RSR 3.0. It must be remembered, however, that any increase in boost pressure also increases the exhaust back pressure and the exhaust gas temperature. In the Porsche engine the exhaust back pressure at full load ranges from about 1 to 1.2 bar (14-17 psi) for boost pressures ranging from 1.3 to 1.4 bar (18.5 to 20 psi), while the exhaust gases reach the turbine wheel at a temperature of 950 to 1,000°C.

Turbocharging entailed a further development of the Bosch six-plunger injection pump which, in normally aspirated engines, meters the fuel according to throttle opening and engine speed. In the turbocharged engine a third factor affecting the weight of the charge filling the cylinders is the boost pressure and an appropriate membrane-type corrector had to be added, while the plunger diameter was increased in view of the larger quantities of fuel to be injected. On the other hand, the higher rate of flame travel in the denser charge filling the cylinders of the turbocharged engine made it possible to simplify the capacity discharge ignition system by deleting the spark advance mechanism.

Above *In 1973, the factory ran a Carrera RSR in Group 4 GT form in many races as a development exercise. Here Herbert Müller drives it into first place of the GT contingent in the Dijon 1,000 km race.*

Below *In prototype form, the 1973 works Carreras used extra-wide rear wheels and a full-width spoiler. The cars were also extensively lightened. Müller and Van Lennep finished fifth overall in the Nürburgring 1,000 km race.*

Above *First outing of the 2.8 litre Carrera RSR brought it outright victory in the Daytona 24 hours race of 1973. Drivers were Peter Gregg and Hurley Haywood. They had a repeat performance with a 3 litre RSR in 1975.*

Below *Men who matter: development engineers Norbert Singer (right), responsible for the development of the racing Carrera and the racing Turbo of 1973/74, and Peter Falk discuss matters with drivers George Follmer and Willy Kauhsen.*

Above *The 2.14 litre turbocharged racing engine in its early 1974 version with the standard racing cooling blower. The pressure limiting valve is seen nearest the camera and the turbocharger is at the extreme rear of the engine, under the heat shield. The intercooler fits between the compressor outlet and the plenum chamber inlet, where the blow-off valve, opening when the accelerator is released, can be seen.*

Below *Later version of the turbocharged racing 2.14 litre engine, with horizontal cooling blower.*

Above left *Businesslike cockpit of the 911 R (1967).* **Above** *Functional layout of a G/H-series racing Carrera cockpit.* **Left** *Racing valve rocker made of steel and without adjusting screw.* **Centre left** *In the Carrera RS 3.0, a cross bar between the front strut anchorages adds rigidity. Note folding tyre spare wheel moved as far off-centre as possible. Battery is in opposite corner.*

Below *Front view of the racing 2.14 litre turbocharged engine (911/76) with horizontal cooling blower. The relocation of the latter necessitated relocating the injection pump. Note the standard-size diaphragm spring single plate clutch transmitting a torque of more than 400 lb/ft!*

Above *Racing version (RSR) of Carrera 3 litre uses Type 917 front brake with perforated and ventilated disc. Note extra air scoop and Type 917 centre lock hub.* **Above right** *Type 917 rear brake, standard on Carrera RS 3.0. This is a Group 4 car, however, as indicated by the auxiliary coil spring around the damper.* **Right** *Standard and racing cylinder heads differ only by the second plug hole in the racing head.*

Below *Quick and fruitless search for a lost fifth gear: the 2.14 litre turbocharged Carrera nevertheless finished second overall at Le Mans in 1974.*

Above *Outright win for Peter Gregg/Hurley Haywood's Carrera RSR 3.0 in the 1975 Daytona 24 hour race.*

Below *A 3 litre Carrera RSR in the Nürburgring's famous 'Karusell' curve. Note the air outlets at the rear of the front wings. Jürgen Barth, 1977 Le Mans winner, is at the wheel. He was a great help to the author in compiling data for this book.*

Above *Front wings similar to those of the previous RSR models (see next page) were soon replaced by forward-sloping wings, made possible by a loophole in the Group 5 regulations and producing some down force. The air/air intercooler can be seen through the rear spoiler. Driver is Jochen Mass at Vallelunga.*
Below *To compensate for the compulsory 16-inch maximum tyre width, the 935 uses 19-inch diameter rear rims. At the end of the 1976 season wheel discs with radial vanes were added for centrifugal air circulation over the brakes.*

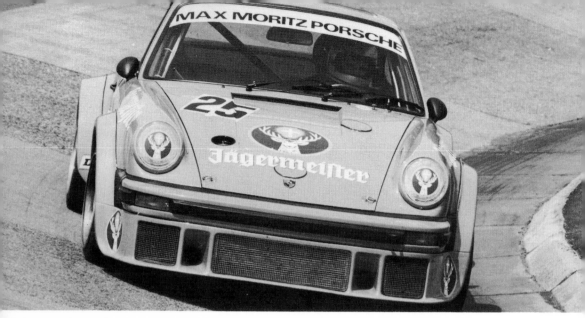

Above *The 1976 Turbo RSR, to 1976 Group 4 specification. The front spoiler incorporates the engine oil radiator (centre), flanked by the brake cooling air inlets and the two small radiators through which the intercooler cooling water circulates. The rear spoiler is standard Turbo 3.0.*

Below *Wings and front spoiler of the 1976 Group 5 Turbo are a single detachable glass fibre unit. The tubular aluminium stays across the front bay, the safety fuel tank and the oil tank can also be seen. The front bay layout of the Group 4 Turbo RSR is similar, but the standard external sheet metal is retained. Note the cooling openings for the rear brakes.*

As developed at the end of the 1974 racing season, the 911 ATL engine, as it is known (ATL stands for Auspuff-Turbolader) developed 490 bhp at only 7,600 rpm and 46 mkg (339 lb/ft) of torque at 5,400 rpm, these figures being obtained with a 1.4 bar (20 psi) boost. Note that the torque figure is higher than that delivered by the unsupercharged 4.5 litre flat-12 which powered the all-conquering 917 Coupés in 1970.

Surprising as this may sound, the standard size (225 mm diameter) single plate clutch was perfectly up to its frightful job, helped by sintered metal linings and an appropriately strong diaphragm spring but, thanks to the over-centre spring device adopted from the standard production models, the clutch pedal was not unduly heavy by racing car standards. The Type 915 gearbox was another problem, but little could be done about it. Its five ratios were retained, but a reinforced differential housing cover was used to resist the much increased axial thrust. The Turbo-Carrera would most probably have won outright the 1974 Le Mans 24 hours race if it had not been left without fifth gear several hours from the end. Unfortunately, the new Type 930 transmission, used on the production Turbo together with a 240 mm clutch, was not ready in time to be used.

In some races, following the lead set by the turbocharged Type 917s, the Turbo-Carrera was run with solid drive to the driving wheels instead of the more usual limited slip differential with an 80 per cent locking factor. In practice it does not make much difference to the handling and it certainly allows the driver to use a lot of power coming out of a corner. In this context, it should be remembered that tests carried out on the Weissach circular pad with a Type 917 racing car in 1969, using differentials with various locking factors, had indicated that the best results were obtained with the highest locking factor which made the car behave more consistently under varying throttle positions. This is probably due to the fact that the higher the locking factor and the pre-loading, the higher the tendency for the car to proceed in a straight line and the less likely it is to oversteer on the over-run.

For the first time, too, in a 911-based Porsche, non-standard half shafts were used. For the Turbo the constant velocity half shafts were replaced by tubular Type 917 ones, made of titanium and with a titanium Hooke joint at either end. The shaft itself is divided to incorporate a Giubo-coupling (doughnut) which serves both to take up the half shaft length variations, caused by suspension movements, and to preserve the transmission from heavy shocks, as may be caused by spinning wheels on a rough surface.

With some 500 bhp available, a speed potential of approximately 190 mph and direct competition from pure racing cars, it had become essential to use even more efficient aerodynamic aids than those developed for the 1973 works Carrera prototype or the RSR 3.0. Wind tunnel tests on racing 911s had indicated that the air flow on the roof line remained smooth up to the top of the rear window, where a perturbation was created by the slight step incorporating the cockpit air outlet vents. This is thus where the low pressure and turbulent zone starts, which develops behind any car, accounting for an important part of the total drag. In addition the turbulence creates conditions unfavourable to the efficiency of any spoiler or aerofoil located in that zone.

As the racing Turbo-Carrera had to run as a sports prototype anyway, there was no reason not to modify the body shape accordingly, and the perspex rear light was moved up to be flush with the roof line and was, in addition, set slightly flatter, so that the air flow continues unperturbed until the air opening in the engine cover is reached. The cover itself has two lateral fins directing the air flow on to a large outrigged aerofoil set approximately at the same level as the bottom of the rear window — which is as high as the regulations governing sports prototypes will allow. To compensate for the overhung down-force created by the large rear aerofoil, a deep front air dam with a large 'running board' is used which just about manages to cancel out the lifting forces.

Wind tunnel data obtained for the car as it was used in most of the races of the 1974 season, the frontal area being $S = 1.923$ sq m (17.3 sq ft), is as follows:

$C_d = 0.42$ $C_{Lf} = +0.09$ $C_{Lr} = -0.46$

For Le Mans a trim reducing the drag at the expense of down force was used, providing:

$C_d = 0.396$ $C_{Lf} = +0.026$ $C_{Lr} = -0.276$

The huge frontal area of nearly 2 square metres is, of course, due to the enormous rear wings necessary to cover the 17 inch wide wheels and their racing tyres. Neither is their shape beneficial to the drag coefficient, and the fact that the latter is rather *better* than for the 1973 Targa Florio car or the Carrera RSR 3.0 indicates that the rear end modifications to the body (flush and flatter rear window, aerofoil instead of spoiler) are very worth while.

It would be reasonable to ask what effect the modifications incorporated in the 2.14 litre racing Turbo had on its handling, for the entire turbocharging installation is overhung at the extreme rear end of the car, while moving the fuel tank from the front end of the body to a position behind the front seats has also shifted some weight rearwards — a lot of it for cars with a full tank. Indeed the weight distribution of the racing Turbo is very near 30/70, but this is no more drastic than was the case of the 917-10, and that is one of the best handling racing cars ever made. Admittedly the problem was even more difficult to solve in the case of the Turbo-Carrera, in which a large part of the weight is overhung, which has inevitably a higher centre of gravity than a full blooded racing car and which does not use racing suspension systems. Carefully selected suspension geometries, efficient aerodynamics and a large difference in front and rear tyre and rim widths (front rims 10.5 inch, rear rims 17 inch) provided the solution, of which the success was proved at Le Mans where official timings through some curves — both fast and slow — showed the Turbo-Porsche driven by Herbert Müller and Gijs van Lennep to be among the very fastest, on the same level as the V12 Matra-Simcas, the most successful cars of the 1973 and 1974 seasons. And this was achieved with know-how to spare, as the Turbos ran without any front anti-roll bar in most of the races!

Though at the time of going to press, the 911 is heading for its twelfth year of production, it will, for several years to come, remain Porsche's main and no doubt very successful weapon at all levels of motoring sport, just as, thanks to ceaseless development by a handful of perfectionists drilled by the high school of racing, it has remained the pace setter among road-going sports cars.

New cars for new sporting regulations: the Porsche 934 and 935

For 1976, Appendix J of the CSI sporting regulations was extensively modified. The modifications permissible in Group 4 (GT cars) were drastically limited. More freedom was given in the new Group 5 for 'modified production cars' which became the basis for the World Championship of Makes and for which only cars homologated in the Groups 1 to 4 were eligible. This implies that prototypes were not eligible in this Group and must run in Group 6.

After gaining experience with the extensively modified Turbo-Carrera in 1974, Porsche pulled out of racing at factory level in 1975 in order to prepare for the 1976 season. The task in hand was quite enough to keep the development engineers busy, as two completely new racing models, both based on the Turbo, were to be developed: one for the new Group 4, to be sold to private customers, and one for the new Group 5 for racing at factory level, though replicas were built for customers after the 1976 season. In fact, the number of new models developed and built turned out to be three, for as late as September 1975 the management decided to go ahead with the design and development of a Group 6 prototype, using the turbocharged 2.14 litre engine, which finally proved to be Porsche's most successful weapon. But that is another story . . .

The new rules in short
Group 4 (GT cars)

In order to qualify for this Group, 400 identical cars of a given type must have been built in no more than two years. Weight must not be homologated any more (which means that the weight of the production model is no longer the minimum at which the vehicle must weigh-in before a race). Instead, a minimum weight related to the engine capacity is required. This ranges from 495 kg (1,091 lb) for a 500 cc car to 1,270 kg (2,800 lb) for a 6 litre car.

Another important change in the rules is the limitation of the width of the complete wheel-and-tyre assembly, also in relation to the engine capacity. Permitted modifications from the standard car are drastically reduced, compared with the previous Group 4. Main components may, in many cases, be modified, but their replacement with a different basic component is forbidden. This applies not only to such parts as cylinder heads, gearbox, clutch, etc, but also to the suspension and running gear, even if the manufacturer makes a certain number of the special parts available to customers. The engine capacity may be modified only within the limits of the class to which the car belongs, but only to the extent of increasing the bore by no more than 0.6 mm or linering down.

Wings (fenders) may be modified only by widening them by up to 50 mm around the wheel opening, but no other changes and no additional openings for ventilation are allowed.

Group 5 (modified production cars)

Any car homologated in Groups 1 to 4 is eligible for racing in Group 5, on which the World Championship of Makes is based. In this Group the cars may be modified much more extensively than is permissible in Group 4, though the body and such major components as the cylinder block, the crankcase and all other major housings (clutch, gearbox, differential, etc) must originate from the production car and remain in their original location. Special suspension parts and non-standard fulcrum points may be used, but the basic principle of the suspension must remain as in the homologated car. Additional aerodynamic devices are allowed, but are limited in size and overhang. In this Group, too, a minimum weight scale and a maximum width scale for the complete wheel-and-tyre assembly are applicable. The cylinders may be bored out or sleeved down without limits, provided the original cylinder casting is used.

The Porsche 934

As previously mentioned, the Group 4 and 5 racing models are derived from the 930 Turbo, which was originally developed so as to provide the best possible base for its racing derivatives. The semi-trailing arm pivot angle of the rear suspension, the anti-dive front suspension geometry, the widened track and the very wide rims and wings (fenders) were not all adopted in view of the 260 bhp of the standard Turbo engine: their main purpose was to provide the basis for competitive Group 4 and 5 cars, the latter with more than twice as much power as the standard model. This also applies to the type 930 gearbox and the enlarged clutch which were not mandatory with the normal production engine. In contrast with previous 911 models specially developed in view of their conversion for racing (as for example the Carrera RS), Porsche never produced a lightweight version of the Turbo, which would have had no justification, the minimum weight of the racing version not being ruled any more by the homologation weight of the standard model. A few died-in-the-wool enthusiasts regret this, one of them being the famous conductor Herbert von Karajan who had a special Turbo made for his own use around a lightweight Carrera RS body shell.

To avoid any confusion, the RSR designation of the racing versions has been dropped, beginning with 1976: the Group 4 version of the 930 Turbo is called 934 and the Group 5 version 935. Similarly, the open Group 6 prototype is called 936, even though only its engine can claim to be of 911/930 derivation.

The 934's running gear and brakes are generally similar to those of the 1974/75 Carrera RSR, though with the anti-dive and anti-squat characteristics of the standard Turbo and its wider main rear suspension arms providing an increased track. The front and rear torsion bars are retained, as required by the rules, but they are supplemented by coil springs concentric with the dampers with provision for quick adjustment of ride height. The rear trailing arms pivot on needle bearings. The type 917 brakes and the centre-lock hubs remain as before and a safety bag-tank, protected by an aluminium sheet box, replaces the standard tank in the nose of the car. This is reinforced by an aluminium tube linking the front McPherson strut consoles as well as by two diagonal tubes running across the front 'luggage' compartment.

At first sight, the engine looks unfamiliar, due to the cooling blower lying flat on top of the engine, as in the 1974 Turbo-Carrera 2.14 litre racing car, but otherwise it is its usual self. Twin ignition being forbidden, unless it is featured in the homologated model, the 934 is the first racing Porsche of 911 derivation with single ignition. Valve sizes (inlet 49 mm, exhaust 41.5 mm) are as in the standard engine, but the ports have been considerably enlarged to 43.5 and 36.5 mm respectively. The camshafts are also new and provide the following timing:

Inlet opens/closes	45°btdc/90°abdc
Exhaust opens/closes	95°bbdc/49°atdc

Towards the end of the 1976 racing season, higher cams were used, increasing the valve lift from 10.5 to 11.5 mm, but the timing remained unchanged.

For the first time the K-Jetronic continuous flow injection system was used for a racing engine. This was made possible by the turbo which damps the blow-back caused by the large valve overlap in the lower engine speed ranges and which would otherwise cause the metering unit disc to vibrate and upset the fuel delivery. The new location of the cooling blower, flat on top of the engine, made it necessary to relocate the metering unit to a position in the rear right-angle of the engine bay. Both this and the turbocharger are, of course, larger than in the standard Turbo.

The K-Jetronic injection system requires that when the 934's six separate throttle valves are closed, the air going through the blower is recirculated to its inlet, as in the production Turbo, so that no air is aspirated through the metering unit. In contrast to the standard car which has a vacuum-operated by-pass valve, the 934 operates the latter through the throttle linkage.

As on the other Porsche air-cooled turbocharged engines, the 934 has a 6.5:1 compression ratio. The maximum permissible boost pressure is 1.4 bar (20 psi). Before the compressed air is fed to the six separate intake pipes, it is led through intercoolers, also serving as plenum chambers, on top of each group of three intake pipes. As there is no room for an air-cooled intercooler under the engine cover (which the rules do not allow to be modified), the intercoolers are water-cooled. Circulation is by an engine-driven pump and the water must go all the way to the two front-mounted radiators, flanking the central oil cooler in the front air dam. Going through the intercoolers drops the temperature of the intake air from about 150 to 50°C. The 934 is thus the first car in Porsche history in which water is used as a cooling medium. At the beginning of the racing season, the legality of the water-cooled intercoolers was questioned, but Porsche pointed out that, according to Appendix J, 'the intake system is free' and that the intercoolers, complete with their cooling system, are part of the intake system — which was eventually accepted.

Maximum power of the 934, as claimed by the factory, is 485 bhp at only 7,000 rpm, with a maximum torque of 60 mkg (434 lb/ft) at 5,400 rpm.

The engine bay lid used for the 934 comes from the standard Turbo fitted with air conditioning, featuring a large air inlet within the spoiler which, in the racing car, is used to duct cooling air to the turbocharger and to the transmission oil cooler. The latter necessitates the use of a gearbox end cover incorporating an oil pump, but otherwise, except for ratios and a differential with an 80 per cent locking factor, the gearbox and final drive unit is standard. The standard size (240 mm) single plate clutch is also retained, but sintered metal linings are used. Those who witnessed the many half shaft failures experienced by Carrera RSR drivers at Le Mans in 1974 may be surprised to find that, with nearly twice as much power as the standard car, the racing 934 retains its original half shafts and constant velocity joints. These have, in fact, proved to be fully up to their task, development having eliminated the cause of the Le Mans failures of previous years: this was found to be the collapse of the dust cover due to the very high and persistent centrifugal force generated on the long Le Mans straight, with resultant loss of lubricant and seizure of the Rzeppa joints.

According to the CSI rules, the nominal capacity of any supercharged engine (except in Formula 1) was considered to be 1.4 times its actual capacity. This brings the 934 into the 4,001 to 4,500 cc capacity class in which the maximum permissible width of a complete wheel (with tyre) is 14 inches. In practice, this restricts the rim width to 12.5 inches, more than enough for the front wheels (which have 10.5 inch rims), but rather inadequate in the case of a 500 hp car having most of its weight on the rear axle. Consequently Porsche decided to make up for at least a part of the rubber contact area they lost in width by increasing its length, and replaced the 15 inch diameter wheels they had been using both on the standard cars and for racing with 16 inch wheels. The same step was taken in the case of the 1977 version of the production Turbo, but for a different reason: the 16 inch wheels fitted with 50 series Pirelli P7 tyres became interchangeable with 15 inch wheels and 60 series tyres without having to alter the final drive ratio and without infringing American bumper height regulations.

There being no Porsche magnesium racing wheels of 16 inch diameter, built-up BBS magnesium wheels were specified for the 934. Despite their increased diameter, however, they still set a limit to the performance of the car, of which the cornering power is still further limited by the rules forbidding the use of a larger than standard rear spoiler which is too small to cancel the rear end lift at speed, as indicated by wind tunnel tests:

$$C_d = 0.440 \quad C_{Lf} = -0.007 \quad C_{Lr} = +0.101$$

with a frontal area S=1.98 sq m. At 187 mph (300 km/h), this results in a lifting force on the rear axle of 166 lb (75 kg).

For the 4,001 to 4,500 cc class to which the 934 nominally belongs, the minimum weight required is 1,120 kg (2,490 lb), which does not require any drastic lightening measures to the standard body shell. Only the trim is simplified, while the rear occasional seats, some accessories and the sound deadening material are left out. This makes the 934 one of the most luxurious racing cars ever seen on a starting grid and certainly the first ever to feature electric windows. The minimum weight requirement is in fact so high that even a completely equipped car would be quite near the limit, but the factory preferred to strip the car to a weight below the limit and put the required weight back by screwing up 40 kg of lead into the nose of the body to lower the centre of gravity and modify the weight distribution as an alternative to using wider rear tyres and rims, which are ruled out. This allows the car to be lightened accordingly by removing the ballast when it is entered in Group 5, where the wider tyres and additional aerodynamic aids provide much improved handling without recourse to weighting the front end.

As had been done in the case of the Carrera RSR 3.0, Porsche decided to build 30 934s from scratch instead of modifying existing standard Turbos. Due to the fact that a normal production body shell could be used, the car was offered, in full racing trim, at a price of DM97,000, which is less than the price asked, two years earlier, for a Carrera RSR with corresponding equipment including the roll-over cage, the centre-lock hubs, the auxiliary coil springs, etc.

In spite of the limits imposed by the rules, the 934s were virtually unbeatable in GT racing in 1976. They suffered their only serious setback in the Le Mans race, for which — as in most other races — a host of 934s had been privately entered but where most of them fell victims of the intense 24 hours rivalry between the various teams, leaving victory in the GT class to an older Carrera RSR 3.0. But for the fourth consecutive year, a Porsche driver — Dutchman Toine Hezemans, driving a 934 — won the European GT Championship, while George Follmer became Trans-Am champion, driving a 934 in the United States.

Due to the decreasing popularity of the GT class and the lack of competition, the 934 was not further developed after 1976, but it won the Group 4 classification at Le Mans in 1977, 1979 and 1980, finishing fourth overall in 1979.

The Porsche 935

Although the Group 5 rules are much stricter than those under which the Turbo-Carrera of 1974 was developed, the experience gained with the earlier car was a great asset in developing the 935, even if originally the latter was a lot closer to the basic model than its forerunner.

Structurally, the original 935 was almost identical with the production Turbo.

Floorpan and rear suspension arms were standard and the fuel tank is still in the car's nose. Though the similarity with the production car is to some extent dictated by the rules, this is not the case for the suspension, of which the standard fulcrum points (which are free in Group 5) were retained, except at the rear of the front wishbones. Here the pivot was raised to provide increased anti-dive. As the Group 5 rules do not require the original type of springs to be retained, the torsion bars were deleted altogether in favour of variable rate titanium coil springs concentric with the dampers carrying an adjustable abutment plate for quick ride height adjustment. The deletion of the torsion bars saves weight not only in itself, but also because the front wishbones are no longer submitted to bending stresses and can thus be made of thin steel tubes. At the rear, the trailing arms were also relieved of bending stresses and were pivoted on spherical joints and adjustment for length allowed quick toe-in modifications. A new feature was the 'while you drive' adjustable rear anti-roll bar, made up of three main parts: the bar itself and its two arms. Either of the latter takes the form of a spring steel blade which can be turned through 90 degrees by means of a Bowden cable operated by a hand lever within the driver's reach. When the blades are upright, they have virtually no flexibility and the only resilient part is the anti-roll bar itself; when they lie flat, their flexibility adds up to that of the bar, and roll stiffness is decreased. Any intermediate position can be used, enabling the driver to adjust the handling to compensate for fuel consumption, track conditions and tyre characteristics. The front wheels were given as much as 2° negative camber, but only 10' negative camber was used at the rear.

The opportunity provided by the rules to reduce (or increase) the cylinder bore without any limitation was exploited by Porsche to reduce the engine's capacity to 2,856 cc by using a 92.8 mm bore instead of 95 mm. This reduces the nominal capacity of the turbocharged engine (actual capacity × 1.4) to less than 4 litres, allowing the car's weight to be lowered to 970 kg (2,155 lb), 55 kg (122 lb) less than the minimum prescribed in the next higher class. The choice was an obvious one, as the maximum allowed wheel-and-tyre width is 16 inches in either case, while lightening the car to the 970 kg limit was no problem at all. In fact the car was originally lightened to weigh 880 kg (1,940 lb) and then weighted with lead in the 'nose' and on the floor in the 'passenger's' foot room, in order to lower the centre of gravity and get the best possible weight distribution.

Aluminium tubes are used to stiffen up the front end of the car, containing the 120 litre safety fuel tank, as in the 934, but in spite of its reduced capacity, the Group 5 engine produces over 100 bhp more than its Group 4 counterpart. Mainly responsible for this are higher engine speed, the twin ignition system and the plunger-type injection pump replacing the K-Jetronic unit. Valve sizes and camshafts are the same as for the 934, but power claimed for the original 935 was 590 bhp at 7,900 rpm.

The fuel injection plant and the turbocharging installation were initially very similar to those on the 1974 Turbo-Carrera, but the intercooler had to be modified during the season, following a decision taken by the CSI. Originally, the air-cooled intercooler was located under the rear airfoil, within the engine compartment where it was housed inside a support bulging out from the engine bay lid to carry the load acting on the airfoil. The cooling air was ducted from the opening normally used, in the production car, to cool the air conditioning condenser. Whereas it was clear that, in Group 4, the engine bay cover could not be modified, Porsche had taken advantage of the greater freedom in the use of aerodynamic aids in Group 5 to use a much simpler and lighter air-cooled intercooler. But at the race in Imola, the scrutineers decided that the airfoil support could not be used to house any mechanical devices, and their judgement was upheld by the CSI who gave Porsche five weeks to make their car legal, according to their interpretation of the rules. The two existing cars (only two were built for the entire season) were modified to take water-cooled intercoolers, similar in their general layout to those used in the 934, but of a larger size. As in Group 5 the rear wings (fenders) are wider than in Group 4 and may incorporate air in- and outlets, advantage was taken of this to locate the radiators in the rear wings (fenders), just ahead of the wheels, which saved a lot of weight compared with the front radiator layout of the 934, but still added some 10 kg (22 lb) compared with the air/air intercooler.

Porsche were rather upset by the CSI's decision. Five weeks were just not enough to design, build and develop the new turbocharging installation for which many components had to be built specially or obtained from outside suppliers. They say the whole episode cost them no less than half a million DM (approx £125,000) and it certainly nearly cost them the Manufacturer's World Championship: they had lost a round to BMW in the Silverstone Six Hours race, when Ickx burned the clutch out on the starting line (the car restarted nearly two hours later, after the clutch had been replaced, and still finished within the time schedule), and they lost the next two, at Nürburgring and Zeltweg, because the new intercooling system was insufficiently developed (at Nürburgring they used type 934 intercoolers and at Zeltweg one of the new throttle shafts broke). Fortunately, the new installation worked in the last two races, in Watkins Glen and Dijon, which were won by Stommelen-Schurti and Ickx-Mass, respectively, but not until the last race was the Manufacturer's World Championship safely back in Zuffenhausen.

The new intercooling installation had no ill-effects on the engine's maximum power, but the drivers say that it made it less flexible, reducing its useful range.

As in the 1974 Turbo-Carrera, the boost could be adjusted by the driver through a knob within his reach. Normally a 1.5 bar (21.4 psi) boost was used, but for Le Mans this was reduced to 1.2 bar (17 psi) for reliability, which reduced the maximum power from 590 to about 540 bhp. Even for such enormous outputs, a production crankshaft is used, after thorough checking, though the conrods are made of titanium. In fact, it can be calculated that the actual bearing loads in the turbocharged engine are not higher than in the corresponding unsupercharged versions in which the maximum load is caused by inertia and occurs around top dead centre on the exhaust stroke. In the turbocharged engine, this load is actually reduced by the exhaust back pressure, while the maximum load during the expansion stroke is not higher than the inertia load.

Even the 60 mkg (434 lb/ft) torque, produced at 5,400 rpm, is transmitted through the basically standard single plate clutch in which sintered metal linings are used for racing. The type 930 transmission is similar to the version used in the 934, except for the fact that no differential is fitted. In this case, however, the production half shafts are replaced by 917 type two-piece titanium half shafts incorporating a Giubo coupling as a damping and length adjusting element, with a titanium Hooke joint at either end, as in the 1974 Turbo-Carrera.

Even with a large part of the total weight carried by the rear axle, rear wheel adhesion proved to be a problem with tyres not exceeding 16 inches overall width (implying the use of rims no wider than 15 inches), and these also proved too narrow for optimum handling. Consequently the same way was chosen as with the 934, but going a lot farther: co-operation with Dunlop culminated in the use of 19 inch diameter rear wheels, while 16 inch diameter and 10.5 inch wide wheels were used at the front.

Compared with the 934, the 935's wider and larger rear wheels and tyres provide a decisive handling advantage, but this also results, to a considerable extent, from the more liberal Group 5 rules about aerodynamic aids. Except for the first two races of 1976, Porsche also made clever use of a loophole in the rules to use front wings (fenders) sloping downwards and producing more aerodynamic downthrust than the standard shaped ones. These are part of a quickly removable one-piece glass fibre front section and are of particular advantage in side winds, when the standard shaped front wings partly shield the car's sloping nose and reduce the aerodynamic down force.

The type 917 brakes have very wide calipers, able to take 19 mm thick pads, with four pistons, each 43 mm front and 38 mm rear. The discs themselves are ventilated and their diameter is 300 mm. Except for Le Mans, they were transversely drilled for lighter weight, better cooling and better wet weather response.

The large rear wheels and square shaped rear wings (fenders) result in a frontal area larger than ever before, exceeding 2 sq m for the first time with a figure of 2.06 sq m. Several wind tunnel tests finally led to a combination of front spoiler and rear airfoil providing the following figures:

$C_d = 0.435$ $C_{Lf} = -0.05$ $C_{Lr} = -0.26$

Corresponding down forces are:

at 200 km/h (125 mph): front 20 kg (44 lb), rear 105 kg (233 lb)
at 300 km/h (187 mph): front 45 kg (100 lb), rear 235 kg (522 lb)

Comparing these figures with those obtained for the 1974 Turbo-Carrera, we note that some front down thrust is obtained which could not be created with the standard shaped front wings (fenders). On the other hand, stricter rules have not made it possible to give the 935 as much rear down thrust as in the older car. Only in the case of the 934, some slight down force could be obtained with the standard shaped front wings (fenders), but this only reflects the fact that the rocking moment created by the rear end lift around the rear axle results in a down force at the front end.

Again, a different aerodynamic compromise was chosen for the 935 when it ran at Le Mans. The rear down force was reduced to lower the drag and the front spoiler was made somewhat smaller to maintain the front/rear balance. These adjustments reduced the drag by over 10 per cent:

$C_d = 0.390$ $C_{Lf} = -0.04$ $C_{Lr} = -0.14$

The limitations imposed on tyres and aerodynamic aids by the new Group 4 and 5 rules and the comparatively high weights imposed result in reduced cornering speeds, compared with the Carrera RSR models of 1974-75. Even for the less handicapped 935, the lateral g-force measured on the Weissach proving ground's steering pad is 0.1 g (6.9 per cent) lower than for the two years older Turbo-Carrera. On most racing circuits this is more than compensated for by the higher power available. On the 5.810 km (3.61 mile) Paul Ricard circuit, the 934 development prototype lapped some 3 seconds quicker than the fastest time recorded by an unsupercharged Carrera 3.0 RSR, while the 935 development car was 1.6 seconds faster than the 2.14 litre Turbo-Carrera had been on the occasion of the Paul Ricard 1,000 km Race of 1974. The gains are 2.5 and 1.4 per cent respectively.

Also of interest is a comparison of the performance of the three racing models of

911 derivation entered by the Martini Racing Team on behalf of the Porsche factory in various long-distance races in 1973, 1974 and 1976. To better understand the figures quoted, it should be noted that they were all obtained with the overall gearing resulting in the highest straight line speed, as used at Le Mans, and that the maximum speed figures quoted are those actually registered on the Hunaudières straight during practice.

		Max speed at Le Mans	0-200 km/h (0-125 mph)	Lateral 'g' force on circular pad of 193 m diameter
1973	911 RSR prototype 3 litre u/s 890 kg	270 km/h (168 mph)	13.5 sec	1.259 g
1974	911 RSR Turbo-Carrera 2.14 litre turboch 825 kg	304 km/h (189 mph)	8.8 sec	1.450 g
1976	935 2.8 litre turboch 980 kg	336 km/h (209 mph)	8.2 sec	1.350 g

It should further be mentioned that the type 936 open prototype using the 2.14 litre turbocharged 911 engine producing 520 bhp at 8,000 rpm, which won both the Sports Car World Championship and the Le Mans 24 Hours Race in 1976, reached a maximum speed of 325 km/h (200 mph) on the Le Mans straight and records a 0 to 200 km/h (0-125 mph) time of 7.1 seconds.

Not only did a model of direct 911 derivation win the World Championship of Makes for the Zuffenhausen factory, but its engine also won for Porsche a championship in which it had to face highly specialised prototypes, including cars built and prepared by no less a manufacturer than the French state-owned Renault.

Following the successful season, a batch of 13 replicas of the factory's 935 in its latest form was built for the use of private owners in 1977.

The Porsche 935/77

At the end of 1976, the Group 5 regulations were slightly relaxed, mainly to give front- and rear-engined cars more equal chances. Permission was given to raise the floor up to the level of the door sills (to better accommodate the exhaust system, with possibly an added turbocharger in front-engined cars), and to move the bulkhead between engine and cockpit 20 cm into the cockpit. Additionally, the 'body structure' was defined as the part between the front and rear bulkheads, which gave the manufacturers freedom to modify or replace the structural parts outside these limits as they wished, with dramatic consequences, as will be seen later.

For 1977, Norbert Singer, the engineer responsible for the 935 project, made use of the bulkhead rule modification to fit a larger (still water-cooled) intercooler set across the car, replacing the two smaller intercoolers surmounting the intake pipes in the 935/76, while the new definition of the structure allowed him to modify the front end slightly to raise the front suspension wishbone pivot points, which made the camber variations nil up to 30 mm either side of the static position, allowing a reduction of the static negative camber to less than 2°.

On the same occasion, the basically standard front suspension struts of the 935/76 were replaced by an aluminium strut carrying a bolt-on magnesium hub carrier of a design similar to the 917 and 936 models. The remote control adjustable anti-roll bar was moved to the front where stiffness variations have a greater effect, due to the use of lighter springs.

Some development also took place on the engine, where the single KKK turbocharger was replaced with two smaller ones, each with its own waste gate: Porsche now used their own, basically standard, Turbo waste gate and two were used to provide a sufficient capacity. The lower inertia of the smaller turbochargers improved the throttle response, but the figures for power and torque remained as at the end of 1976, after the introduction of the higher lift cams: 630 bhp at 8,000 rpm and 60 mkg (434 lb/ft) at 5,400 rpm, respectively. These figures were obtained with 1.4 bar (20 psi) boost pressure.

The most striking difference with the 1976 car, however, is the body, of which especially the rear end shape was completely redesigned by a new glass fibre tail covering the standard body to include the production Turbo's rear spoiler and extending to the maximum overhang allowed by the regulations: a clever interpretation of 'aerodynamic aids'.

Another novelty was the brake servo, used for the first time in a racing Porsche, with the balance bar interposed between the servo and the twin master cylinders. It turned out, however, that the brake pad wear was considerably increased, possibly because the pads remained in slight contact with the discs with the brakes off, and the servo was eventually discarded. After the removal of the servo, lighter operation was obtained by the use of the same calipers, each with four 43 mm pistons, at the rear as at the front, the balance bar being readjusted accordingly.

Aerodynamically, the body modifications were well worth while: for almost the same downforce figures as those obtained with the 935/76, the drag coefficient dropped from 0.435 to 0.393, a gain of exactly 10 per cent.

Three cars were built to 935/77 specifications, chassis Nos 935/77-003 to 005, of which 004 was destroyed in its first race, the Mugello 6 Hours, when the driver omitted to 'pump' the brakes after a pad change, while 005 ran in all the World Championship of Makes events of 1977, winning three of them and materially contributing to Porsche's fourth victory in the Championship. It retired in the others, which were all won by privately owned 935/76s from the batch of 13 cars made at the end of the 1976 season. In all cases but one the retirement was caused by a cylinder head gasket failure which also caused the car's retirement at Le Mans. This indicated that the combination of thermal and mechanical stresses had reached a point where any further increase in power was bound to cut into the engine's reliability, unless a drastic redesign was undertaken, though the practice and race times achieved on most circuits clearly demonstrated the 935/77's superiority over the 1976 version.

At the end of 1977, Porsche again built a batch of 'customer's cars'. Fifteen were made, outwardly similar to the cars built one year earlier, but incorporating some important developments, such as the twin turbochargers and the raised front wishbone pivots. In America, some of them were converted back to single turbo specification, following a new national regulation penalising twin turbocharged engines.

The Porsche 935/2 'Baby'

Thanks to the CSI's decision to ban Porsche's air/air intercooler on the 935 in 1976, forcing Porsche into hectic development work, BMW had had a fair chance of winning the World Championship of Makes. But in the following year, they saw no chance for their ageing 3.0 CSL, even with the addition of a turbocharger, and

222   Porsche 911 Story

switched to the 2 litre class, mainly concentrating on the German National Championship, dominated by quick Ford Escorts. The World Championship of Makes thus
became virtually a Porsche family affair in which the lone factory 935/77 fought it
out with a horde of privately owned 935s which won when the factory car, mostly
driven by Ickx and Mass, struck trouble. The press was not always very kind to
Porsche for not joining the Ford-BMW battle, sometimes even implying that they
were afraid to do so — which was rather unfair, as Porsche clearly had no car of that
capacity class. But when Prof Fuhrmann learned that German television had decided
to broadcast the Division 1 (2 litre) race of the German National Championship
meeting on the Norisring, on July 3 1977, rather than the Division 2 in which the
Porsches were running, he decided 'to show them all'.

After discussing the situation with the engineers responsible for the Group 5
activities, mainly Hans Mezger in charge of racing car design and more specially
concerned with the engine development, and Norbert Singer, in charge of the 935
project, he signed an order to develop a car for the 2 litre class. This was on April 5,
less than two months before the race. In that time, a 1.4 litre turbocharged version of
the 911-based flat-six was to be developed and no less than 245 kg (540 lb) had to
come off the weight of the existing 935/77 (in fact, thanks to the ballast carried by the
bigger car, they were 'only' 155 kg — 342 lb), to get down to the minimum weight of
725 kg (1,598 lb) for the 2 litre class.

The weight target was eventually achieved both by re-evaluating every single
component and a drastic measure consisting of chopping off the structures outside
the front and rear bulkheads and replacing them with light aluminium tube subframes. The rear suspension was completely redesigned too to incorporate semi-
trailing arms fabricated from aluminium sheet, both the subframes and the suspension being based on the experience gained with the Turbo-Carrera of 1974.

The weight saving operation was not facilitated by the fact that the basic 911
engine, of which the bore and stroke dimensions were reduced to 71 x 60 mm, is
grossly oversize for a 1.4 litre, but weight could be saved on the intercooler which,
being smaller, could be of the air-to-air type and enclosed under the standard engine
cover. Air circulation through the installation was cleverly activated by the so-called
'jet system', energised by the exhaust gases. This consists of a venturi surrounding
the end of the exhaust pipe, in which the partial vacuum created by the exhaust gas
stream is used to aspire the air through the intercooler. With no radiators to cool any
more, the engine and transmission oil coolers could be moved into the openings
ahead of the rear wheels, and the shorter pipes saved weight too.

More weight was saved by using the lighter type 915/50 gearbox which had the
further advantage of having five speeds. As in the other Group 5 models, no differential was fitted. It was replaced by a solid titanium shaft. To comply with the
regulations, the rear wheels were narrowed down to a rim width of 13.5 inches.

Port and valve sizes were reduced to match the engine's 1,425 cc capacity. With a
compression ratio of 6.5:1 and a single turbocharger providing a 1.4 bar (20 psi)
boost, it developed 370 bhp at 8,000 rpm.

Eventually, the complete car turned the scales at 710 kg (1,565 lb) — 15 kg (33 lb)
underweight! This was enough margin for eventual local reinforcements and 20 kg
(44 lb) of ballast was bolted into the 'nose' before Jacky Ickx turned a few laps of the
Weissach test track and the car was loaded into the transporter, and sent off to
Nürnberg for the race, the first practice scheduled for the next morning, July 1.

Unfortunately, the schedule had been too tight. The engine had been bench tested

Right *Power and torque curves of Group 5 and Group 6, single blower 'two-valve' engines (1976).*

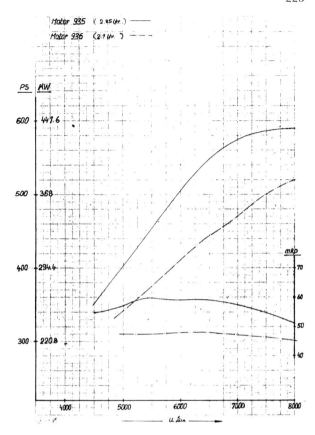

Below *Acceleration chart of Porsche racing models of 911 derivation from 1973 to 1976, compared with production 3-litre 'Turbo' acceleration curve. All cars with Le Mans gearing. Later 935 2.85- and 3-litre models improved on the 1976 model mainly above 200 kph (125 mph) and only by a comparatively small margin.*

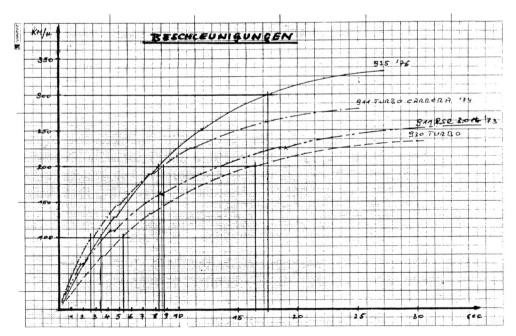

This page *The air/air intercooler of the original 935 was declared illegal by the CSI, as it interfered with the original contours of the engine cover. It had to be hastily replaced by the water/air installation shown below.*

Above *In the 935/77, 'aerodynamic aids' included the complete enclosure of the rear parts with a glass fibre cowl housing a flush-fitting, steeply raked perspex rear window.* **Below** *Engine of the 935/77. The twin turbochargers and waste gates are clearly seen, as well as the water/air intercooler surrounding the cooling blower.*

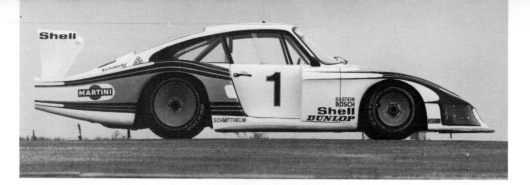

Top *The 935/78 with its lowered central section, 'four-valve' engine and hardly 'legal' partially cowled doors represents the final stage of 911 development for racing. Only one was built.* **Above** *The 935/2.0 'Baby' had an air/air intercooler and dispensed with any front radiator. Lightening included the use of front and rear aluminium tube subframes.* **Below** *The Kremer-prepared 935 driven by Klaus Ludwig won 12 out of the 15 races for which it was entered in 1979, including the Le Mans 24 Hours Race.*

only and turned out to lack flexibility to the point of being almost undriveable, which was made worse by gear ratios that were much too high — even when 16 inch diameter rear wheels were fitted instead of the planned 19 inch wheels. Cockpit ventilation was quite inadequate and on a blazing hot day Ickx eventually gave up the struggle. So Prof Fuhrmann had to postpone his demonstration, but in the following race, on the Hockenheim Ring, he proved his point with a vengeance and, after being some two seconds a lap quicker than anything in sight, Ickx walked away with the race, finishing half a lap ahead of his nearest follower.

The 'Baby', as it was called, never raced again. From the track, it headed straight for the Porsche museum where it now rests with only a nominal mileage to its credit.

The 935/78 'Moby Dick' and the four-valve engine

In 1977, numerous head gasket failures and the piston failure in the winning 936, 45 minutes before the end of the Le Mans 24 Hours race had forcibly reminded Hans Mezger and his engine development team that the still basically standard 911/930 engine was nearing the end of its development potential for racing. The higher power outputs obtained had been reached mainly by using a high super-charging pressure, but the piston crown and cylinder head temperatures had reached a level that could not be exceeded without loss of reliability. More power could only be obtained reliably by using four valves per cylinder and these in turn, for reasons of space, could only be cooled efficiently by the use of a liquid coolant which would also reduce the head temperature.

In order to incorporate these modifications, the engine was extensively redesigned to take entirely new, much flatter, watercooled individual cylinder heads sur-mounted by a common camshaft housing, each with twin overhead camshafts operating four valves per cylinder, all hollow and sodium-cooled. Gear trains replaced the timing chain, but the cylinders remained air-cooled and both the crank-shaft and crankcase remained standard 930 Turbo. Much less cooling air being required than before, a reversion was made to a normal vertical 911-type cooling blower, though of smaller size, making room for accessories on top of the engine. One reason for not cooling the cylinders with water as well as the heads was that the Group 5 regulations required the use of the standard cylinder castings, while the combination of the air-cooled cylinders and individual cylinder heads made it pos-sible to do without a head gasket, the two components being electron beam welded to form a single unit. This was impossible with the two-valve heads as the larger and more inclined valves cannot be inserted after welding.

The 'four-valve' engine was laid down in several sizes, of which the 2.1 litre and a 3.2 litre version were first built for use in the Group 6 prototype (936) and in the Group 5 (935) car, later followed by the 2.65 litre, methanol burning 'Indianapolis' engine. The 3.2 litre engine has bore and stroke dimensions of 95.8 x 74.4 mm, the crankshaft being a selected standard part from the 3.3 litre Turbo. Compared with the two-valve engine, the compression ratio is raised from 6.5 to 7.1 and the valves, which have an included angle of 30°, have a lift of 10 mm and a head diameter of 35 mm for the intake valves and 30.5 mm for the exhaust valves. The single plug per cylinder is located at the top of the pent roof combustion chamber and the fixed timing, high capacity discharge electronic ignition system has its contactless trigger driven off the driven end of the right-hand intake camshaft, while the distributor is driven symmetrically off the left-hand camshaft.

The 210 mm diameter cooling fan is belt driven at 1.34 times crankshaft speed and absorbs only 4 bhp at the engine's maximum speed of 8,200 rpm.

The twin turbo turbocharging installation is similar to the fully air-cooled engine's, but with the intercoolers back on top of the intake stacks, as in 1976, because the plenum chamber effect of the installation had proved beneficial to the throttle response, and the valve timing too is very similar to the two-valve engine's, in which both the intake and exhaust valves remain open for 358 crankshaft degrees.

Compared with the fully air-cooled engine, the boost pressure is raised from 1.4 to 1.5 bar (from 20 to 21.4 psi) at which the 3,211 cc engine develops 750 bhp at 8,200 rpm. At the request of private entrants contesting the German National Championship, Porsche eventually built fully air-cooled 'two-valve' engines of almost the same size in 1979, which could be operated with a boost pressure of 1.6 and even 1.7 bar for short periods, such as a fast practice lap, producing around 800 bhp in that condition. But the big advantage of the 'four valver' is that, for an identical power output, the highest cylinder bore temperature is reduced from 280 to 200°C, which leaves the engine with a much greater safety and development margin, which Porsche used only partly by adopting a boost pressure only 0.15 bar (2.2 psi) higher than in the two-valve engines. Powering the lone 935/78 entered for the Le Mans race of 1978, it ran with the leaders most of the time, consistently leading the Group 5 contingent, but eventually lost a lot of time during the last six hours, when the pit

Power and torque curves of type 935/71, 3.2 litre 'four-valve' engine, with 1.3 bar (18.6 psi) boost, used in the Porsche 935/78 (left) and 2.14 litre 'four-valve' engine with same boost used in the Porsche 936/78 (right).

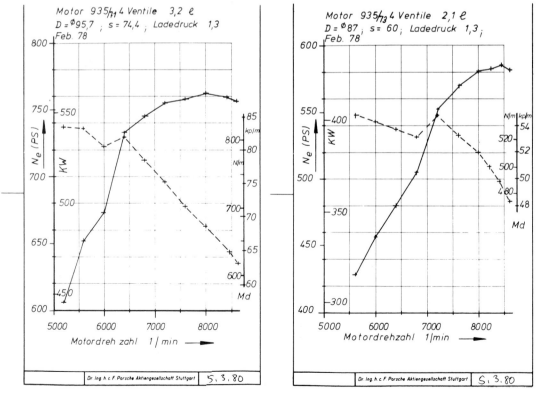

crew tried to locate an oil leak and the many pit stops and orders to drive gently because of a suspected crack in the crankcase dropped it to eighth place overall, headed in Group 5 by three other 935s of the older model. Only when the car was dismantled in the factory was it discovered that the leak was an insignificant one and the engine was, in fact, in excellent condition!

Specifications of the 2.1 litre four-valver, which in the Porsche 936 finished second overall that year at Le Mans and which uses a special short stroke (60 mm) crankshaft with 87 mm bore cylinders, will be found in the appendix.

A completely new sort of 935, called the 935/78, was built to take the new engine which the 1.4 turbocharging factor imposed by the regulations put in the 4,000 to 4,500 cc class. The choice of a 3,211 cc capacity was a deliberate one, for though it implies a minimum weight of 1,025 kg (2,260 lb), the car was specifically designed for Le Mans, where a high maximum speed on the long straight was considered to more than offset the 65 kg (143 lb) of ballast which eventually had to be carried.

The car itself, which had right-hand drive to make the best of the clockwise running on most circuits, made much better use than before of the facilities provided by the regulations, especially the rule allowing the floor to be raised up to door sill level. Full use could not be made of it, otherwise the headroom would have been insufficient, but Singer cut off the entire floor pan, replaced it with aluminium tubes welded to the roll cage to make a very rigid structure and added a glass fibre floor about three inches higher than the original steel floor. As the structures fore and aft of the bulkheads are free, Singer then dropped the body between the front and rear structures by the amount chopped off the bottom to lower the entire car by some three inches compared with the previous 935 version. It was a stroke of genius, quickly copied by many others, against which the ruling body was helpless.

He did not get away quite as successfully with another bright idea, when he discovered that the rules did not stipulate any limit to the forward extension of the rear aerodynamic aids and added cowls to the doors, widening them to be flush with the widened front and rear wings (fenders). In answer to this, the CSI decided that the rear of the car did not extend forward beyond the middle of the wheelbase. Finally a compromise was agreed on, leaving only the forward part of the cowl which had proved indispensable to obtain adequate rear down thrust with the body shape adopted, though the full width airfoil, mounted low to meet the frontal area regulation (the airfoil to be within the frontal area of the car) had to be abandoned, having proved inefficient with the reduced door cowlings. To meet the rules the new, higher mounted airfoil had to be reduced in width.

With the cylinder head radiators located ahead of the rear wheels, the dislodged intercooler radiators were replaced by a single radiator at the front of the car, just ahead of the engine oil radiator.

Though type 917 large diameter titanium drive shafts, incorporating very large Giubo couplings (doughnuts) were used on the 935 from the beginning, many 935s suffered drive shaft trouble in the 1977 Le Mans 24 Hours race, mainly caused by the large angles at which the rubber couplings had to transmit the driving torque. This was a direct consequence of the combination of a low ride height and the use of 19 inch diameter wheels, of which the hub was very high relative to the final drive output shaft. This was avoided in the 935/78 by turning the entire transmission upside down, which put the final drive shaft above instead of below the gearbox input shaft. The modification required new bell housing and transmission castings, as the crown wheel position could not be inverted in the existing one.

The front suspension geometry remained virtually unaltered, but the track was increased 125 mm to 1625 mm, allowing the static negative camber to be reduced to 1° 20′. At the rear, the production aluminium semi-trailing arms and steel trailing arms were replaced by single, forked fabricated aluminium semi-trailing arms of which the pick-up points were raised in accordance with the requirements of the 19 inch diameter wheels to reduce squat under acceleration.

More power, more weight and, as will be seen, a lower drag coefficient did nothing to facilitate stopping the car. Especially at Le Mans, for which the 935/78 had been specifically developed, brakes are submitted to a very severe test and this is the only race where the radially ventilated *and* transversely perforated discs were known not to last to the end. Porsche wanted to use perforated discs on the 935/78 at Le Mans because their lower temperature reduces the pad wear and because they are lighter. To achieve this, a long development programme was undertaken, taking advantage of the fact that the existing type 917 brakes had been developed to fit 15 inch wheels while the 935's front wheels were one inch larger. The final solution was a new, type 935 brake having a one-piece light alloy caliper, each with four 43 mm pistons, and a ventilated and perforated disc of 332 mm diameter and 32 mm thickness, mounted floating on the hub. These brakes, using Raybestos pads, proved to be absolutely trouble-free and at Le Mans their pads lasted longer than those of the type 917 brakes used in the much lighter type 936 cars.

Both the inverted transmission and the type 935 brakes were fitted to the batch of cars built by the factory for private teams at the end of 1978, but otherwise basically still twin turbo-engined 2.85 litre 935/76 models. Some of these were fitted with a 3 litre engine of 95 mm bore and ballasted accordingly and in the course of 1979 a 3.2 litre engine — still two-valve, air cooled — became available. Both were developments made by Porsche's racing service department in cooperation with Mahle, the cylinder and piston suppliers — not by the Experimental Department in Weissach.

The 935/78 is the fastest version of the 911 (technically, it is based on the 911 SC homologation rather than on the Turbo's, of which the rear spoiler puts limitations to the shape of the added rear glass fibre aerodynamic structure) made to date and it will probably remain so, though it must be admitted that very little remains of the basic model. Even with the only partial door cowling, the car had a drag coefficient $C_x = 0.358$ in Le Mans trim, 8.9 per cent better than the 935/77, and as the frontal area was also slightly less, the total drag was reduced by almost 10 per cent, with admittedly little front down force but notably more rear down force ($C_{Lf} = -0.01$ and $C_{Lr} = -0.375$), compared with the previous model. With an advantage of over 100 bhp over its 2.85 litre predecessor, the 1978 car was some 20 mph (32 km/h) faster on the Le Mans straight, having been timed at 227.5 mph (366 km/h) in practice and 222 mph during the race.

Performance of factory entered Porsche 935 in the Le Mans 24 Hours race

	935/76	935/77	935/78
Lap time in practice (min)	3.41.7	3.39.3	3.30.9
Lap time in race (min)	3.51.0	3.43.0	3.38.0
Speed on straight in practice (mph)	—	205.7	227.5
Speed on straight in race (mph)	199.5	201.0	222.0
Fuel consumption (mpg)	4.6	5.2	4.25
Place (overall)	4th	Retired	8th

Kremer's Le Mans winner

Though the 935/78, of which a single car was built, remains the most advanced elaboration on the 911 theme, it was a privately owned and prepared 935 which achieved what, for a long time, had been Porsche's greatest ambition: to win Le Mans with a production-derived model. In past years, the 120 litre fuel tank imposed on Group 5 cars had proved to be an excessive handicap and when Porsche decided to make a last-minute entry for the 1979 Le Mans race, only two Group 6 936 models with the four-valve engine were entered. Both were considerably delayed in the opening phases of the race and eventually retired, while the other Group 6 cars, including the official Ford entries powered by the Cosworth-Ford Formula 1 engine, which also ran into trouble, were no match for the very fast 3 litre engined 935 of the Kremer and Gelo teams. The latter eventually retired, but the Kremer cars finished first and third, with four Porsches — three 935s and one 934, all cars of 911/930 derivation — taking the first four places.

Though the winning car, driven by Klaus Ludwig and the brothers Don and Bill Whittington, is basically a 935 to 'customer' 1979 specification, the Kremer brothers, who specialise in the preparation of Porsche cars for racing, had actually built it themselves from bare components, trying to improve on the factory specifications wherever possible. The most visible modification made to the basic car is a complete redesign of the plastic material components grafted to the basic shell to improve the car's aerodynamics, mainly with the object of getting more down force, and the replacement of glass fibre with Kevlar which is both stronger and lighter, but also much more expensive. The most obvious feature of the new body are the 'fences' running along the outside edges of the front and rear wings to prevent lateral spilling of the air flow, and the 935/77-like tail extension.

A second important modification is the further increase in structural stiffness obtained by extending the aluminium tube roll-over cage to the front and rear suspension anchorages, which also allowed cutting off the rear cross member of the original body shell to replace it with bolt-on cross-braced aluminium tubes, greatly simplifying removing the engine and putting it back.

A third major modification is the reversion to an air-to-air intercooler which the Kremer brothers managed to fit, thanks to the revised bulkhead regulations of 1977. It is lighter than the water-to-air intercooler of the normal 935 and it provides a higher and more stable temperature drop, which is helped by the fact that the engine's cooling blower aspirates some of the air it circulates through the intercooler. To compensate for the pressure drop, it turns at a slightly higher speed than in the original car.

This, however, is the only modification made to the engine which, for Le Mans, was a 3 litre unit chosen for its anticipated greater reliability than the 3.2 litre's which was already available at the time and which the Kremer cars, called 935-K3 (K3 stands for Kremer Mk 3) used in many of the 1979 German National Championship races of which their driver Klaus Ludwig won 11 out of 12!

The 3.2 litre 'two-valve' engine is obtained by the combination of the 95 mm bore of the 3 litre and the 74.4 mm stroke of the production Turbo 3.3, which gives an exact capacity of 3,164 cc. With the 1.7 bar boost permissible for short periods, this engine develops a healthy 800 bhp, though 1.5 bar (21.4 psi) is the normal boost in a short or medium distance race, probably dropping the power to around 750 bhp. It is with a 3.2 litre engine using the normal 1.5 bar boost pressure and with the gearing used for typical modern circuits that the German magazine *Auto, Motor & Sport* obtained the acceleration figures for Ludwig's 935-K3, with Ludwig at the wheel. Though they were all taken from a 60 km/h (37 mph) rolling start in order to save the single plate clutch, the following standing start figures can easily be calculated:

                        0 to   60 mph in 3.0 sec
                        0 to 100 mph in 5.8 sec
                        0 to 120 mph in 8.1 sec

No new cars were built by Porsche for the 1980 season, but all parts and components remained available to anyone wanting to build up a new car or modify an existing model to 1980 specifications, which include the replacement of the water-to-air intercooler by an air/air intercooler similar to the one used in the Kremer car and the plastic body components required by the modification and comprising the appropriate air ducts. Some further development work was also done on the two-valve, fully air-cooled engine to solve the head gasket problem. Of the cars built outside the Porsche factory, two 935/78 'Moby Dick' replicas, but using a 'two valve' engine, built by the Joest Racing organisation, must be mentioned. One was successfully driven by Bob Wollek in German Racing Championship races and the other was bought by John Fitzpatrick who raced it in many endurance races of the 1982 season with David Hobbs as co-driver, the pair finishing fourth overall at Le Mans, behind the three works 956s, using a 2.65 litre version of the four-valve engine. This still 911-based engine won six Le Mans races in a row, though in 1987 it had been developed into a 3 litre, fully water-cooled unit.

The fully air-cooled, two-valve engine, however, still had not ended its racing career. As the type 956 Group C car did not meet the IMSA regulations, Porsche developed the type 962 racing car which, apart from its engine, was similar to the 956, but had a 12 cm longer wheelbase (2.77 m) to accommodate the pedals behind the front wheel centre line, as required by the regulations. As, however, the American regulations severely handicapped four-valve and twin-turbo engines, the 962 was originally powered by a single-turbo 2.85 litre, fully air-cooled engine developing 680 bhp at 8,200 rpm and a maximum torque of 660 Nm (487 lb/ft) at 5,800 rpm with a 20 psi boost. It was followed by a 3.16 litre yielding 720 bhp at 7,300 rpm and a massive 612 lb/ft torque at only 4,500 rpm, also with a 20 psi boost. A 3 litre version was developed when the rules limited the engines to that capacity. From 1977 to 1987, 911-derived two-valve, fully air-cooled engines won 11 Daytona 24 hours races consecutively.

The Group B 930 Turbo

All these efforts, however, were only stopgaps in expectation of the 1982 season, when completely new regulations were to be introduced by FISA. Under these regulations, three major Groups stand out:

1 Group A for production touring cars with at least four seats, a minimum yearly production of 5,000 units and a minimum weight based on the engine's capacity.

2 Group B for two-seater GT cars with a minimum yearly production of 200 units and a minimum weight based on the engine's capacity.

3 Group C for prototypes with a minimum weight of 800 kg (later increased to 850 kg) and a set of minimum and maximum dimensions. Engine type and size are free, power being governed solely by the 100 octane petrol allowance for the race distance.

Group B and C cars are allowed to take part in the Endurance Races of the World Championship series, which imposes no engine type or capacity limitations, as long as they use petrol of an octane rating not exceeding 100 and can finish the race on the maximum fuel allocation. In the years 1982 to 1985, the allocation was 600 litres for 1,000 km or

2,600 litres for 24 hours, reduced from then on to 510 and 2,210 litres respectively (but increased to 2,550 litres for 24 hours from 1987 on).

After the Porsche 956 had established its supremacy in Group C, the factory was anxious to provide its customers with a competitive Group B car. At long term, this was intended to be the four-wheel drive prototype exhibited at the Frankfurt Motor Show of 1983 (which later became the Porsche 959), but with cu.tomers knocking at the door, a quicker solution had to be found. The only possible one was to develop a car based on the 911 Turbo. Six of them were built for the beginning of the 1983 season and were entered for the Le Mans 24 Hours Race which four finished, winning Group B, one finishing eleventh overall. The winner was driven by the all-British crew of John Cooper, Paul Smith and David Ovey. At the end of the year, the FISA Group B Cup also fell to Porsche, in spite of strong competition from the faster, but less reliable BMW M1. In the following year, a Group B 911 Turbo finished second in the Group, behind a BMW M1, but with the advent of Group C2 (similar to Group C—which became C1—, but with a lower consumption and weight limit), the interest for Group B soon faded and the Group B 911 Turbo was not further developed. It served, however, as a base for an uprated version of the road-going 911 Turbo, developing 330 bhp, available from Porsche's 'Special Requirements' department. The modifications involved are described in Chapter 3.

Group B does not allow major modifications to be made and if these are applied to a 'bona fide' production car, rather than a 'homologation special', one ends up with a pretty near standard car. Consequently the 'interim' version of Porsche's 930 Turbo Group B car is a very close parent to the production 911 Turbo (or 930 Turbo as it is known internally) from which it is externally almost undistinguishable, except for its wider wheels and for the large oil cooler under the front bumper, replacing the smaller cooler normally mounted inside the right hand front fender.

Turbocharged Group B cars suffer a severe weight handicap, due to the fact that the turbocharger is technically supposed to increase the engine capacity by 40 per cent. This brings the 3.3-litre Turbo into the 5-litre class for which a minimum weight of 1,235 kg is required. This would allow the Group B Turbo to be raced with its full de luxe equipment, including radio and air conditioning, and still be not far off the weight limit. Consequently, little attempt is made at reducing weight, though the rear emergency seats are removed, the trim is simplified and floor mats are deleted, but some of the cars which ran at Le Mans still had the electric window lifters in place. Saving weight is, however, justified by the fact that ballast can be added in the right place to improve the weight distribution, and according to the saving 80 to 100 kg of ballast is carried in the passenger space's footwell, as far forward as possible. The only other body modifications are the fitting of the compulsory aluminium tube roll-over cage and the 100-litre safety fuel tank in the front 'luggage' compartment in which the McPherson towers are braced by a cross bar and to which the oil tank is also transferred.

The modifications to the engine, restricted by the regulations, are of a minor nature, the most important ones being the use of a larger intercooler and of a camshaft providing more valve overlap, but unchanged valve lift (intake 9.7 mm, exhaust 8.9 mm), no increase in lift being allowed by the regulations. The camshaft timing is as follows:

Inlet opens	60° btdc, closes 75° abdc
Exhaust opens	85° bbdc, closes 80° atdc

In addition, the wastegate is set to provide a 0.1 bar (1.4 psi) higher boost pressure than standard, the reference figure being 0.72 bar (approximately 10.5 psi) at 6,000 rpm and, as previously mentioned, the standard oil cooler located in the right front fender is replaced by a larger cooler under the front bumper. A further refinement is an air intake pipe aspirating the air directly under the grill provided in the (standard) rear spoiler and, to avoid cylinder head gasket problems, type 935 gaskets are used. Thus modified, the engine develops 320 bhp at 4,500 rpm, 364 bhp at 5,500 rpm and 354 bhp at 6,500 rpm, the maximum torque of 500 Nm (51 mkg or 369 lb/ft) being obtained at 4,500 rpm. This tremendous torque is transmitted through a type 935 clutch (with sintered metal linings) to a basically standard type 935 transmission incorporating either a limited slip differential or a solid drive and an oil pump circulating the lubricant in a cooler, as in the type 934. For more sensitive control and better reliability, the entire engine and transmission unit is solidly mounted in the body shell.

The alterations to the running gear permitted by the Group B regulations are few: the wheels and tyres must not protrude beyond the original fender openings; auxiliary springs are forbidden and the anchorage points of the suspension must remain unaltered in their location, although rubber may be replaced with solid material. Any alteration to the standard settings must be within the adjustment range provided by the manufacturer. For Porsche the fact that no auxiliary springs may be used is a problem insofar as torsion bars should never be thicker than the diameter of their splines, otherwise a stress concentration and consequent breakage will occur. Neither can the splines be enlarged, as any modified spring must be interchangeable with the standard one. In the case of the Group B car, the torsion bar diameter is increased at the front from 19 to 22 mm and at the rear from 26 to

Rothmans sponsored a three-car team, lead by Jacky Ickx, on the 10,000 km Paris-Dakar rally early in 1984. The specially prepared 911s had four-wheel drive and extra ground clearance.

27.5 mm. The standard front anti-roll bar is replaced by a bar with connecting links as used on early 911 and on the Turbo 3.0, but with the diameter increased from 18 (for the original Turbo) to 22 mm, while an adjustable bar of 18 mm diameter (as standard) is used in the rear suspension.

Porsche recommend Dunlop Racing tyres 245/575-16 front and 300/625-16 rear to be fitted to 9.5 x 16 ET and 11 x 16 ET wheels respectively. Measured with 50 litres of fuel in the tank and a weight of 80 kg on the driver's seat, the recommended suspension settings compare as follows with those of the standard car:

	Group B	**Standard**
Front		
Camber	−1°10′	0°
Toe-in	0°	0°
Castor	4°	6°5′
Height of wheel centre over torsion bar centre	135 mm	94 mm (racing car lowered by 41 mm)
Rear		
Camber	−45′	0°
Toe-in	15′ per wheel	10′ per wheel
Height of wheel centre respective to torsion bar centre	22 mm over	12 mm under (racing car lowered by 34 mm)

Obviously, stiffer dampers are fitted, with the rebound stiffness about half the compression stiffness at the front and two thirds at the rear.

Originally, the wheel brakes remained unaltered but, from the second half of 1983, larger brakes with 330 mm diameter discs of the type 935 became eligible with or without perforated discs. Porsche's recommendation was to disconnect the vacuum servo (which the regulations require to remain *in situ*) for better feel, but not every customer agreed with this recommendation and kept it working. An advantage of disconnecting it, however, was that parallel master cylinders operated through an adjustable balance bar could be used. The recommended brake pads were Ferodo DS 11.

The limitations of the regulations certainly made it impossible to obtain handling characteristics comparable to those of a full-blooded racing car or even a 935, but in this configuration, Roland Kussmaul, responsible for the car's development and also Porsche test driver, obtained a time of 60.9 seconds on Weissach's 'CanAm' circuit and the car's average time on the 193 m diameter skid pad was 19.95 seconds, equivalent to a lateral acceleration of 0.97 g. With the appropriate gearing, the car has a maximum speed of around 185 mph.

In April 1983, *Auto, Motor & Sport* took a set of acceleration figures on the first car to be completed, which eventually finished 13th overall at Le Mans and second in Group B, behind a similar model. Here is an extract from the set obtained, compared to the figures I had obtained for an earlier standard 3.3 Turbo:

0-100 km/h (62 mph)   4.5 sec (5.2 sec)
0-160 km/h (99.5 mph) 9.8 sec (11.4 sec)
0-200 km/h (124.3 mph) 15.8 sec (17.7 sec)

Unfortunately, the test does not indicate which gear ratios were fitted for the test, but as the car was raced at Monza in that period, it is most likely that the ratios most appropriate to that fast track were used.

Chapter Eight

The fabulous Porsche 959/961

Undoubtedly the most spectacular development of the 911 concept is the Porsche 959, together with its competition pendant, the 961. The car made its first appearance as an undeveloped prototype called 'Group B Studie' at the Frankfurt Motor Show of 1983, provisionally fitted with an engine of the type 935/77, as used in the Group C racing car. Its main technical features were announced as follows:

Base 911.
Four-wheel drive with variable torque split.
Rear mounted flat-six, 2.85 litre engine with air cooled cylinders, liquid-cooled cylinder heads with four valves per cylinder, twin compound turbochargers, 400 bhp.
Six-speed gearbox.
Double wishbone suspension front and rear with variable ride height.
Four shock absorbers per wheel.
Dunlop SP Sport 'Denloc' safety tyres on 17 in diameter wheels.
Widespread use of highly resistant plastic materials for body panels.
No-lift body shape with 0.32 drag coefficient.

Though the car was designed with the Group B regulations in mind, it was to be fully legal for road driving and as tractable as any other road-going Porsche. Two hundred units of the model were to be built, that being the minimum number required for homologation in Group B by FISA. It was expected that the road-going version would top 300 km/h (186 mph) and those who cared to enquire were told that the price would be around DM400,000 (approx £133,000), but long before the optimistic delivery date of late 1985 had been reached, 200 customers had put down the DM50,000 deposit required for an order to be taken into consideration. Meanwhile the final price had been fixed at DM420,000 (£140,000), and customers had to wait more than two years longer than expected, as the first cars were not delivered before the end of 1987. But what they got was worth waiting for: the car was even more powerful and sophisticated than originally announced . . . and meanwhile people who had not ordered the car before the 200 units were sold offered prices of up to one million Mark (£335,000) to those who had a firm contract. Initially, Porsche had intended to retain a certain number of the 200 cars built for further development purposes, but in view of the number of orders reaching them, they decided to sell the 200 cars and build a few more for their own use and for competition purposes.

There is little doubt that even at the astronomic price asked, the 200 Porsche 959s do not cover the development and manufacturing costs of the model. But a car which is not only the fastest offered by any established manufacturer for road use, but also by far the most technically advanced, brings considerable prestige. This is not only reflected on other

The Porsche 959 was developed from the 911 on the lines suggested by the 'Group B Study' shown in the 1983 Frankfurt Motor Show.

Porsche production cars, but is also bound to attract orders from the industry world wide for the Weissach Development Centre. Furthermore, a lot of development work which went into the 959 will be put to good use in future Porsche models.

The structure

As has been said, the 911 served as the base for the development of the 959 which retained its basic shape. But even with its aerodynamic accessories—the flexible front air dam and the rear spoiler—the 911 has a drag coefficient of just under 0.4, excellent for a shape designed in 1963, but not really up to date for a high grade sports car. Even with its aerodynamic aids, it is subject to—admittedly quite low—aerodynamic lift which was considered undesirable for a car which was to exceed 185 mph by a useful margin. It was also clear that the new suspensions and the proposed four-wheel drive would require a considerably modified floor pan, and to compensate for the weight of the technical sophistication, the largest possible number of body panels was to be manufactured either in aluminium or in highly-resistant plastic materials.

Most of the modifications to the body shape were developed in Porsche's own wind tunnel, first using scale models and then, at a more advanced stage, on full-size prototypes. First requirement was to achieve zero lift, even at the expense of increased drag. The aerodynamically unfavourably shaped 911 front bumper was replaced by a rounded shield of resilient polyurethane foam, as successfully used in the Porsche 928, and the integral rear aerofoil was shaped as a direct result of these tests. Drag was further reduced by bonding the windscreen flush with the body structure, the exterior mirror was optimised in shape, the rain gutter was deleted and the front fenders were reshaped around the headlights. The lower part of the wide front and rear fenders is linked by an aerodynamic 'running board' and the bottom of the car is aerodynamically optimised. While the zero-lift target has been achieved, the drag coefficient of 0.31 of the final model betters the predictions by 1 point. The width of 1.84 m (72.4 in) dictated by the width of the tyres exceeds that of the 911 Turbo by 65 mm (2.5 in), but as the ride height is automatically lowered as the car gathers speed, it is also 30 mm lower than the Turbo, so that its frontal area of 1.92 m^2 (20.66 sq ft) is very similar and the air drag is reduced by some 25 per cent. In its final form, the car is even subject to a slight aerodynamic down force.

As in the 911, the structural shell of the 959 is made of zinc-coated sheet steel and forms a highly crash-resistant cell. The doors and front compartment lid, however, are aluminium, while the rest of the exposed parts is moulded in Aramid and fibreglass reinforced resins, except for the aforementioned polyurethane foam front shield. In the complete, dry car, steel accounts for only 49 per cent of the total weight. This compares with an average of 72 per cent of steel in European passenger cars built in 1985.

The interior is almost identical to that of the 911, except for the higher central 'tunnel' over the propeller shaft driving the front wheels, standard leather upholstery and some additional instruments and controls.

The engine

The engine of the 959 was essentially developed from the successful type 935/76 engine powering the Group C racing cars 956 and 962C. As all Porsche flat-sixes, it is based on the 911/930 engine of which the crankcase, the crankshaft and the air-cooled cylinders were adopted almost unmodified. But the liquid-cooled, four-valve cylinder heads, the titanium connecting rods and the four gear driven camshafts are specific to the racing engine. In order to adapt the racing engine for road use, it had to be modified to achieve more silent operation and easier maintenance. Apart from increasing the capacity from

Porsche 959 engine shown without turbochargers and air metering unit. The alternator is concentric with the cooling fan but driven at higher speed by a separate V-belt.

2.65 to 2.85 litre by the adoption of slightly increased bore and stroke dimensions, the most important differences between the Group C and the 959 engine are the following:

The four camshafts are chain-driven, in a way similar to the drive in the type 911/930 engines.

The individual cylinder heads, electron-beam welded to the cylinders in the racing engine are replaced with one-piece heads with three combustion chambers for each row of three cylinders. A ring gasket is used between the combustion chambers and their cylinder and the heads are liquid-cooled, as in the racing engine.

The valves are operated via hydraulic self-adjusting tappets.

In view of the three-way catalyst to be fitted to some of the cars delivered, all the engines are tuned to use 95 octane, lead-free 'Eurosuper'.

The most remarkable feature of the engine, however, is its compounded turbocharging installation. To describe it in a few words, the principle is that the engine is fed by two turbochargers towards one of which the exhaust gases of all six cylinders flow as long as the engine speed lies below approximately 4,000 rpm, after which the gases of one row of three cylinders are rerouted towards the turbine of the second turbocharger.

By directing the engine's entire exhaust gas energy to the turbine of only one comparatively small turbocharger in the lower engine speed range, a quick build-up of the boost pressure is obtained together with short turbo response. This results in good low and medium speed torque characteristics. In the higher speed ranges, however, the volume of the exhaust gases would be more than the single small turbocharger could deal with, resulting in a loss of efficiency due to excessive exhaust back pressure and inefficient pressure build-up in the compressor. Before this condition is reached, as the engine revolutions rise, the second turbocharger is progressively brought into action by rerouting the exhaust gases of one group of cylinders towards its turbine. At full throttle, from about 4,200 rpm on, the two turbochargers, located on the left and right hand side of the engine, are each fed from the corresponding bank of three cylinders. A balance pipe connects the pressurised intake pipes feeding the two banks. The vacuum operated valves controlling the route taken by the exhaust gases and the wastegate are governed by a microprocessor.

The following example illustrates the advantage provided by the compound system: if, at a steady engine speed of 2,500 rpm in 3rd gear (50 mph), the accelerator pedal is suddenly floored, the boost pressure rises to the maximum, wastegate controlled pressure of 1 bar (14.2 psi) within only 2 seconds while, with the more usual parallel twin turbo installation, it takes 6.5 seconds to achieve the same pressure build-up.

The two turbochargers have water-cooled bearings and the compressed air is fed from each turbocharger to an intercooler located in the rear part of the rear wheel arches. The precise working mode of the installation is described hereafter.

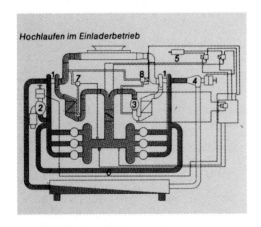

Porsche compound turbocharging installation. 1. Turbocharger. 2. Wastegate. 3. Compressed air valve. 4. Turbine valve. 5. Damping valve. 6. Exhaust cross pipe. 7. Recirculating valve. 8. By-pass valve.

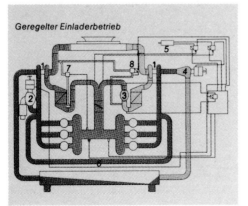

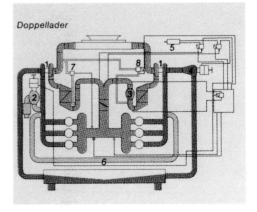

First cycle—lower revolution range

The entire exhaust gas volume and the entire air intake volume flow through the left hand turbocharger until the required boost pressure is reached. The turbine (4) and compressed air valves (3) are closed. The exhaust gases of the right hand row of cylinders flows through the cross-pipe (6) towards the left hand turbine. The right hand turbocharger idles. The wastegate (2) is closed.

Single turbo operation

If the required boost pressure has been obtained, but more exhaust energy is available than required by the turbocharger, the turbine valve (4) opens to allow the passage of the excess exhaust gases as required not to exceed the maximum permissible boost pressure. At this stage, it assumes the function of the wastegate (2) which remains closed. Thanks to the opening of the turbine valve (4), exhaust gases flow through the turbine of the right hand side turbocharger, which begins to rotate. However, as the compressed air valve (3) remains closed, the air flow from the right hand compressor is fed to the intake side of the left hand compressor.

From single to twin turbo operation

When engine revolutions and load are sufficient to feed both turbochargers with enough exhaust energy, the right hand turbo is put into action by opening the turbine valve (4) completely and closing the by-pass valve (8). The right hand turbocharger accelerates to full speed and the pressure built-up by the right hand compressor opens the compressed air valve.

Twin turbo operation

The two turbochargers share the exhaust energy and the compressed air output equally. The redundant exhaust energy is released by the wastegate (2) which controls the boost pressure by releasing exhaust gases as required. The turbine (4) and compressed air (3) valves are fully open. The by-pass valve (8) is closed.

Within the limits dictated by its overall measurements, adjusting the engine capacity of 911-type or derived engines is easy, thanks to the individual cylinders. For the 959, the 2.85 litre capacity was chosen because, for incorporation in the various capacity classes, at the time the car was designed, FISA's equivalence formula multiplied the actual capacity of a supercharged engine (however the intake pressure is obtained) by 1.4. This meant that with a real capacity of 2.85 litres, the 959 fitted into the 4 litre class for which a minimum weight of 1,100 kg was required. Exceeding that capacity would have pushed the minimum weight required to 1,235 kg which, in the case of a stripped and lightened racing version, the Porsche engineers felt confident they could undercut. From 1988, the equivalence factor was changed from 1.4 to 1.7 and the weight scale was revised.

To obtain the 2.85 litre capacity, bore and stroke dimensions of 95×67 mm were chosen (the dimensions of the 2.65 litre Group C engine were 92.3×66 mm). As in the racing engine, the connecting rods are titanium forgings and entirely polished. The forged crankshaft is made of chrome-molybdenum steel (31 Cro Mo V9) and gas-nitrided. The very short forged aluminium alloy pistons carry three rings of which the lower one is an oil scraper. The two 35 mm intake and two 32 mm exhaust valves per cylinder form an included angle of 28° and are closed by twin concentric springs. The exhaust valves are filled with sodium for better heat dissipation. The valve gear includes maintenance-free hydraulic tappets which operate reliably up to 8,400 rpm. As the large diameter valve heads leave little room for the sparking plugs, this led to the use of a 12 mm instead of the more

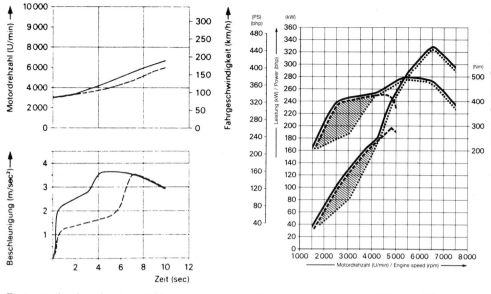

Engine speed and acceleration with Porsche compound turbochargers, compared with parallel twin turbochargers (4th gear).
Plain line: compound turbochargers
Dotted line: parallel turbochargers.

Power and torque curves of Porsche 959 engine compared.
Plain line: Porsche compound system.
Dashed line: single turbocharger.
Dotted line: Parallel twin turbochargers.

usual 14 mm brand. Valve lift is 10 mm for both intake and exhaust and the timing is as follows:

Intake opens/closes	28° before tdc/68° after bdc
Exhaust opens/closes	72° before bdc/24° after tdc

The four camshafts are driven by two two-row chains (one chain per head), each chain having its own guiding rail and hydraulic tensioner. Surprisingly, the development of the chain drive was the hardest task the engineers had to face in the development stages of the engine. The plugs are exactly in the cylinder centre line and, as in the racing engine, two injectors per cylinder inject the fuel into the intake pipes. The quantity of fuel injected is controlled by a Bosch digital electronic processor (Motronic) with overrun cut-off, governed by an air pressure sensor in the tranquillisation chamber of the intake system, and corrected by inputs from various sensors recording the engine oil temperature, the intake air temperature, the coolant temperature, the barometric pressure and other parameters. The ignition timing is controlled by the Motronic in a similar way and also reacts to a knock sensor.

The dry sump lubrication system comprises one pressure and five scavenge pumps (two of them for the twin turbos) with seven pick-ups in order to obviate oil splash under the hardest longitudinal and lateral accelerations. There are two oil coolers in the front of the car while the oil tank of the dry sump system is housed behind the right hand door, as in 1972 model 911s.

With a 8.3:1 compression ratio and 0.9 bar (12.8 psi) boost, the engine develops 331 kW (450 bhp DIN) at 6,500 rpm and a highest torque of 500 Nm (51 mkg or 369 lb/ft) at 5,500 rpm:

The transmission

The Porsche 959's four-wheel drive system allows instant torque split variations to be performed manually or automatically to suit the prevailing driving conditions. In contrast to most permanent four-wheel drive systems, there is no differential to split the torque—equally or not—between the front and rear wheels. In the 959, the engine torque is transmitted through a dry single plate clutch and a newly developed 6-speed gearbox with Borg-Warner synchronizers to the rear axle differential of which the slip can be limited by an hydraulically operated multi-plate clutch (of which more later). So far, the transmission does not differ in principle from the standard 911 transmission. But in the 959, the forward end of the gearbox output shaft drives a propeller shaft, itself driving a front differential unit of which the housing is connected to the front end of the gearbox by a large diameter tube through which the propeller shaft runs (what Porsche call the 'transaxle tube'). But before the torque reaches the front crown wheel and pinion unit, it goes through a multi-plate clutch of which the pressure between the discs can be varied from zero to fully locked. This clutch has two distinct functions: it adjusts the amount of torque transmitted to the front wheels, and by slipping it allows the front and rear axles to run at different speeds when the car corners.

If, in a straight line, the front and rear wheels were running at exactly the same speed,

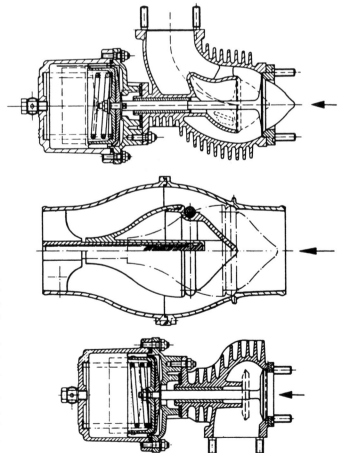

Top: *Turbine cut-in valve in Porsche two-stage turbo controls charge-air pressure when only one turbocharger is operating, and cuts in second turbocharger by opening.* **Middle:** *Compressor cut-in valve in Porsche two-stage turbocharging system. It operates as a non-return valve, opening when pressures up- and down-stream of the valve are equal.* **Bottom:** *Wastegate in Porsche two-stage turbocharging controls charge-air pressure when both turbochargers are operating.*

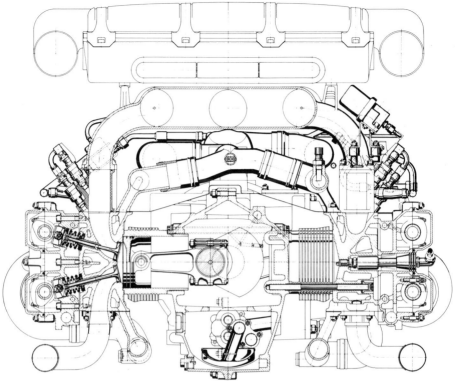

Above *Cross-section of type 959 engine.*

Below *Longitudinal section of type 959 engine.*

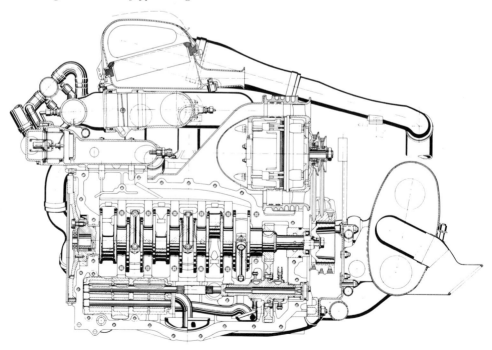

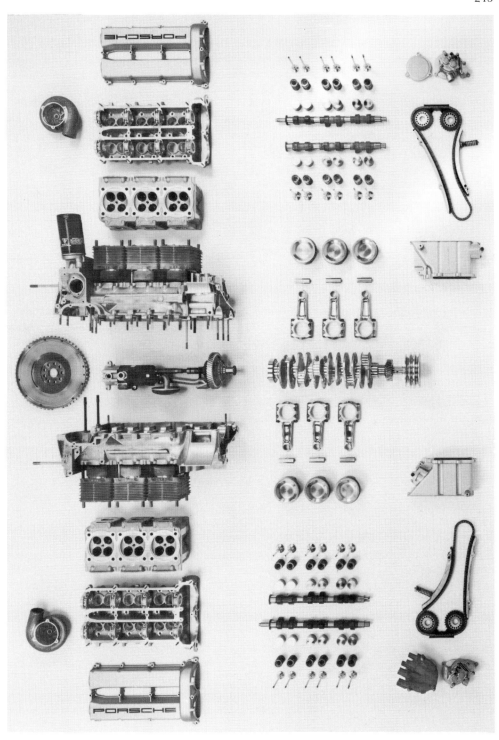

Components of 959 engine.

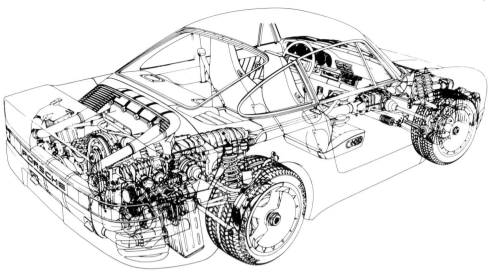

'Ghost' drawing of Porsche 959

varying the pressure on the plates of this clutch would have no influence on the torque transmitted to the front wheels. For the pressure variation to have an effect, the front wheels must always be positively driven, which means that they must run slower than the rear wheels. Under hard acceleration, this would always be the case, due to the slip of the directly-driven rear wheels, but to achieve this under all circumstances, the Porsche uses front tyres with a rolling radius approximately 1 per cent larger than the rear tyre radius. In a straight line, the driving plates of the clutch run thus at a speed at least 1 per cent higher than the driven plates. There is consequently a minimal permanent slip and varying the pressure between the plates allows continuously variable adjustment of the torque transmitted. The permanent clutch slip obviously causes wear and produces heat, an obvious indication that power is being wasted. However, except when the driver selects 'Traction' in a case of emergency, the torque transmitted to the front wheels is governed never to exceed 40 per cent of the total, so the 1 per cent difference in the rotational speed of the driving and driven plates results in a power absorption which, in the worst conditions, never exceeds 0.4 per cent of the power developed by the engine. This is considerably reduced under full acceleration, when only 20 per cent of the torque is transmitted to the front wheels. As for the wear, the clutch is so dimensioned that—according to Porsche—it is negligible.

The hydraulic pressure required to operate the front drive clutch as well as the clutch controlling the rear differential is provided by an engine driven pump and a conventional membrane pressure accumulator. The pressure governing the clutch action is controlled both manually and by a microprocessor. A stalk under the steering wheel gives the driver a choice of four modes. In the 'Traction' mode, both the front drive clutch and the clutch controlling the rear differential are fully engaged, locking the transmission solid. It should be used only in emergencies, to get the car out of deep snow, mud and other difficult situations. In the 'Ice + Snow' mode, the torque distribution is 40/60 front/rear, which approximately matches the car's static weight distribution and remains constant, as under those conditions little dynamic influence can be expected. With this distribution the best traction is obtained without interference from a solidly locked transmission. In the 'Rain' and 'Dry' modes, the basic torque distribution remains 40/60, but is varied as acceleration causes dynamic weight transfer, increasing the load on the rear and decreasing it on the front wheels. Under full acceleration, the torque transmitted to the front wheels is decreased to 20 per cent with 80 per cent of the torque transmitted by the rear wheels, but the law governing the variations is different in the two modes.

The torque split variations are governed by a microprocessor which calculates the acceleration from the throttle opening, the engine revolutions and load and the gear ratio engaged. Nevertheless, should the rear wheels begin to spin, this is instantly detected by the sensors carried by the wheel hubs and combined with the brake anti-lock sensors, which, whatever the mode engaged, feed the excess torque to the front wheels. Even at constant speeds, the microprocessor matches the torque split to the power transmitted, as for instance when the car is driven up a steep slope. The clutch limiting the freedom of the rear differential is also activated in function of the torque transmitted and immediately reacts to spin. At very low speeds and light load, the two clutches are completely released, so as not to interfere with manoeuvring. Gauges on the instrument panel give information on the operation of the two controlling clutches.

Running gear
a) Anti-lock brakes

The 959 is not only by far the fastest, but also the heaviest member of the 911 family, which puts very high requirements on the braking system. As for the 911 Turbo, Porsche has met them with techniques developed for racing. The 8 in wide front and 10 in wide rear magnesium wheels of 17 in diameter have made possible the use of front brake discs of 322 mm diameter and 32 mm thickness, the rear discs being of 308×28 mm. They are

Dry sump lubrication of 959 engine. 1. Pressure pump. 2. Scavenge pump. 3. Pressure relief valve. 4. Oil filter. 5. Pressure limiting valve. 6. Camshaft. 7. Cam lubrication jet. 8. Hydraulic tappet. 9. Crankshaft. 10. Jet to piston bottom. 11. Layshaft. 12. Piston. 13. Chain tensioner. 14. Sensor for thermometer. 15. Sensor for oil pressure gauge. 16. Turbocharger. 17. Scavenge pump for turbo. 18. Scavenge pump for cam box. 19. Thermostat. 20. Oil cooler. 21. Oil tank.

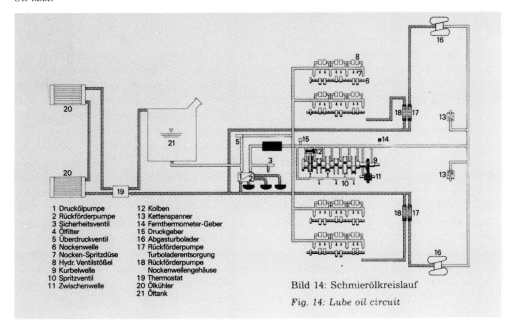

1 Druckölpumpe	12 Kolben
2 Rückförderpumpe	13 Kettenspanner
3 Sicherheitsventil	14 Fernthermometer-Geber
4 Ölfilter	15 Druckgeber
5 Überdruckventil	16 Abgasturbolader
6 Nockenwelle	17 Rückförderpumpe
7 Nocken-Spritzdüse	Turboladerentsorgung
8 Hydr. Ventilstößel	18 Rückförderpumpe
9 Kurbelwelle	Nockenwellengehäuse
10 Spritzventil	19 Thermostat
11 Zwischenwelle	20 Ölkühler
	21 Öltank

Bild 14: Schmierölkreislauf

Fig. 14: Lube oil circuit

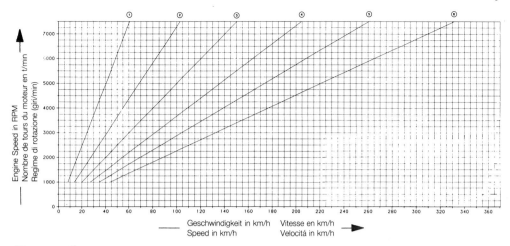

Engine speed/car speed diagram for Porsche 959.

internally ventilated, but holed only in the 'Sport' version of the 959 because the perforated discs are noisier. The four-piston aluminium calipers are Porsche's own development and are identical front and rear.

There are twin diagonal high pressure brake circuits with separate pressure accumulators fed from an engine driven pump. They incorporate an electronic anti-lock system developed by Wabco (Westinghouse patents) in co-operation with Porsche, with sensors on all four wheels. Its sensitiveness is such that it operates even when all clutches are locked, the elasticity of the transmission components being sufficient for the sensors to operate. Thanks to the slight aerodynamic down force acting on the car at speed, Porsche have measured on dry, grippy asphalt, an average deceleration of 1.27 g from 300 km/h (186.5 mph), corresponding to a stopping distance of 279 m (915.5 ft.).

b) Suspension

Quite early in the development period it became clear that to reduce the torque/steer effects, the offset of the wheel centre plane to the pivot axis at hub level would have to be kept small, which is impossible with a strut-type suspension when very wide wheels and tyres are used. This led to the adoption of a double wishbone suspension which was tried out as early as January 1984 in the successful Paris–Dakar cars. A similar suspension is also used at the rear, the 911-type semi-trailing links being considered an inadequate compromise solution for such a fast car which was also to have a suspension travel long enough to provide adequate comfort, without the penalty of toe-in changes.

The performance of the 959 requires firm suspension damping at high speeds, but Porsche was reluctant to put up with excessive harshness at low speeds. The problem was solved by the use of manually and automatically adjustable dampers, also providing for manual and automatic ride height adjustment. Normal ride height is 12 cm (4.7 in), but ride heights of 15 and 18 cm (5.9 and 7.1 in) can be selected manually in case the car is driven over very bad roads or high snow or ruts. But for safety reasons, whatever the height chosen, the car automatically returns to 15 cm as its speed reaches 50 mph and to 12 cm as 100 mph is attained, as the higher ride heights impair the stability and increase air drag.

Each wheel is controlled by two dampers. One of them contains an electric motor operating the damper's valve system of which the base adjustment can be chosen by the driver from three different positions, but is automatically varied electronically according to the car's speed. The second damper takes care of the ride height adjustment, in addition to its normal damping function. The hydraulic power is provided by an engine driven four-piston pump feeding the fluid to pressure accumulators and maintains the system at a pressure of 120 bar (1,700 psi). The ride height is also automatically adjusted in function of the load carried, but a quicksilver switch sensitive to lateral acceleration prevents corrections when cornering, so that roll control is achieved exclusively by the metallic road springs and the anti-roll bars. A further advantage of the twin damper system is that each damper does only half the work, and thus has a longer life. Anti-roll bars are provided front and rear, both of the link-type, the front bar arrangement being very similar to that of early 911 models. As a suspension medium, the 911's torsion bars have been replaced with coil springs, concentric with one of each wheel's damper, which saves weight.

c) Wheels and tyres

When the 959 project was initiated, tyres for road-going cars capable of around 200 mph—independent tests proved the 959 to be 197 mph fast—just did not exist. Racing tyres would certainly have met the speed but would not have met the comfort requirement and would have had a much too short life. As Porsche was determined to use Dunlop's 'Denloc' system which prevents a flat tyre from leaving the rim and allows driving on a deflated tyre over a distance of around 100 miles at moderate speed, Dunlop was approached to develop an appropriate tyre. But some time later, on its own initiative, the Japanese Bridgestone company took up the development, using an uprated 911 Turbo, weighted to simulate approximately the weight distribution of the 959, as a development car. As they came up with a satisfactory solution earlier than their competitor, the Bridgestone R 71 tyre was chosen as original equipment, though the Dunlop brand was eventually approved at a later date. The 'Denloc' patent problem was easily solved because both Dunlop and Bridgestone are now part of the Sumimoto Bank empire.

The tyres have a very low profile, almost as low as racing tyres, their exact sizes being 235/45 VR 17 front and 255/40 VR 17 rear, mounted on 8J 17 and 10J 17 rims respectively. The rims have the special 'Denloc' cross section and the possibility of driving the car over a reasonable distance on a flat tyre is very important as, in the interests of the luggage accommodation, the 959 does not carry a spare wheel. A very important safety feature originally developed for racing and used by Porsche at Le Mans from 1981 on, is the tyre pressure monitor. It comprises two membrane pressure switches per wheel, mounted on the inside of the rim. Every time the pressure switches pass across the field of a high frequency emitter in the wheel housing, a microprocessor gets a signal. If the pressure drops 0.2 bar below par, the switch opens and as the signal frequency is halved, the microprocessor triggers both an acoustic signal and a warning light indicating which tyre is at fault.

As the spokes of the magnesium alloy wheels are hollow and communicate with the rim, any leak caused by a crack in the spokes is also immediately signalled. As the hollow spokes increase the volume of air on which the car rolls, they should also provide a small increase in ride comfort.

Steering and accessories

The three piece, safety steering column is similar to that of the 911, but the pinion of the rack and pinion steering mechanism, borrowed from the Porsche 928 S, is offset to the left to make room for the power steering pistons. The system is entirely conventional and has its own engine driven hydraulic pump.

It was not an easy task for Manfred Bantle (of Porsche 908/03 racing car fame) who led the 959 project, to accommodate so much technology in a car of a 911's size. Even with the

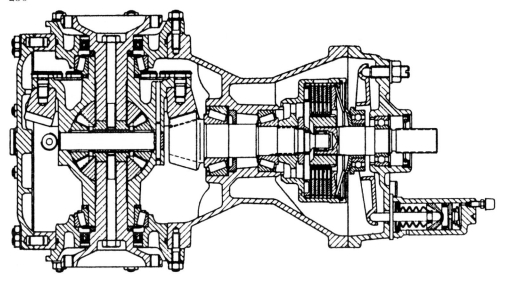

Above *Variable pressure multidisc clutch controlling torque transmitted to front wheels in type 959.*

Below *Left: Dunlop-Denloc safety wheel. Top: Cross-section of the safety tyre. Middle: Anchoring of the uninflated tyre on the rim when cornering. Bottom: Tyre geometry when uninflated. Right: Porsche 959 safety wheel with central screw connection and air pressure control system for tyre and wheel.*

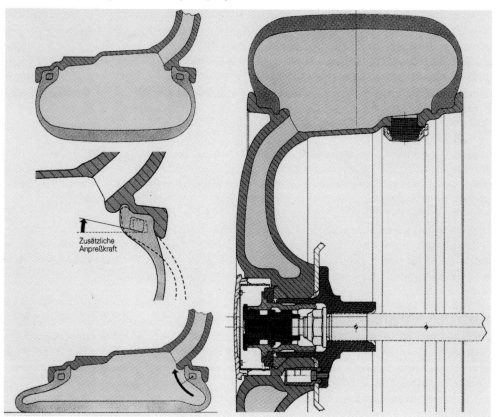

spare wheel deleted, the front luggage compartment is rather smaller than in a 911 as the water radiator with its twin fans and the large condenser of the air conditioner all had to find a place in the 'nose' of the car, not to mention the space taken up by the front clutch and differential unit. The fuel tank too had to be increased in capacity to 90 litres in view of the higher consumption when use is made of the available performance. The only simplification, compared to the 911 comes from the heating system which benefits from the availability of the water cooling system of the cylinder heads.

The 959 Sport

Whatever care is taken to save weight, a car carrying such an amount of advanced technology cannot be a lightweight. Originally, Porsche predicted a weight of 1,450 kg with full tanks, but this eventually turned out to be optimistic by anything between 150 and 200 kg. At a quite early development stage, however, it was decided to build two versions of the car, both featuring the sophisticated four-wheel drive and braking systems which are the 959's essential features, but of which one, called 959 Sport, would forsake the variable ride height and damping, the air conditioning, the electric window mechanism, the central door locking system and the right hand external mirror, and which would have lighter sports seats, operated manually rather than electrically. This model, which has stiffer springs and dampers to compensate for the lack of ride height adjustment and has a lower load carrying capacity, is supposed to weigh nearly 100 kg less than the fully equipped model—both selling for the same price. However, few customers felt inclined to sacrifice those comfort items to even higher performance, and only six 959 were ordered in the Sport version.

When it was tested by *Auto, Motor & Sport*, even this lighter model turned the scales at 1,566 kg (3,452 lb) with a full tank, the weight distribution being 41.1/58.9 front/rear. The performance figures obtained by the author and fully confirmed when *Auto, Motor & Sport* tested a different example are nevertheless devastating, with a maximum speed of 197 mph obtained by two-way electronic timing on Volkswagen's fabulous high speed test track and a standing start kilometre in 21.6 seconds. The full set is worth studying:

Maximum two-way speed 317 km/h (197 mph)
0–100 km/h (62 mph)   in 3.7 s.
0–160 km/h (99.5 mph) in 8.3 s.
0–200 km/h (124 mph) in 13.0 s.
Standing start km   in 21.6 s.
Standing ¼ mile   in 11.9 s.

On the same day, a fully equipped 959 did 314 km/h (195 mph), 0–99.5 mph in 9.5 sec and the standing kilometre in 22.2 seconds, but when the car went back to the factory, a fault was found in the compound turbocharging installation which caused the engine not to develop its full potential.

Racing for development

The development of the Porsche 959 took two years more than originally estimated—understandable as many of its features were still completely unknown quantities when development began. For Porsche it was unthinkable to start production before every one of the new features had been thoroughly tested in the most arduous conditions. And what better test than the strenuous Paris–Dakar rally—8,000 miles driving against the clock across the Sahara and African forests under the tropical sun? Fortunately, this is a rally for which prototypes are eligible and, encouraged by its star driver Jacky Ickx and helped by

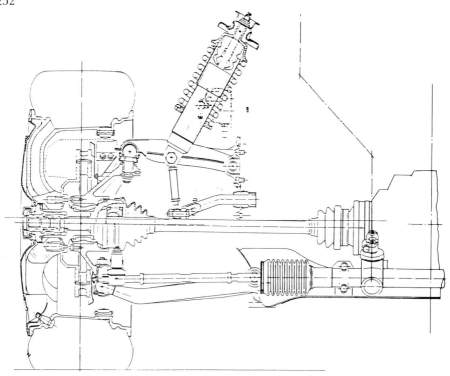

Front (top) and rear suspension of type 959.

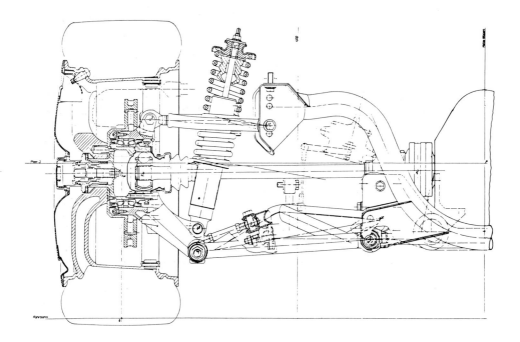

Above *As part of the final testing programme, a modified prototype of the 959 (type 961) was entered for the 1986 and 1987 Le Mans 24 Hours race. In 1986 it won IMSA classification and finished 7th overall (headed only by Group C Porsches), driven by Metge and Ballot-Léna, but it crashed in 1987. The photo shows the car in 1986.*

Below *The fully-enclosed engine keeps impeccably clean but access is difficult.*

Above *A pre-production 959 photographed in the French Alps during a 3,000 miles road test by the author in April 1987.*

Below *The cockpit and instrument panel of the 959 is almost pure 911, but instruments and controls are more numerous. The tyre pressure alarm with wheel identification can be seen in the second dial from left. On the right is the instrument indicating the drive programme (dry, rain, ice or traction) selected by operating a stalk on the right of the steering column. On the console, the switches for damper setting and ride height selection can be seen.*

The steeply-raked headlight glasses require comparatively high mounted washers. For aesthetic reasons, these are recessed and are raised by water.

the sponsorship of Rothmans, Porsche entered three cars for the event in three consecutive years. They were all development cars which, every year, came closer to the 959's final specification, except for the necessary adaptation required by the special desert conditions, such as a much increased ground clearance.

The first participation took place in the 1984 event with cars which were still essentially 3.2 litre 911 Carreras modified to four-wheel drive, as described in the previous chapter. In these cars, the system still featured a 'central' torque splitting differential. One of them, driven by René Metge, won the event and the others finished sixth and twenty-sixth overall. Except for an electrical short which left Ickx stranded for several hours, the cars displayed a remarkable reliability. The cars which started in the 1985 event were already much closer to the final model, not only in shape, but also as regards transmission (which featured the variable pressure clutch driving the front wheels) and suspension, but were still powered by a virtually standard Carrera 3.2 engine. Rear suspension failures delayed all three cars early in the event and two of them retired, one following an accident in which the car was not at fault. The faulty suspension part was quickly redesigned and flown in to be fitted to Metge's car which had regained the lead, when the oil pipe to the timing chain tensioner broke and the engine lost all its oil—a stupid breakdown, as the engine would have run without problem without this oil supply, which could have easily been cut by closing the pipe with a pair of pliers.

In the 1986 rally, the cars were almost to final specification, though extensively lightened and featuring the basically 'Sport' suspension without ride height control, but increased ground clearance. The twin turbocharged engines were slightly detuned in view of the inferior quality of the fuel available in the heart of Africa, but still developed 400 bhp. Metge and Ickx had no difficulty in finishing first and second, while Dipl Ing Roland Kussmaul who had been responsible for the development of the competitions versions, and drove a car burdened with spares for the entire team, still managed to finish fifth.

As a last test before the model went into production, one car was prepared to run in the Le Mans 24 Hours Race of 1986. Bearing the type number 961 (the competition version of the 959), it had been considerably lightened and weighed in at 1,169 kg with an empty fuel tank, which is approximately 330 kg less than the standard model. Apart from the deletion of the entire interior trim, it had a fixed ride height suspension, no damper remote and automatic control, no ABS, direct brake operation without power system, no power steering and—as all Porsche racing cars—no rear differential. Further weight had been saved by the use of almost paper-thin plastic body panels, Perspex rear and side windows etc. Externally, the car differed from the standard model mainly by a larger rear aerofoil, but under the plastic rear cover, the 2.85 litre engine was virtually to Group C specification, except for its one-piece cylinder heads topping three cylinders each. To save development time, the twin turbos operated in the parallel—not compound—mode, as in the Group C engine and the power was quoted as 680 bhp.

Though there had been no time to submit the car to an endurance test (as is current Porsche practice before a new model tackles an endurance race) and the car had been entered for the 24 hours race essentially as a development exercise, it acquitted itself extremely well. Driven by Paris–Dakar winner René Metge and Le Mans veteran Claude Ballot-Léna, it finished seventh overall, winning the IMSA classification. Its longest pit stop had taken 15 minutes when a rear drive shaft had to be replaced and it was headed only by Porsche 956 and 962C Group C cars. On its fastest lap it averaged 133.3 mph after eight hours racing (for comparison, the fastest race lap by a Group C Porsche was turned at 148.8 mph). On the straight, it was timed at a speed of 204.4 mph and its fuel consumption for the race was 51 l/100 km (5.53 mpg).

The Le Mans exercise was resumed in 1987, but with less fortunate results. Not only did the car retire, following an accident after 16 hours running, but also both its fastest lap and maximum speed were slightly inferior to those obtained at the first attempt.

Going into production following sporting successes in competitions so widely different as a trans-Sahara rally and an ultra-fast endurance race, the Porsche 959/961 has shown itself a worthy descendant of the 911, the most versatile sports car of all time.

Chapter Nine

The 911 Carrera 4 and future developments

A quarter of a century of painstaking development has not only kept the Porsche 911 in the running, but has made it one of today's most coveted and prestigious sports cars. Part of the credit for its lasting success must be given to the body's timeless shape, the brilliant work of Ferdinand Alexander Porsche, Professor Ferry Porsche's son, who has been just as successful in quickly establishing his own company, Porsche Design.

Meanwhile, there have been technical evolutions which could not be forecast a quarter of a century ago and which are not compatible with the current 911's structure, such as four-wheel drive and anti-lock brakes. Therefore, in its second quarter-century and without any major alteration to its external shape, the 911 will undergo a major redesign. The atmospheric models will be available with two or four wheel drive, though both models will share a common platform with a higher central tunnel to accommodate the transmission to the front wheels in cars so equipped. The higher tunnel will further increase the body's stiffness. In the suspension, small diameter coil springs wound around the front struts and the rear dampers will replace the torsion bars for the sake of reduced weight and easier serviceability. The revised steering geometry will feature a zero scrub radius to reduce brake steer effects for better compatibility with anti-lock brakes and the front wishbones will be cast in aluminium. The rear semi-trailing arms, also cast in aluminium, are of a completely new design and pivot around bushes automatically compensating for the toe-in variations caused by the deformation of the rubber. The rack and pinion steering is also new, the steering pinion having been moved from the centre to the side (left in left hand drive cars) of the aluminium housing to allow the incorporation of hydraulic power assistance which will be standard. In the four-wheel drive version, a high pressure brake system will replace the vacuum assistance and the future 911 will at last get rid of the cast iron brake calipers which it had to accept under Ernst Fuhrmann (from 1974 models on), to revert to aluminium calipers.

The general layout of the four-wheel drive system in the cars so equipped will be generally similar to the 959's, a so-called 'transaxle tube' linking the front differential housing to the front of the 5-speed gearbox. But it will not feature the 959's variable torque split system. Instead of this, the system features an epicyclic, torque splitting differential controlled by a multidisc hydraulically operated and electronically controlled clutch. The sensors signalling eventual wheel spin are combined with those of the anti-lock braking system. The torque split provided by the differential is 31/69 front/rear and the system implies the use of a hollow gearbox output shaft through which the shaft driving the rear wheels is led. In turn, this has required the central differential housing to be bolted to the nose of the gearbox instead of being combined with the front differential housing, as in the case of the multidisc clutch of the 959. An electronically controlled multidisc clutch is also used to limit the slip of the rear differential and a driver-operated switch locks both the rear and central differentials if necessary.

A lot of development work has also gone into the engine of the second generation 911, internally known as the type 964. The bore has been further increased to 100 mm and the stroke to 76.4 mm to raise the capacity to 3.6 litres, which in turn has required a redesign of the crankcase and a relocation of the studs holding the cylinders down. A further step towards raising the power to compensate for the increased weight of the new car and for the catalytic exhaust system is the adoption of twin ignition, as has been used in all racing engines of 911 derivation, except when regulations specifically forbade it. This together with improvements in the engine management system will raise the power to 250 bhp DIN with a maximum torque of 31.6 mkg (229 lb/ft).

The redesigned body structure also provides for a much improved heating and ventilation system, but optically, above bumper level, it remains the car Ferdinand Alexander Porsche designed more than 25 years ago. The only striking changes are to the bumpers, made of resilient plastic material, and integrated front air dam and rear skirt which have been reshaped to reduce aerodynamic drag. This, together with a few other detail improvements like the optimization of the floor pan and the closing of the rain gutters running along the windscreen pillars, has reduced the drag coefficient from 0.395 to 0.32, a considerable improvement indeed. But probably the most striking identification feature of the second generation is the 16 in diameter polished aluminium ventilated disc wheels, rather similar in style to those of the Porsche 928 S4. They will finally replace the famous five-spoke spider 'Fuchs' wheels which, ever since they appeared on the 911 S of 1966, were *the* wheels to have on a 911. As their offset is apparently not compatible with the new front end geometry, they will not be available on the second generation cars.

The existing 911 Carrera in all its forms will continue to be produced.

In the new car, Porsche have finally solved the problem of combining the much better high speed stability of spoiler equipped cars with the clean lines of those not so equipped. In the second generation models, the engine room's air intake grill assumes the function of the rear spoiler. In the lower speed ranges, it is flush with the engine room cover, but at higher speeds, an electric motor raises it to act as an effective spoiler.

The 911 Carrera 4 is to be announced in autumn 1988 in four-wheel drive version and will be built in a completely new, largely automatized body factory in Zuffenhausen. Meanwhile, the Carrera 3.2 litre will continue to be built in the existing body shop until the new one is fully operational. The two-wheel drive new generation car will be added at a later date, replacing the 3.2 Carrera and should become known as '911 Carrera 2'.

Meanwhile, the current 911 Turbo will be further developed, as the second generation Turbo is not scheduled to follow immediately into the atmospheric model's footsteps. Internally known as the 965, it will be based on the 2nd generation floorpan, but will differ much more from the atmospheric model than does the current 911 Turbo. It will incorporate many features developed in the Porsche 959, of which its shape will be reminiscent. Four-wheel drive will be standard while the power output of its twin turbocharged engine should be at least 350 bhp DIN which, thanks to the improved aerodynamics, should ensure a top speed of around 185 mph . . . with a price tag to match. This will also probably be the first car to be offered with the PDK twin clutch gearbox, with a control enabling it to be used in both automatic and manual mode. The drive through the PDK is entirely mechanical, which reduces power absorption, and ensures full two-pedal control and changes up and down without interrupting the drive, as is the case with current automatics but it is unlikely to be available at the time the car is launched.

As the 965 pursues its development, the most important modification to the 911 Turbo for 1989 is the adoption of a much needed five-speed gearbox, developed from the Carrera's type G.50 box as described in Chapter 4, while a minor suspension change is the replacement of the 26 mm rear torsion bars with 27 mm bars, the anti-roll bar being correspondingly reduced from 20 to 18 mm diameter.

Epilogue

When I wrote the epilogue to the 2nd edition, I did not think that there would ever be a third, let alone a fourth: the future of the 911 looked pretty grim in spite of the continued demand. After 16 years of production, Professor Fuhrmann who, at the time, was Porsche's Managing Director, had decided that it must make room for more recent Porsche designs such as the 928, the 924 and the soon to be announced 944. The 911 did not fit into his standardisation programme and he thought that there was no room in it for an air-cooled, rear-engined car. In our over-ruled, computerised world, ever stricter laws do not take such exceptions as rear-engined cars into consideration, cars leaving little space for such hardware as catalysts and in which the concentration of the engine and exhaust noise at one end of the vehicle makes it more difficult to meet existing and future regulations.

Meanwhile, however, the management has changed. Peter W. Schutz took over from Ernst Fuhrmann at the onset of 1981. He had the full confidence of Dr Ferry Porsche and suddenly the future of the 911 looked bright. The greatest part of the development budget for 1982 went to the 911 which, for the last four years, had been neglected. First the 'Cabriolet' version was produced, then intense development work started on new versions for road and track. The demand for the 911 is as intense as ever and the production is back to some 60 cars per day, more than two thirds of the Zuffenhausen production. Only the Neckarsulm-built 944 can rival it. I can personally vouch for the vivid attraction the 911 still exerts, for the two previous examples I have owned were stolen long before I ever thought of parting with them.

After more than 25 years of production, the plans for further developments are such that even before the fourth edition of *Porsche 911 Story* is printed, I feel sure that there will be a fifth. The enormous commercial success which the 911 has enjoyed during its long and continuing career, and its unique sporting successes, testify that conventional designs are not necessarily the best and only way to supreme achievement. What matters is logical thinking, intelligent development and the touch of genius without which no outstanding achievement has ever come about.

The Porsche 911 has become a classic in its lifetime. This ultimate development of the VW Beetle concept will stand in history as a tribute to the genius of three Porsche generations — remember Ferdinand Alexander Porsche gave the 911 its timeless shape — and to the team which developed it to become one of the world's truly great cars. I feel convinced that, under the management of Heinz Branitzki with Porsche for more than 20 years, the tradition will be upheld.

Paul Frère
Vence, France, 1988

Appendices

Above *The mechanical units of the 911 Carrera 4, showing the tube linking the power unit to the front differential. The torque splitting differential is contained in the 'nose' of the gearbox. Note the coil spring units.* **Below** *The 911 Carrera 4 has been aerodynamically optimized without any notable alteration of its basic shape.*

1 Porsche 911 genealogy, 1963–88

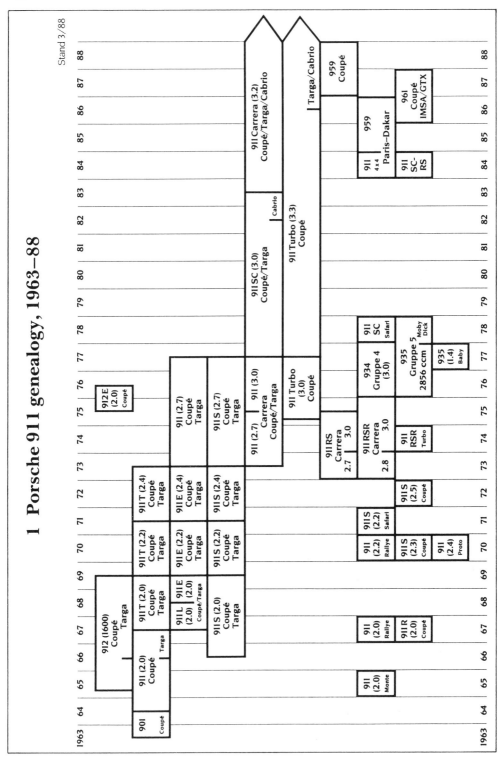

Stand 3/88

2 Porsche 911 genealogy — Production models

Model year	Type	cm³	hp	Number made	Description
12.9.63	901	1,991	130		Successor to type 356 announced at Frankfurt Motor Show.
1965–67	911 (2.0)	1,991	130	10,723	Type number changed to 911 following protest by Peugeot. 4.5 in wide rims. Wiper arms park on right. Oblique 911 script. Bumper overriders f & r. Six Solex overflow carbs. 5-speed gearbox. Round external mirror. *From model year 1967*: Targa body with soft rear window. Weber carbs.
1965–69 1967–69	912 Coupé Targa	1,582	90	30,300	Type 911 body and running gear with simpler equipment and 4-cylinder engine from type 356 SC with power reduced from 95 to 90 hp for increased flexibility. Max speed 112 mph.
1967–69	911S (2.0) Coupé/ Targa	1,991	160	5,056	As 911 (2.0), except engine (App 4), forged alloy wheels (Fuchs), anti-roll bars f and r, ventilated brake discs. *From model year 1968*: Semi automatic 'Sportomatic' 4-speed transm optional, black wiper arms, bumper horns replaced with rubber lining, 5.5 in wide wheels. *From model year 1969*: Plunger pump fuel inj, 170 hp, oil cooler in rh front fender, wheelbase increased to 2,268 mm, 6 in wide wheels, wider fenders, halogen headlights. Targa has fixed rear window and air exit louvres in rollover bar.
1968–69	911T (2.0) Coupé/ Targa	1,991	110	6,618	Replaces 911 (2.0), equipment and running gear as 912. No anti-roll bars. 4 speeds. *From model year 1969*: 5-speed gearbox.
1968	911 (2.0) Coupé/ Targa	1,991	130	11,610	Similar to previous 911 (2.0), but with equipment similar to 911S (2.0). 4- or 5-speed gearbox or Sportomatic.
1969	911E (2.0) Coupé/ Targa	1,991	140	2,826	Replaces 911L. Equipment similar to 911S (2.0). Plunger pump fuel inj hydropneumatic ride height control incorporated in front shock absorbers. No anti-roll bars.
1970–71	911T–2.2 Coupé/ Targa	2,195	125	15,082	Development of previous model with 4 ventilated brakes, 2 three-choke carbs. 4-speed or Sportomatic gearbox.
1970–71	911E–2.2 Coupé/ Targa	2,195	155	4,927	Replaces 2 litre version. Equipment as 911S–2.2. 4- or 5-speed or Sportomatic box.

1970–71	911S–2.2 Coupé/ Targa	2,195	180	4,691	5-speed gearbox, no Sportomatic, optional limited slip diff. USA with fuel tank vent and alarm system.
1972–73	911T–2.4 Coupé/ Targa	2,341	130	16,933	Third capacity generation. Runs on Regular fuel. New 4- or 5-speed gearbox, Sportomatic optional. 2 three-choke carbs. Oil filler behind r/h door (only 1972). No front bumper overriders. *USA*: Plunger pump fuel inj, 140 hp. *From 1973 model*: Black trim, rectangular ext mirror. Wheelbase 2,271 mm, rustproof exhaust. *USA*: K-Jetronic.
1972–73	911E–2.4 Coupé/ Targa	2,341	165	4,406	Equipment as 911T–2.4. Regular fuel, fuel inj. 6 in steel wheels. *From model year 1973*: front air dam.
1972–73	911S–2.4 Coupé/ Targa	2,341	190	5,094	Equipment as 911E–2.4. Regular fuel. Plunger pump fuel inj. 6 in alloy wheels, front air dam.
1973	911 Carrera RS 2.7 Coupé	2,687		1,590	Developed from 911S–2.4. First 911 'Carrera'. Three variants: Sport, Touring, Racing. Widened rear fenders, 6 in front, 7 in rear alloy wheels, 'Duck-tail' rear spoiler and front dam, rust-free exhaust.
1974–77	911–2.7 Coupé/ Targa	2,687		17,260	Replaces T and E models. Shock resistant bumpers, safety steering wheel, seats with integral headrest. K-Jetronic, 4-speed gearbox, clutch release aid spring, seat belts. 80 l tank. *From model year 1975*: Modified heat exchangers, 6 in cast alloy wheels. *From model year 1976*: 165 hp, 5-blade cooling fan, automatic cold start system, ext mirror, electrically adjustable and heated. Fully galvanized body shell carrying 6-year anti-rust warranty.
1974–77	911S–2.7 Coupé/ Targa	2,687	175	17,124	Equipment as 911–2.7. *From model year 1976*: Name 911S only in USA with 165 hp engine.
1974–77	911 Carrera Coupé/ Targa	2,687	210	3,353	Similar to Carrera RS 2.7, but with full equipment as 911–2.7, plus electric window lifter, ext mirror and headlight surrounds in car's colour. Wheels and fenders as RS 2.7, black trim. *For certain markets*: front dam and rear spoiler as Turbo. *From model year 1975*: headlight washers.
1974	911 Carrera RS 3.0 Coupé	2,994	230	109	Evolution of Carrera RS 2.7. Widened f and r fenders, as Turbo. 50 cars were modified to RSR spec for competition purposes.

1975–77	911 Turbo (3.0) Coupé	2,994	260	2,173	First turbocharged production sports car. Breakerless capacity discharge ignition system. Fuchs alloy wheels, 7 × 15 in f, and 8 × 15 in rear. Widened f and r fenders, large front air dam, rear 'tray' spoiler. 4-speed gearbox, 3-spoke steering wheel. *From 1977 model*: wheels 7 × 16 front and 8 × 16 rear with ultra-low aspect ratio tyres, brake servo, clutch release aid spring.
1975	912 E Coupé	1,971	90	2,092	New edition of the 912 after 6 years of production interruption. 2 l, 4-cyl pushrod engine with fuel inj comes from VW—Porsche 914-4. For export only.
1976–77	911 Carrera Coupé/ Targa	2,994	200	3,691	Replaces 911 Carrera 2.7. K-Jetronic 4-speed gearbox. 5-speed manual and 3-speed Sportomatic optional. *From model year 1977*: All three transmissions standard. Brake servo. Automatic heater control.
1978–83 1982–3	911 SC Coupé/ Targa Cabrio	2,994	180	57,972	Replaces 911–2.7 and Carrera 3.0. Power initially 180 hp. Fixed rear quarter windows, 11-blade fan. Cast alloy wheels 6 × 15 front, 7 × 15 rear, Fuchs forged alloy 6 × 16 front and 7 × 16 rear optional. *1980 model*: 188 hp. *From model year 1981*: Premium fuel, 204 hp.
1978– From 1986 Cabrio/Targa	911 Turbo Coupé	3,299	300	14,969*	Replaces 911 Turbo (3.0). Intercooler. Basic equipment as 911 SC and 911 Carrera (3.2). Higher rear spoiler. 4-speed gearbox. Fuchs wheels 7 × 16 front. 8 × 16 rear. *From 1980 model*: Twin exhaust pipes. *From 1985 model*: 4-spoke steering wheel. *From 1986 model*: 9 × 16 rear wheels. *From 1989 model*: 5-speed gearbox.
1984–	911 Carrera Coupé/ Targa Cabrio	3,164	231	61,327*	Replaces 911 SC. Foglights recessed in front dam. Low front dam and rear tray spoiler optional. Turbo-look option for Coupé with catalyst 207 hp. *From model year 1985*: Electric seat adjustment. Turbo-look option for Targa and Cabrio. *From model year 1986*: With catalyst 217 hp. *From model year 1987*: New 5-speed gearbox, hydraulic clutch operation. Integrated rear foglights.
1987–88	959 Coupé	2,848	450	200	Development exercise for future Porsche models. Production limited to 200 units.

* End March 1988.

Water-cooled, forged, cyl heads with
4 valves/cyl, air-cooled cyl, twin
compound turbochargers, polished
titanium conrods, hydraulic valve tappets,
4WD with electronically controlled torque
split, speed sensitive ride height variation.
6-speed gearbox.

Year	Model/Type	cm³	hp		Description
1989	911 Carrera 4	3,600	250	—	Redesigned 4WD version of 911. Coil spring suspension. Twin ignition.

3 Porsche 911 genealogy — Racing models

Year	Model/Type	cm³	Bore/Str	c/r	hp	Description
1965	911–2.0	1,991	80 × 66	9.8	160	First sporting event in which the 911 took part was the Monte Carlo Rally of 1965, driven by development engineer Peter Falk and test driver Herbert Linge. The car was homologated in the GT class and mild tuning had increased the power from 130 to 160 hp. A 100 l tank, larger brakes and a limited slip differential were fitted. The crew finished 5th overall. This was the beginning of the 911's exceptional sporting career.
1967	911S–2.0 'Rallye'	1,991	80 × 66	10	170	Rally version of 911S. Red finish, black interior, heated rear window with wiper, Catacolor glass, reclining co-driver's seat, 100 l fuel tank, exterior thermometer, Koni dampers.
1967	911R–2.0	1,991	80 × 66	10.5	210	Special 911 built exclusively for racing in small numbers. Carrera-6 engine. Weight 830 kg, thanks to spartan equipment.
1970	911S–2.2 'Rallye'	2,195	84 × 66	9.8	180	Rally version of 911S–2.2. Scored great successes in Monte Carlo Rally, Swedish Rally, Austrian Alpine Trial, RAC Rally. Winner Manufacturers Rally World Championship, 1970.
1970	911S–2.3	2,247	85 × 66	10.3	240	Circuit racing version of 911S–2.2 with 1 mm larger bore and 240 hp. Twin electric fuel pumps, plunger pump fuel injection, forged alloy 7 and 9 in wide wheels. A favourite of private entrants.
1970	911S–2.4 'Proto'	2,395	85 × 70.4	10.3	260	Specially built for Tour de France 1970. Dry weight 790 kg, twin Weber triple choke carbs, transistor ignition.
1971	911S–2.2 'Safari'	2,195	84 × 66	9.8	180	Special car for 1971 East African Safari.

Year	Model					Notes
1973	911 Carrera RSR (2.8)	2,806	92 × 70.4	10.3	300	Group 4 version of RS 2.7. These mostly privately-entered cars dominated the GT scene and won 7 out of 9 races.
1973–74	911 Carrera RSR (3.0)	2,994	95 × 70.4	10.3	315/330	Replaced the RSR 2.8. 50 units of the Carrera RS 3.0 were modified for racing and rallying. Major successes: 1st overall Targa Florio 1973 European GT-Champion, European Hill-Climb GT-Champion.
1974	911 Carrera RSR Turbo	2,142	83 × 66	6.5	450/500	In view of the forthcoming Group 5 based on production models, Porsche developed this turbocharged version from which the 935 was to be derived. One turbocharger, intercooler, mechanical port injection, 5-speed gearbox, no diff. Max. speed 187 mph. 2nd overall Le Mans and Watkins Glen.
1976–77	934 Turbo	2,994	95 × 70.4	6.5	485	Replaced Carrera RSR 3.0. Group 4 racing version of 911 Turbo 3.0. Limited number built for private entrants. *US version 1977*: 540 hp.
1976–77	935	2,857	92.8 × 70.4	6.5	590	Group 5 production racing car. Turbocharger and intercooler, mechanical port injection, 4-speed gearbox, no diff. Max speed 211 mph. *1977*: Twin turbochargers, 630 hp. Won Manufacturers World Championship for Porsche 1976 and 1977. A privately-entered (Kremer) 935 won Le Mans 24 Hr outright in 1979.
1977	935 Turbo 'Baby'	1,425	71 × 60	6.5	320	Developed from 935 to participate in 2 litre class of German Racing Championship. Weight 750 kg. Only two starts. J Ickx won in Hockenheim.
1978	935/78 Turbo 'Moby Dick'	3,211	95.8 × 74.4	7.0	750	Final development stage of 935 making the best of Grp 5 regulations. Improved aerodynamics, water-cooled 4-valve cyl heads, 4 camshafts, air-cooled cylinders.
1978	911 SC 'Safari'	2,994	95 × 70.4	9.1	250	For factory entries in 26th East African Safari Rally 1978. Plunger pump fuel inj, limited slip diff. Ground clearance 28 cm (11 in), reinforced running gear. Result: 2nd and 4th places.
1984	911 Carrera 'Paris-Dakar'	3,164	95 × 74.4	9.5	225	4WD Carrera specially modified for Paris-Dakar Rally. Plastic doors, front and engine bay lids and fenders. Fuel

						tankage 260 l. Result: 1st, 2nd and 26th, plus team prize.
1984	911 SC/RS	2,994	95 × 70.4	10.3	255	Twenty cars built as 'evolution' of 911 SC for competition purposes, mainly rallies. Plunger pump fuel inj. 40 per cent limited slip diff, aluminium front fenders, doors and front lid, GFK bumpers and air dam.
1985–86	959 Paris-Dakar					After failing in the 1985 Paris–Dakar Rally, the 1986 event was a triumph for
1985		3,164	95 × 74.4	9.5	230	the future 4WD Porsche 959. The
1986		2,847	95 × 67	8.0	400	three cars entered finished the gruelling event in 1st, 2nd and 5th places.

All competition versions of the 911 and derivatives were Coupés.

4 Major steps in the development of normal production 911 models

Model year (begins in August of previous year)

1964 911 production begins with single 2 litre, 130 hp Coupé model.

1967 Introduction of the 911 S.

1968 Wider (5.5 in) wheels. Targa introduced.

1969 Wheelbase lengthened from 2.211 to 2.272 m. Wheels widened to 6 in (except 911 T with steel wheels). Plunger pump fuel injection for 911 S and E.

1970 2.2 litre models.

1972 2.4 litre models. All cars detuned for 91 octane fuel. Floor pan partly galvanised.

1973 Introduction of Carrera RS 2.7 litre with widened rear wheel housings to accommodate 7J×15 wheels. First model with rear spoiler (duck's tail).

1974 2.7 litre models. K-Jetronic replaces plunger pump, except on Carrera.

1975 Introduction of 3 litre Turbo (running on 96 octane).

1976 Carrera 3.0 with K-Jetronic introduced. All cars with fully zinc-coated body (except roof for short period. Only one 2.7 model continued (165 hp).

1977 Air vents on dashboard.

1978 Range reduced to single 911 SC 3 litre model with Carrera-type rear wheel housings and 7 in wide rear wheels.
Introduction of 3.3 litre Turbo (98 octane).

1981 911 SC engine uprated for 98 octane. Power up from 188 to 204 hp.

1983 Introduction of 911 Cabriolet.

1984 Introduction of Carrera 3.2 litre, 231 hp.

1989 Introduction of 911 Carrera Speedster (first shown in prototype form at 1987 Frankfurt Motor Show) and of 4WD, 250 hp, 3.6 litre Carrera 4.

5 Main external identification points of various 911 series

Equipment varies slightly according to models, but the various series can easily be identified by some common features. Targa models keep pivoting front quarter panels up to I-series included.

O-series (Sept '64-July '67)

Short wheelbase (cover giving access to rear torsion bars, at tangent to wheel arch). 4.5 inch rims. Circular external mirror. Simple push-button door handles. Pivoting front quarter panels. Chromium plated wipers parking on rh side of screen. Steering wheel with bare metal spokes. Front bumper over-riders. Heater outlets in door sills.

A-series (Aug '67-July '68)
5.5 inch rims. Black wiper blades parking on lh side of screen. Targa without air vents in roll-over arch.

B-series (Aug '68-July '69)
Long wheelbase. Flared wings. 911 E and S with 6 inch rims and fuel injection. Fixed front quarter panels on Coupé. Raised door handles protecting push-button against accidental opening. Steering wheel with padded spokes. Dashboard part-covered by perforated metal. Targa with air vents in roll-over arch. Heater outlets under dash. Electrically heated rear window to which warm air ducts are deleted.

C- and D-series 2.2 litre models (Aug '69-July '71)
Door handles with internal trigger lever.

E-series 2.4 litre models (Aug '71-July '72)
Oil tank filler in rh body side panel. Black air intake grille on engine cover. Rectangular external mirror. Front air dam on 911 S (optional on others). No front bumper over-riders. No metal grille on dash panel.

F-series (Aug '72-July '73)
Oil tank filler back in engine room. Front air dam on all models. Black front air intake grilles and parking/flashing light surrounds. Inertia reel seat belts. Carrera 2.7 with wider rear wings, 7 inch rear rims, 'duck's tail' spoiler (not for certain markets). K-Jetronic on 911 T USA cars from January 1973.

G-series (Aug '73-July '74)
Higher and more protruding aluminium bumpers. Deeper rocker panels. Modified rear panel. Stainless steel exhaust system.

More deeply padded steering wheel with safety boss (3 spokes on Carrera). Light-weight seats with integral headrest. 911 and 911 S with K-Jetronic. Fixed rear quarter windows. Carrera Targa introduced.

H-series (Aug '74-July '75)
Hinged rear quarter windows. Twin heater control levers on floor. Additional flexible tubes and ventilator for heating system in engine room. 930 Turbo with extra-wide wings and large front and rear spoilers. 'Tray' rear spoiler on Carrera, if fitted.

I-series (Aug '75-July '76)
Electrically controlled external mirror. 5-blade cooling fan (except Turbo). Body made of zinc coated steel.

K-series (Aug '76-July '77)
Fresh air vents on dash. Rotating interior door lock release buttons. Turbo with 16 inch wheels (optional on other models). Adjustable rear trailing arms.

1978-79 mod. (Aug '77-July '79)
Fixed rear quarter windows. Turbo (3.3) with higher rear spoiler. Three-spoke steering wheel also on standard 911 SC. All cars with 11-blade cooling fan.

1980 mod. (Aug '79-July '80)
Turbo with twin exhaust pipes.

1981-83 mod. (Aug '80-July '83)
Additional directional lights on body side panels.

1984–86 mod. (Aug '83–July '85)
911 Carrera with holed cast alloy wheels and fog lights recessed in air dam. Four-spoke steering wheel.

1987–89 mod. (Aug '86–   )
Twin rear foglight integrated in rear light panel.

6 Principal dimensions of 911/930 models

Wheelbase

O-and A-series	2,211 mm
B- and later series	2,271 mm

Track

Rim size	Front track	Model
4.5J 15	1,337 mm	All O-series models.
5.5J 15	1,353 mm	All A-series models.
	1,360 mm	B- and later series 911 T, G-series 911.
5.5J 14	1,362 mm	B-series 911 E Sportomatic.
		B- and C-series optional on 911 T.

Track

Rim size	Front track	Model
6J 15	1,372 mm	B- and later series 911 E (except Sportomatic), 911 S, Carrera (except RS 3.0), H- and later series 911, 911 S, 911 SC and Carrera 3.2
6J 16	1,372 mm	Opt. on Carrera 3.0, 911 SC and Carrera 3.2.
7J 15	1,398 mm	Option on Carrera 3.0, 911 SC and Carrera 3.2. Standard Carrera 3.2 from 1988 mod.
	1,432 mm	H- and I-series 930 Turbo.
7J 16	1,432 mm	K- and later series Turbo.
8J 15	1,413 mm	G-series Carrera RS 3.0.

Rim size	Rear track	Model
4.5J 15	1,317 mm	All O-series models.
5.5J 15	1,321 mm	All A-series models.
	1,342 mm	B- and later series 911 T, G-series 911.
5.5J 14	1,344 mm	B-series 911 E Sportomatic. B- and C-series optional on 911 T. Comfort Kit K-series 911.
6J 15	1,354 mm	B- and later series 911 E (except Sportomatic) and 911 S, H- to K-series 911.
7J 15	1,380 mm	F- and later series Carrera (except RS 3.0), 911 SC and Carrera 3.2
8J 15	1,405 mm	Option on I-series Carrera 3.0, 911 SC and Carrera 3.2. Standard Carrera 3.2 from 1988 mod.
	1,501 mm	H- and I-series 930 Turbo.
8J 16	1,501 mm	K- and later series Turbo up to 1985 mod. Option on Carrera 3.2 from 1988 mod.
9J 15	1,501 mm	G-series Carrera RS 3.0.
9J 16	1,501 mm	Option on K- and later Turbo and Carrera T-look. Standard from 1986 mod on.

Overall length

O- to D-series	4,163 mm	
E- and F-series	4,147 mm	(no front bumper overriders)
G- and later series	4,291 mm	(high impact bumpers)

Overall width

All cars up to 911 SC except Carrera and Turbo	1,610 mm
Carrera and 911 SC	1,652 mm
Carrera RS 3.0 and 930 Turbo and Carrera T-look	1,775 mm

Weight (with full oil & fuel tanks)

All models up to H-series, except Carrera RS models and Turbo 3.0	1,050-1,100 kg	
I- and K-series, except Turbo	1,120 kg	
Carrera RS (F- and G-series)	980 kg	Average
Turbo 3.0	1,205 kg	road
911 SC	1,180 kg	test
Turbo 3.3	1,300–1,335 kg	figures
Carrera 3.2	1,200–1,250 kg	
Carrera 4	1,450 kg	

Tyre sizes

Front	Rear	Model
165 HR 15	165 HR 15	All O- and A-series models, all 911 T, G-series 911.
185 HR 14	185 HR 14	B-series 911 E Sportomatic, opt B- and C-series 911 T. Comfort kit K-series 911/2.7.
185/70 VR 15	185/70 VR 15	All B- and later series 911 E (except Sportomatic) and 911 S, H- to K-series 911.
185/70 VR 15	215/60 VR 15	F- and later series Carrera (except Carrera RS 3.0), H-series 930 Turbo (opt on I-series Turbo), 911 SC and Carrera 3.2
205/60 VR 15	215/60 VR 15	Carrera RS 3.0.
205/50 VR 15	225/50 VR 15	I-series 930 Turbo (opt on I-series Carrera 3.0).
205/55 VR 16	225/50 VR 16	K- and later series Turbo. Opt on all K- and later atmospheric models.
205/55 VR 16	245/45 VR 16	Turbo and T-look from 1986 mod on.

7 Evolution of the 901/911/930 engine (European Models)

O-series (Sept '64-July '66)

911

6 cylinders, 80× 66 mm, 1,991 cc. Biral cylinders, 9:1 comp ratio. 8 bearing forged crankshaft, cast alloy pistons. 6 Solex single choke carbs, replaced by two triple choke Webers in Feb '66. 901/01 camshafts, valves 39/35 mm. 490 W alternator. 215 mm dia clutch. 130 bhp at 6,100 rpm, 17.8 mkg at 4,200 rpm. Octane requirement 98 Res.

O-series (Aug '66-July '67)

911

As above until Nov '66, when new heat exchangers (as 911 S) were introduced, together with 'softer' camshafts (901/06 engine). 2 Weber triple choke carbs.

911 S

As 911, except: 9.8:1 comp ratio. Forged alloy pistons. 2 Weber triple choke carbs. 901/02 camshafts, valves 42/38 mm. New heat exchangers. 160 bhp at 6,600 rpm, 18.2 mkg at 5,200 rpm.

A-series (Aug '67-July '68)

911 T
As 911 L, except: cast iron cylinders. 8.6:1 comp ratio. Simplified 8-bearing crankshaft. 901/03 camshafts. Valves 42/38 mm. 110 bhp at 5,800 rpm, 16 mkg at 4,200 rpm.

911 L
As late O-series 911 with Weber carbs and type 901/06 camshafts.

911 S
As O-series.

B-series (Aug '68-July '69)

911 T
As A-series, except: magnesium crankcase, 770 W alternator.

911 E
As 911 L, except: 9.1:1 comp ratio. Plunger pump fuel injection. Original 901/01 camshafts. Magnesium crankcase. 770 W alternator. 140 bhp at 6,500 rpm, 18.2 mkg at 4,500 rpm.

911 S
As O-series, except: plunger pump fuel injection. Magnesium crankcase. Oil cooler in rh front wing. 770 W alternator. 170 bhp at 6,800 rpm, 18.5 mkg at 5,500 rpm.

C- and D-series (Aug '69-July '71)

911 T/2.2
As B-series, except: B/S 84×66 mm, 2,195 cc. Valves 46/40 mm. Clutch dia 225 mm. 125 bhp at 5,800 rpm, 18.0 mkg at 4,200 rpm.

911 E/2.2
As B-series, except: B/S 84×66 mm, 2,195 cc. Camshafts type 901/06. Valves 46/40 mm. Clutch dia 225 mm. 155 bhp at 6,200 rpm, 19.5 mkg at 4,500 rpm.

911 S/2.2
As B-series, except: B/S 84×66 mm, 2,195 cc. Valves 46/40 mm. Clutch dia 225 mm. 180 bhp at 6,500 rpm, 20.3 mkg at 5,200 rpm.

E- & F-series (Aug '71-July '73)

911 T/2.4*
As 911 T/2.2, except: B/S 84× 70.4 mm, 2,341 cc. Oil jets for piston cooling. 7.5:1 comp ratio. Fully counterweighted crankshaft. New camshafts (911/51). 130 bhp at 5,600 rpm, 20 mkg at 4,000 rpm. Octane requirement 91 Res.

911 E/2.4
As 911 E/2.2, except: B/S 84× 70.4 mm, 2,341 cc. Oil jets for piston cooling. 8:1 comp ratio. Revised camshaft timing. 165 bhp at 6,200 rpm, 21 mkg at 4,500 rpm. Octane requirement 91 Res.

911 S/2.4
As 911 S/2.2, except: B/S 84× 70.4 mm, 2,341 cc. Oil jets for piston cooling. 8.5:1 comp ratio. 190 bhp at 6,500 rpm. 22 mkg at 5,200 rpm. Octane requirement 91 Res.

911 SC/2.7 (Carrera)
As 911 S/2.4, except: B/S 90× 70.4 mm, 2,681 cc. Nikasil cylinders. 210 bhp at 6,300 rpm, 26 mkg at 5,100 rpm. (F-series only.)

* US engines with plunger pump fuel injection until Dec '72, and with K-Jetronic as from Jan '73. 140 bhp at 5,600 rpm and 20 mkg at 4,000 rpm.

G-series (Aug '73-July '74)

911/2.7
As E/F-series 911 T, except: B/S 90× 70.4 mm, 2,681 cc. Nikasil, later Alusil cylinders. New camshafts (911/97). K-Jetronic CF injection. 150 bhp at 5,700 rpm, 24 mkg at 3,800 rpm.

911 S/2.7
As E/F-series 911 E, except: B/S 90× 70.4 mm, 2,681 cc. Nikasil, later Alusil cylinders. New camshafts (911/98). Oil cooler in rh front wing. K-Jetronic CF injection. 175 bhp at 5,800 rpm, 24 mkg at 4,000 rpm.

Carrera/2.7
As F-series Carrera.

Carrera RS 3.0
As Carrera 2.7, except: B/S 95× 70.4 mm, 2,994 cc. Valves 49/41.5 mm. 9.8:1 comp ratio. 230 bhp at 6,200 rpm, 28 mkg at 5,000 rpm. Octane requirement 98 Res.

H-series (Aug '74-July '75)

911/2.7
As G-series, except: Alusil cylinders only. Revised heat exchangers. Alternator 980 W.

911 S/2.7
As G-series, except: Alusil cylinders only. Revised heat exchangers. Alternator 980 W.

911 SC/2.7
As G-series.

911 Turbo
As 911, except: B/S 95×70.4 mm, 2,994 cc. Nikasil cylinders. 6.5:1 comp ratio. Forged alloy pistons. Aluminium crankcase. Different camshafts (930/51) with 4 bearings. Valves 49/41.5 mm. K-Jetronic injection and turbocharger (0.8 Bar boost). Clutch 240 mm. 260 bhp at 5,500 rpm, 35 mkg at 4,500 rpm. Octane requirement 96 Res.

I- and K-series (Aug '75-July '77)

911/2.7
As H-series 911 S, except: Larger oil pressure pump. 5 blade cooling fan. Automatic cold start system. Power re-rated at 165 bhp at 5,800 rpm.

Carrera 3.0
As 911, except: B/S 95×70.4 mm, 2,994 cc. Nikasil cylinders. Aluminium crankcase. Different (930/02) camshafts with four bearings. Valves 49/41.5 mm. Larger K-Jetronic. 200 bhp at 6,000 rpm, 26 mkg at 4,200 rpm.

911 Turbo
As H-series.

1978-79 mod. (Aug '77-July '79)

911 SC **911 Turbo 3.3**

As I-K-series Carrera 3.0, except camshafts advanced 6°. Larger dia main and big end bearings. Air pump. 11-blade cooling fan, 226 mm. 180 bhp at 5,500 rpm, 27 mkg at 4,100 rpm.

As H-series, except: B/S 97×74.4 mm, 3,299 cc. Larger diameter main and big end bearings. 7.0:1 comp ratio. Intercooler. 300 bhp at 5,500 rpm. 42 mkg at 4,500 rpm.

1980 mod. (Aug '79-July '80)

911 SC **911 Turbo 3.3**

As above, except: Larger oil pump, 245 mm, 11-blade fan. 8.6:1 comp ratio. 188 bhp at 5,500 rpm.

As above. Identification by twin exhaust pipes.

1981–83 mod. (Aug '80-July '83)

911 SC **911 Turbo 3.3**

As 1980, except: 9.8:1 comp. ratio, 204 bhp at 5,900 rpm, 27 mkg at 4,300 rpm, camshaft timing as Carrera 3.0. Octane requirement 98 Res.

As 1980 except max torque 44 mkg at 4,000 rpm

1984 and later mod. (Aug '83 onward)

911 Carrera **911 Turbo 3.3**

As 1980 911 SC except: B/S 95×74.4 mm, 3,164 cc, 10.3:1 comp ratio, 231 bhp at 5,900 rpm, 28.6 mkg at 4,800 rpm. Camshafts advanced 3°, ignition and fuel injection by electronic engine management. No air pump. Alternator 1,260W.

As 1983

---

8 Valve timing of production 901/911/930 engines

Timing		Models	Models	Models	Models
Inlet opens	btdc	52° 911 from	43° 911 from Nov	64° All O-to	41° E- & F-series
Inlet closes	abdc	62° Sept '64 to	57° '66, 911 L, C-	76° F-series 911 S,	59° 911 E/2.4.
Exhaust opens	bbdc	64° Nov '66.	65° & D-series	64° Carrera 2.7	63°
Exhaust closes	atdc	44° B-series	31° 911 E/2.2.	44° G-series,	33°
		911 E.		Carrera RS 3.0.	
Inlet opens	btdc	40° A- to D-series,	41° E- & F-series	24° Late F-series	22° G- & H-series
Inlet closes	abdc	56° 911 T (2.0+	55° 911 T/2.4	56° K-Jetronic	58° 911/2.7
Exhaust opens	bbdc	66° 2.2).	67°	54° 911 T 2.4	52°
Exhaust closes	atdc	22°	21°	14° litre for USA.	16°
Inlet opens	btdc	16° G- & H-series	24° I- & K-series	20° All	30° L- & later
Inlet closes	abdc	72° 911 S/2.7,	76° Carrera 3.0.	60° Turbo.	70° series 911 SC.
Exhaust opens	bbdc	47° I- and K-series	66° 1981-83 series	50°	72°
Exhaust closes	atdc	21° 911/2.7.	26° 911 SC.	18°	20°
Inlet opens	btdc	27° 911 Carrera			
Inlet closes	abdc	73° (1984-)			
Exhaust opens	bbdc	69°			
Exhaust closes	atdc	23°			

Valve head diameter

Inlet	Exhaust	Models
39 mm	35 mm	2 litre 911, 911 L and 911 E.
42 mm	38 mm	2 litre 911 S and 911 T models.
46 mm	40 mm	All 2.2, 2.4 and 2.7 litre models.
49 mm	41.5 mm	3 and 3.2 litre models, Turbo 3.0 and 3.3.

9 Evolution of the brakes

	Single/twin circuit	Caliper front	Caliper rear	Ventilated discs
O-series 911	Single	M — cast iron	L — cast iron	no
O-series 911 S	Single	M — cast iron	L — cast iron	yes
A-series 911 L 911 S	Twin	M — cast iron	L — cast iron	yes
911 T	Twin	M — cast iron	L — cast iron	no (Sporto-matic yes)
B-series 911 T	Twin	M — cast iron	M — cast iron	no (Sporto-matic yes)
B- to F-series 911 E	Twin	M — cast iron	M — cast iron	yes
B- to F-series 911 S	Twin	S — alu	M — cast iron	yes
C- to H-series 911 T and 911	Twin	M — cast iron	M — cast iron	yes
G- and H-series 911 & 911 S	Twin	M — cast iron	M — cast iron	yes
F- to H-series Carrera 2.7	Twin	S — alu	M — cast iron	yes
G-series Carrera RS 3.0	Twin	917 — alu	917 — alu	yes
H- to K-series 930 Turbo	Twin	S — alu	M — cast iron	yes[1]
All I-series and later atmospheric models	Twin	A — cast iron	M — cast iron	yes[1]
All Turbo 3.3 and Carrera T-look	Twin	917 — alu	917 — alu	yes[2]

L — caliper=40 sq cm brake pad area.
M — caliper=52.5 sq cm brake pad area.
S — caliper=78 sq cm brake pad area and 13 mm thick lining material.

A — caliper=78 sq cm brake pad area and 10 mm thick lining material.
917 — caliper=94 sq cm brake pad area.

[1] Hydrovac 7″ from K-series (L-series for rhd mod), except K-series basic 911. From 1984 model 911 Carrera on: Hydrovac 8″ vacuum pump, rear pressure limiter, front disc thickness increased from 20.5 to 24 mm, rear from 20 to 24 mm.
[2] Hydrovac 8″.

10 Porsche 901/911/930/935 racing engines
(All engines have twin ignition except 930/71 and type 935)

Type and year	901/20 901/25 1965-68	901/21 1967-69	911/20 911/22 1970	911/21 1970	911/70 1970-71	911/73 1972	911/72 1972	911/74 1973	911/75 1974
Bore × stroke (mm)	80× 66	80× 66	85× 66	87.5× 66	86.7× 70.4	89× 66	92× 70.4	95× 70.4	95× 70.4
Capacity (cc)	1,991	1,991	2,247	2,380	2,494	2,466	2,808	2,994	2,994
Compression ratio	10.5	10.5	10.5	10.5	10.5	10.5	10.5	10.5	10.5
Max power/ rpm	210/ 8,000	220/ 8,000	230/ 8,000	250/ 8,000	275/ 8,000	275/ 8,000	308/ 8,000	315/ 8,000	330/ 8,000
Valve dia Inl/ Exh (mm)	45/39	45/39	45/39	45/39	46/40	46/40	49/ 41.5	49/ 41.5	49/ 41.5

Valve lift Inl/Exh (mm)	12.1/10.5	12.1/10.5	12.1/10.5	12.1/10.5	12.1/10.5	12.1/10.5	12.1/10.5	12.2/11.6	12.2/11.6
Port dia Inl/Exh (mm)	38/38	38/38	—	—	41/41	41/41	43/43	43/43	43/43
Carburettors/Injection	2 Weber 46 IDA3C	Inj	911/20 Inj, 911/22 Twin Weber	Inj	Inj	Inj	Inj	Inj	Inj
Throttle valves/slides	Valves	Slides	Valves	Valves	Valves	Valves	Valves	Valves	Slides
Boost pressure									
Used in Porsche models	901/20 for 906, 901/25 for 911 R	906, 910, 907	911 RSR	911 RSR	911 RSR	911 RSR	Carrera RSR	Carrera RSR	Carrera RSR

Type and year	911/76 1974	930/71 1976	930/72 1976-77	911/78 1976-77	935/71 1978	935/73 1978	935/76 1981-82	935/77 1983	956/962C 1983–84
Bore × stroke (mm)	83×66	95×70.4	92.8×70.4	83×66	95.7×74.4	87×60	92.3×66	92.3×66	95×70.4
Capacity (cc)	2,143	2,994	2,856	2,143	3,211	2,140	2,650	2,650	2,994
Compression ratio	6.5	6.5	6.5	6.5	7.0	7.0	7.2	7.5	9.5
Max power/rpm	490/7,600	485/7,000	590(630)/7,900	520(540)/8,000	750/8,200	580/8,500	620/8,200	620/8,200	660/8,200
Valve dia Inl/Exh (mm)	47/40.5	49/41.5	49/41.5	47/40.5	2×35/30.5	2×33/29	2×35/30.5	2×35/30.5	2×35/31
Valve lift Inl/Exh (mm)	10.5/10.5	10.5/10.5	10.5/10.5 (11.5/11.5)	10.5/10.5	10/10	10/10	10/10	10/10	9.3/9.3
Port dia Inl/Exh (mm)	41/41	43/43	43/43	41/41	—	—	—	—	
Carburettors/Injection	Inj & Turbo	K-Jet & Turbo	Inj & Turbo (+2 turbos)	Inj & Turbo (+2 turbos)	Inj & 2 Turbos	Inj & 2 Turbos	Inj & 2 Turbos	Electronic Inj & 2 Turbos	Electronic Inj & 2 Turbos
Throttle valves/slides	Valves	1 Valve	Valves	Valves	Valves	Valves	Valves	Valves	Valves
Boost pressure	1.4 bar	1.4 bar	1.4 bar	1.4 bar	1.4 bar	1.4 bar	1.2 bar	1.2 bar	1.2 bar
Used in Porsche models	Turbo-Carrera	934	935	936	935/78	936/78	936/81 and 956/82	956/83 – 84	962C

All engines with 4 valves per cylinder have water cooled heads, 935/83 is fully water cooled.

Valve timing	All unturbocharged engines	Turbocharged 2-valve engines: 911/76-78	930/71-72	Turbocharged 4-valve engines: All 935 engines
Inlet opens btdc/closes abdc	104°/104°	80°/100°	78°/98°	58°/78°
Exhaust opens bbdc/closes atdc	100°/80°	105°/75°	103°/73°	78°/58°

11 Power and torque (1973-75 models)

12 Acceleration chart (1973-75 models)

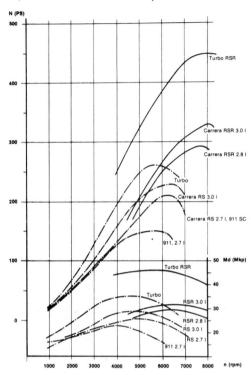

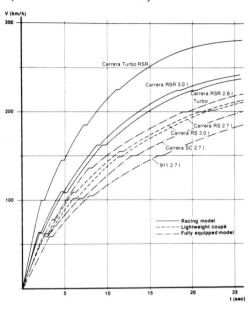

13 Transmissions for 911 and 930 models

Transmission	Models
Type 901/902, 5 speeds	O- to B-series 911, 911 L, 911 E, 911 S.
Distance between shaft centres 68 mm. Aluminium housing, sand cast.	Optional on 911 T.
Type 901/902, 4 speeds	A- & B-series 911 T.
Type 911, 5 speeds	C- & D-series 911 E and 911 S. Optional on 911 T
Developed from 901/902, but reinforced. Die-cast aluminium, later die-cast magnesium housing. 225 mm dia clutch.	
Type 911, 4 speeds	C- & D-series 911 T.
Type 905, 4 speed Sportomatic	Option on all A- to D-series 911 T, 911 L and 911 E, on A-series 911 S and on E-series 911 T, except 911 T/USA.
Developed from 901/902 with torque converter. Conversion ratio 1:2.2.	
Type 925, 4 speed Sportomatic	Optional on all E- to H-series models except Carrera and Turbo.
Developed from 905, but reinforced. Conversion ratio 1:2.0.	
Type 925/10, 3 speed Sportomatic	Optional on all I- and later series (up to 1980) models, except Turbo.
Developed from 925, but reinforced.	
Type 915, 4 speeds	All E- to K-series models, except Carrera RS and 930 Turbo.
New transmission based on Type 916 racing transmission with 77 mm between shaft centres. Die-cast	

Transmission

magnesium housing. Distance between
shaft centres 76 mm. Provision for
forced feed lubrication for racing.
225 mm diameter clutch.

Type 915, 5 speeds

Die cast aluminium housing from 1980 models
on. Oil pump and cooling serpentine from 1984
models on.

Type 930, 4 speeds

Developed from 915, but reinforced.
Die-cast aluminium housing. Provision
for forced feed lubrication, 240 mm
diameter clutch. Four-star differential.

Type G50, 5 speeds

BW synchromesh. 85 mm shaft centre distance.
Cast aluminium housing. 240 mm clutch.

Models

F-series Carrera RS 2.7, G-series Carrera RS
3.0, L- and later series atmospheric models.
Optional on all other E- to K- series models,
except Turbo.

Turbo 3 and 3.3 litre.

911 Carrera from 1987 mod.
Turbo from 1989 mod.

---

14 Selection of road test figures

Model	Year	Source	0-100 kph (0-62.5 mph) (sec)	0-160 kph (0-99.5 mph) (sec)	0-200 kph (0-124 mph) (sec)	1 km from standing start (sec)	Max speed (mph)
911 Coupé 2 litre	1965	Own	8.8	22.3	47.0	29.3	131
911 S Coupé 2 litre	1966	Own	6.8	17.7		27.55	137.8
911 T Coupé 2 litre	1967	*Auto, Motor & Sport*	8.3	22.8		29.0	129.2
911 E Coupé 2 litre Sportomatic	1968	Own	9.4	20.3		29.25	128.7
911 E Coupé 2.2 litre Sportomatic	1969	*Auto, Motor & Sport*	9.7	24.7		29.3	134.9
911 T Coupé 2.2 litre	1969	*Auto, Motor & Sport*	9.5	24.3		29.7	128.7
911 S Coupé 2.2 litre	1970	Own	7.0	17.0	29.1	27.0	143.4
911 S Coupé 2.4 litre	1971	Own	6.6	15.7	26.6	26.9	144.1
Carrera RS 2.7	1973	Own	5.8	12.8	22.0	25.4	149.1
Carrera 2.7 (G-series)	1974	*Auto, Motor & Sport*	6.1	15.2	27.0	26.2	148.1
911/2.7 Coupé	1974	*Auto, Motor & Sport*	8.2	21.9		28.9	130.8
911 S/2.7 Coupé	1974	*Auto, Motor & Sport*	8.5	20.3	41.3	28.7	139.8
Carrera RS 3.0	1974	Own	5.5	13.5	24.2	25.35	148.2
Turbo 3.0 (air condit)	1975	Own	6.5	14.2	22.7	25.15	156.0
911/2.7 (I-series)	1975	*Auto, Motor & Sport*	7.3	18.7		27.9	138.1
Carrera 3.0 (I-series)	1975	*Auto, Motor & Sport*	6.1	15.0	27.9	26.2	146.2
Turbo 3.3	1978	Own	5.2	11.8	17.7	24.0	160.3
911 SC Coupé 188 hp	1979	*Auto, Motor & Sport*	6.3	15.8	29.3	26.6	141.6

Model	Year	Source	0-100 kph (0-62.5 mph) (sec)	0-160 kph (0-99.5 mph) (sec)	0-200 kph (0-124 mph) (sec)	1 km from standing start (sec)	Max speed (mph)
911 SC Coupé 204 hp	1980	*Auto, Motor & Sport*	5.9	14.7	26.3	25.9	149.1
Carrera Coupé	1983	*Auto, Motor & Sport*	5.8	13.9	23.1	25.6	157.5
Carrera Cabrio	1987	*Auto, Motor & Sport*	6.0	14.7	25.6	26.0	154.1
Carrera Club Sport	1987	*Auto, Motor & Sport*	5.9	14.1	23.8	25.7	154.1

15 Porsche 911 competition successes 1965-87

In races counting towards the World Championship of Makes, rallies of the World/European Championship series and other major events

1965
Rallies
5th overall Monte Carlo (Linge-Falk)

1966
Rallies
European GT Rally Champion
(Günther Klass)
1st overall Austrian Alpine
(Wallrabenstein-Müller)
1st overall German (Klass-Wütherich)
1st GT Alpine (Klass-Wütherich)
4th overall Tulip (Gass-Bretthauer)

1967
Rallies
1st overall Austrian Alpine
(Zasada-Dobrzansky)
1st overall Lyon-Charbonnière
(Elford-Stone)
(911s also 2nd, 3rd and 4th)
1st overall Tulip (Elford-Stone)
1st overall Geneva (Elford-Stone)
3rd overall Danube
(Wallrabenstein-Bretthauer)

also
1st overall Marathon de la Route (Elford-
Neerpasch-Herrmann, driving Sportomatic
911 R)

Races
1st GT Sebring 12 hours (Kirby-Johnson)
1st GT Targa Florio (Cahier-Killy)
1st GT Daytona 24 hours (Ryan-Bencker)
1st GT Nürburgring 1,000 km
(Kelleners-Neuhaus)

also
1st overall Spa 24 hours (touring cars)
(Gaban-Pedro)
1st overall Coupes de Spa (touring and GT
cars) (Udo Schütz)

1968
Rallies
European Rally Drivers' Championship:
P. Toivonen (Porsche 911)
1st & 2nd overall Monte Carlo
(Elford-Stone & Toivonen-Tiuhkanen)
1st overall Geneva (Toivonen-Viherrava)
1st and 2nd overall East German
(Toivonen-Viherrava and
Zasada-Leszozuk)
1st overall Danube (Toivonen-Tiuhkanen)
1st overall Spanish (Toivonen-Tiuhkanen)
1st overall Sweden (Waldegaard-Helmer)
1st & 2nd overall German
(Toivonen-Kolari & Zasada-Postawka)
1st overall San Remo
(Toivonen-Tiuhkanen)

also
1st and 2nd overall Marathon de la Route
(Linge-Glemser-Kauhsen & Schuler-
Blank-Steckkönig)

Races
1st GT Nürburgring 1,000 km (Greger-Huth)
1st GT Watkins Glen 6 hours
(Gregg-Everett)
1st GT Le Mans 24 hours (Gaban-Schütz)
1st GT Monza 1,000 km
(Glemser-Kelleners)
1st GT Sebring 12 hours (Johnson-Kirby)

1st GT Targa Florio (Haldi-Greub)

also

1st overall Spa 24 hours (touring cars)
(Kremer-Kelleners-Kauhsen)

1969
Rallies

1st overall Danube (Poeltinger-Hartinger)
1st overall Swedish (Waldegaard-Helmer)
1st overall Acropolis (Toivonen-Kolari)
1st overall Polish
(Zasada-Miss E. Zasada)

also

1st overall Monte Carlo
(Waldegaard-Helmer)
1st overall Tour de France
(Larrousse-Gelin)
1st overall Tour de Corse
(Larrousse-Gelin)

Races

1st GT Le Mans 24 hours (Gaban-Deprez)
1st GT Daytona 24 hours
(Jennings-Watson)
1st GT Monza 1,000 km
(Fröhlich-Neuhaus)
1st GT Spa 1,000 km (Larrousse-Lins)
1st GT Targa Florio (Bonomelli-Guzzi)
1st GT Nürburgring 1,000 km
(Neuhaus-Fröhlich)
1st GT Austrian 1,000 km (Linge-Bauer)

also

1st overall Spa 24 hours (touring cars)
(Chasseuil-Ballot Léna)
(also 2nd, 3rd and 4th overall)

1970
Rallies

European Rally Champions 1970
1st and 2nd overall Monte Carlo
(Waldegaard-Helmer & Larrousse-Gelin)
1st overall Austrian Alpine
(Waldegaard-Nyström)
1st overall Swedish (Waldegaard-Helmer)
1st overall Danube (Janger-Wessiak)
2nd overall Lyon-Charbonnière
(Haldi-Chapuis)
1st Bodensee Rally (Gass-Frey)

Races

1st GT Nürburgring 1,000 km
(Fröhlich-Toivonen)
1st GT Spa 1,000 km (Haldi-Chenevière)
1st GT Monza 1,000 km (Schenetty-Zerbini)

1971
Rallies

2nd overall RAC (Waldegaard-Nyström)

Races

1st GT Le Mans 24 hours (Touroul-Anselme)
1st GT Nürburgring 1,000 km
(Kremer-Neuhaus)
1st GT Spa 1,000 km (Kremer-Huber)
1st GT Monza 1,000 km (Kremer-Huber)
1st GT Austrian 1,000 km
(Schickentanz-Kersten)
1st GT Targa Florio (Chenevière-Keller)

1972
Rallies

2nd overall Monte Carlo
(Larrousse-Perramond)
2nd overall East African Safari
(Zasada-Bien)
2nd overall Swedish (Waldegaard-Helmer)

Races

European GT Trophy (John Fitzpatrick)
1st GT Daytona 6 hours (Gregg-Haywood)
1st GT Targa Florio (Pica-Gottifridi)
1st GT Nürburgring 1,000 km
(Kremer-Fitzpatrick)

1973
Races

Joint European GT Champions
(Clemens Schickentanz and
Claude Ballot-Léna)
1st overall Daytona 24 hours
(Gregg-Haywood)
1st overall Targa Florio
(Müller-van Lennep)
1st GT Targa Florio (Borri-Barone)
1st GT Nürburgring 1,000 km
(Keller-Neuhaus-Schickentanz)
1st GT Watkins Glen 6 hrs
(Keyser-Minter)
1st GT Spa 1,000 km (Jöst-Follmer)
1st GT Dijon 1,000 km (van Lennep-Müller)
1st GT Vallelunga 6 hours
(Follmer-Kauhsen)

1974
Rallies

2nd overall Safari (Waldegaard-Thorzelius)

Races (All Carrera RSR 3.0)

IMSA Championship (USA)
European GT Championship
(John Fitzpatrick)
FIA GT Cup
10 national championships
1st GT Monza 1,000 km (Fitzpatrick-Loos)
1st GT Spa 1,000 km (Fitzpatrick-Loos)
1st GT Imola 1,000 km (Keller-Heyer)
1st GT Nürburgring 1,000 km
(Barth-Pesch-Fitzpatrick-Loos)
1st GT Watkins Glen 6 hours

(Gregg-Haywood)
1st GT Austrian 1,000 km
(Keller-Kremer-Heyer)
1st GT Brands Hatch 1,000 km
(Fitzpatrick-Hezemans)
1st GT Paul Ricard 1,000 km
(Schenken-Stommelen)
1st GT Kyalami 6 hours
(Schenken-Fitzpatrick-Stommelen)

911 Turbo 2.14 litre driven by
Herbert Müller and Gijs van Lennep was:
2nd overall Le Mans 24 hours
2nd overall Watkins Glen 6 hours
3rd overall Spa 1,000 km
5th overall Monza 1,000 km
6th overall Nürburgring 1,000 km
7th overall Paul Ricard 1,000 km

1975
Races (all Carrera RSR 3.0)
IMSA Championship (USA)
European GT Championship (Bertrams)
FIA GT Cup
1st overall Daytona 24 hours
(Gregg-Haywood)
1st GT Mugello 1,000 km
(Schurti-Fitzpatrick-Hezemans)
1st GT Dijon 1,000 km
(Hezemans-Fitzpatrick)
1st GT Monza 1,000 km
(Hezemans-Schurti-Fitzpatrick)
1st GT Spa 1,000 km (Haldi-Béguin)
1st GT Pergusa 1,000 km (Coppa Florio)
(Bertrams-Wisell)
1st GT Nürburgring 1,000 km
(Kelleners-Heyer-Wollek)
1st GT Watkins Glen 6 hours
(Haywood-Hagestad)
1st GT Le Mans 24 hours
(Fitzpatrick-van Lennep)

1976
Races
World Championship of Makes
(Porsche 935)
Trans-Am Championship, USA
(Follmer, Porsche 934)
European GT Championship
(Hezemans, Porsche 934)
1st Mugello 6 hours (Mass-Ickx)
1st Vallelunga 6 hours (Ickx-Mass)
1st Watkins Glen 6 hours
(Stommelen-Schurti)
1st Dijon 6 hours (Ickx-Mass)
(all Porsche 935)
Additionally Gr 6 Porsches powered by the
turbocharged 2.14 litre 911 engine won all

six races counting towards the World
Championship of Sports Cars (Jöst one
race, Ickx-Mass five races), as well as the
Le Mans 24 Hours Race (Ickx-van Lennep
on Porsche 936).

1977
Races
World Championship of Makes
(Porsche 935)
Trans-Am Championship, USA
(Gregg on Porsche 935)
1st Daytona 24 hours
(Graves-Haywood-Helmick on Carrera)
1st Mugello 6 hours
(Stommelen-Schurti on 935)
1st Silverstone 6 hours
(Mass-Ickx on 935/77)
1st Nürburgring 1,000 km
(Stommelen-Hezemans-Schenken on 935)
1st Watkins Glen 6 hours
(Ickx-Mass on 935/77)
1st Mosport 6 hours
(Heimrath-Miller on 934)
1st Brands Hatch 6 hours
(Ickx-Mass on 935/77)
1st Hockenheim 6 hours
(Wollek-Fitzpatrick on 935)
1st Vallelunga 6 hours
('Dino'-Moreschi on 935)
NB: Le Mans 24 Hours won by Ickx-Barth-
Haywood on 911/78-engined Porsche 936.

1978
Rallies
1st Rally Monte Carlo
(Nicolas-Laverne on Carrera 3.0 RS)
2nd Safari Rally
(Vic Preston Jr on 911 SC)

Races
World Championship of Makes
(Porsche 935)
IMSA Championship, USA
(Peter Gregg on 935)
European Hill Climb Championship
(Jacques Almeras on 935)
FIA GT Cup (Palavicini on 934)
1st Daytona 24 hours
(Stommelen-Hezemans-Gregg on 935)
1st Mugello 6 hours
(Hezemans-Heyer-Fitzpatrick on 935)
1st Silverstone 6 hours
(Ickx-Mass on 935/78)
1st Nürburgring 1,000 km
(Ludwig-Heyer-Hezemans on 935)
1st Misano 6 hours
(Wollek-Pescarolo on 935)

1st Dijon 1,000 km
(Wollek-Pescarolo on 935)
1st Watkins Glen 6 hours
(Gregg-Hezemans-Fitzpatrick on 935)
1st Vallelunga 6 hours
(Wollek-Pescarolo on 935)

1979
Rallies
1st Tour of Italy
(Moretti-Schon on 935)

Races
World Championship of Makes
(Porsche 935)
European Hill Climb Championship
(Jacques Almeras on 935)
IMSA Championship, USA
(Gregg on 935)
Trans-Am Championship, USA
(Paul on 935)
1st Le Mans 24 Hours
(Ludwig-Bill & Don Whittington on 935-K3)
1st Daytona 24 hours
(Ongais-Haywood-Field on 935)
1st Mugello 6 hours
(Fitzpatrick-Schurti-Wollek on 935)
1st (Gr 5) Dijon 1,000 km
(Wollek-Ickx-Schurti on 935)
1st Silverstone 6 hours
(Heyer-Wollek-Fitzpatrick-Schurti on 935)
1st Nürburgring 1,000 km
(Schurti-Fitzpatrick-Wollek on 935)
1st (Gr 5) Coppa Florio
(Palavicini-Vanoli on Carrera RSR)
1st Watkins Glen 6 hours
(Bill & Don Whittington on 935)
1st (Gr 5) Brands Hatch 6 hours
(Ludwig-Plankenhorn on 935)
1st (Gr 5) Vallelunga 6 hours
(Calderari-Spatetti-Martz on Carrera RSR)
NB: The Dijon and Brands Hatch races
were won outright by Jöst-Merl driving a
modified Porsche 908/03 powered by a
2.14 litre turbocharged type 911/78 engine.

1980
Rallies
1st Tour of Corsica
(J.-L. Therier on 911 SC)
European Rally Championship
(A. Zanini on 911 SC)

Races
World Championship of Makes
(935 tied with Lancia)
Endurance Racing World Championship
(John Paul Sr on 935)
European Hill Climb Championship

(Groups 1 & 3, R. Biancone on 930 Turbo;
Groups 2 & 4, J. Almeras on 934; Groups 5 &
6, J.–M. Almeras on 935)
Trans-Am Championship
(John Bauer on 911 SC)
IMSA Championship (makes and drivers)
(J. Fitzpatrick on 935)
1st Daytona 24 Hours
(Stommelen-Jöst-Merl on 935)
1st Mosport 6 Hours
(Fitzpatrick-Redman on 935)
1st Dijon 1,000 km
(Pescarolo-Barth on 935)
Le Mans 24 Hours
1st IMSA (5th overall),
(Fitzpatrick-Redman-Barbour) & 1st Group
(8th overall),
(Schornstein-Grohs-Tschirnhaus, both on
935s)

1981
Races
European Hill Climb Championship
(Groups 1 & 3, K. Linnig on 930 Turbo)
Endurance Racing World Championship
(Bob Garretson on 935)
World Championship of Makes (1st Division)
(935)
1st Daytona 24 Hours
(Garretson-Rahal-Redman on 935)
1st Monza 1,000 km
(Doeren-Laessig on 935)
1st Silverstone 6 Hours
(Schornstein-Grohs-Röhrl on 935)
Le Mans 24 Hours
1st Group 5 (4th overall),
Bourgoignie-Cooper-Wood on 935)

1982
Races
FIA Endurance Cup for Group B (GT cars)
(Müller-Memminger on 930 Turbo)
IMSA Championship (makes and drivers)
(John Paul Jr on 935)
European Hill Climb Championship (Division
II)
(Jacques Guillot on 930 Turbo)
1st Daytona 24 Hours
(J. Paul Sr-J. Paul Jr-Stommelen on 935)
Le Mans 24 Hours
1st GTX (4th overall), Fitzpatrick-Hobbs &
2nd GTX (5th overall),
Cooper-Smith-Bourgoignie on 935s)

1983
Races
1st Daytona 24 Hours

(Wollek-Ballot Léna-A. J. Foyt on 935)
Le Mans 24 Hours
(1st Group B (11th overall),
Cooper-Smith-Ovey & 2nd Group B (13th
overall), Memminger-Kuhn Weiss-Müller on
930 Turbo)

1984
Rallies
FISA Middle East Rally Championship for
Manufacturers
(Porsche AG with 911 SC/RS)
FISA Middle East Rally Championship for
Drivers
(Saeed Al Hajri, Porsche 911 SC/RS)
Belgian Rally Championship
(Patrick Snyers, 911 SC/RS)
Swedish Special Production Car
Championship
(Mats Linden, 935)
Spanish Regional Rally Championship
(Carlos Pizeira, 911)

1985
Rallies
FISA Middle East Rally Championship
(Saeed Al Hajri, 911 SC/RS)
German Rally Trophy
(Reinhardt Schülein, 911)

Swiss Sports Racing Car Championship
(A. Salamin, 935)
Finnish and Scandinavian Drag Racing
Championship
(L. Nylund, 911)
Super Saloon Asphalt Championship of
Denmark
(J. Jensen, 911 Carrera)
Belgian National Rally Championship
(Pascal Gaban, 911 SC/RS)
Luxemburg Hill Climb Championship
(J. Welkenbach, 911)
Pharaon Rally
(1st, Saeed Al Hajri, 959)

1986
Races
Le Mans 24 Hours Race
(1st IMSA and 7th overall, R. Metge-
C. Ballot-Léna, 961)

Rallies
Paris-Dakar, 1st, 2nd and 5th overall (Metge-
Lemoyne, Ickx-Brasseur and
Kaussmaul-Unger, 959)

1987
Rallies
Belgian National Rally Championship
(Marc Soullet, 911 RS/SC)

Index